JIMMY
NEUROSIS

JIMMY NEUROSIS

A MEMOIR

JAMES OSELAND

ecco

An Imprint of HarperCollins*Publishers*

JIMMY NEUROSIS. Copyright © 2019 by James Oseland. All rights reserved. Printed in the United States of America. No part of this book may be used or reproduced in any manner whatsoever without written permission except in the case of brief quotations embodied in critical articles and reviews. For information, address HarperCollins Publishers, 195 Broadway, New York, NY 10007.

HarperCollins books may be purchased for educational, business, or sales promotional use. For information, please email the Special Markets Department at SPsales@harpercollins.com.

FIRST EDITION

Designed by Michelle Crowe

Library of Congress Cataloging-in-Publication Data has been applied for.

ISBN 978-0-06-226736-8

19 20 21 22 23 LSC 10 9 8 7 6 5 4 3 2 1

For my mom and dad

JIMMY
NEUROSIS

July 1977 to December 1980

PART I

1

SORRY, CHARLIE

While the credits rolled, I mentally composed my movie review for the *New York Times*. A pithy one-liner to start with, I decided, with the serious criticism to follow.

The house lights went on abruptly, and my daydream vaporized. "We'd better get going, Jim," my mother said. "Daddy will be waiting." As we filed out of the auditorium, she paused to check her reflection in the lobby's mirrored walls.

"You look fantastic, Mom," I told her, trying to hurry us outside. Really, I just wanted to get away from my own reflection. I was fourteen, and so far it wasn't going too well. Mom fluffed her dome of frosted hair.

The Minnesota afternoon summer heat was intense, and I wondered what Dad might be making for dinner in this weather. Some kind of salad? Whatever he was preparing, I looked forward to it, the jumbo box of popcorn we'd polished off during the movie notwithstanding.

When you move as often as we did back then, family is the only real home you've got, the only element that isn't constantly changing. For instance, Dad could be counted on to be in his favorite room when we got back. The Carriage House Estates apartment had a galley kitchen furnished only with a cracked Formica countertop and a broken freezer, but he needed no fancy accoutrements to rustle up an elaborate meal.

He wasn't always in town; he traveled for work. But I loved it when he was. I pictured how his sleeves would be rolled up, his forearms revealing faded tattoos from his navy days. Scotch and soda on a coaster. The drone of *ABC's Wide World of Sports* in the background. I imagined the preoccupied smile he'd give us when we came in.

MOM AND I WADED through the heat, searching for our station wagon in the parking lot. She might've stepped right out of the movie we'd just seen, *Fun with Dick & Jane,* so strongly did she resemble Jane Fonda's slim and glamorous character.

The son in the movie was about my age, too, with sandy hair like mine. Nerdy like me as well. He had a role at the beginning, but then it was as if everyone forgot about him.

She peered over the rims of her sunglasses. "Honey, I'm not seeing the car anywhere!"

"Because all the cars look identical," I pointed out. If it had been up to me, we would've gone to the art-house cinema near downtown Minneapolis, but that would've necessitated a freeway trip, and my mom viewed the prospect of driving in the fast lane the way most people would view leaning out the open door of a cargo plane at thirty-nine thousand feet, so that was out. Of course, I could have taken the bus downtown myself, but it never would've occurred to me to break our standing date.

"Found it, Mom."

She cautiously piloted us out of the parking lot, the air barely stirring inside the car. "I thought that was pretty good, for a regular movie," I said. By "regular" I meant not like the serious ones I preferred, such as *Taxi Driver* or *Rosemary's Baby*. This one had been a satire. It was about an all-American couple who lose everything when the husband gets fired, and to make ends meet they go on a spree of robberies. "I like that they got away with it in the end. Did you?"

"I thought they made a very handsome couple. But"—she pursed her lips into a moue of disapproval—"honestly, I found it a little depressing. I didn't expect it to be so much about *unemployment*."

"Well, but that's real life."

"You don't go to the movies to see real life," she retorted, peering anxiously over the dashboard before making a very wide turn. "I know that Daddy just started his new job, but it made me worry. They're handing out so many pink slips nowadays, it's scary. If he gets fired *this* time, I don't know what we'll do, honey, I really don't."

Since I'd been a little kid, the phrase "getting fired" had given me a mental image of someone being shut into a steel-lined chamber and engulfed in flames. Even now I couldn't rid myself of the association. To combat a surge of uneasiness, I ground my teeth. Because it was Sunday, the seventh day of the week, it had to be done seven times. I hid this by turning my head as though fascinated by the overgrown grass and jack pines of the median strip. If anyone knew about my protective rituals, including my mom, their power would be eliminated.

Now Mom, with much tapping of the brakes, was maneuvering us into a parking space on the main drag.

"Where are we? Oh . . . I see!" We were parked in front of a Fanny Farmer candy shop.

She gave me a sheepish smile. "Just a quick stop?" As vigilant as she was about watching her figure, chocolates were irresistible to her, and candy feasts, like Sunday bargain matinees, were another mother-son custom.

AS WE PULLED IN to the parking garage at our apartment complex, my mom giggled. "Jim, hide the evidence, so Daddy doesn't ask why we didn't bring him any." I played along, making a dramatic show of stuffing the candy wrappers into my pockets.

Inside, I paused to shuck off my sneakers. Even when we were living in a less-than-wonderful place like this, my mother wanted things neat, and protecting the red shag carpeting that smelled like the previous tenant's cigarette smoke was no exception.

It took me a moment to notice that she was standing frozen before the open closet door, one sandal still dangling from an index finger. "Mom, what's wrong?" I asked.

Without a word she marched into the master bedroom. I heard drawers being pulled, the medicine cabinet clicking open and shut.

I had the familiar sensation of anxiety gripping my guts. I ground my teeth again, but I could tell, as I forced myself to walk down the hall after her, that it was too late to rouse any protective forces.

I found her staring at their bed as though it were a dead body. "Your father," she announced, not looking at me, "has taken all his things."

Half of our belongings were still in storage—we had moved

to St. Paul from suburban Chicago just a few weeks prior—but the other half we'd crammed into the small rooms of this temporary apartment. Since Dad kept assuring us that the Carriage House Estates was a temporary situation, none of us had unpacked anything besides clothing and kitchen items yet. And it was immediately obvious that my dad's side of their bedroom closet was bare except for a few coat hangers.

Knowing, with mounting dread, that she had already checked, I pulled out a dresser drawer. Where his socks and underwear usually were, there was nothing but some loose change. His polo shirts and shorts were gone from the second drawer. Dad went away for business all the time, but as a seasoned traveler he was adept at packing light. He certainly wouldn't have taken all his winter coats and every pair of shoes he owned to an office-supply conference. Nor, for that matter, would he forget to tell us if he was leaving. Still, as I ransacked the rooms for his belongings, my mind continued to grope for justifications. But then I checked the liquor cabinet, one of the few pieces of furniture we'd brought with us, and saw that he'd taken everything but a sticky old bottle of schnapps. Then I knew.

Behind me Mom sank onto a chair. "Go on and watch TV, honey," she said after a minute. "I'll make us dinner."

"Where's Daddy?" I managed.

"I don't know."

That night I dreamed of being chased by a tornado, the dark funnel bending toward me as it whirled faster and faster, dragging at my clothes and hair as I tried to flee on slow, heavy legs.

DAD DIDN'T RETURN THE NEXT DAY, or the day after that. Since we'd been in St. Paul a grand total of only twenty-three days, neither of us knew a soul there. The previous tenants had absconded with the air conditioner, and I woke up every morning with my hair stuck to my face with perspiration. In the courtyard below, an old man sat planted in a folding chair from dawn until dusk, cigar clamped between his teeth, transistor radio tuned to baseball.

Mom and I spent the week performing reruns of our daily rounds. Grocery trips with coupons in hand, dinner in front of the TV. Once an ice-cream truck stopped on our block, and we lined up with the little kids to exchange a couple quarters for a pair of Fudgsicles. Nothing seemed real.

NOW THIS SULTRY AFTERNOON STRETCHED before me. Mom had gone to the bank. All our neighbors had retreated indoors, their fans and air conditioners whirring; even the old man with the radio had scooted his chair to catch the shade of the parking garage. Only our ancient pet turtle, Peewee, who lay with his arms and legs splayed atop a rock in his aquarium, looked at ease in the heat.

The television was on, of course. The dial made a snapping noise as it changed channels. Snap! *Campbell's Soup is mm-mm good!* Snap! A grandmother at a wedding was turning the crank of a Polaroid camera. *Imagine instant pictures with color. Color! In minutes you get bright, colorful pictures.* A blank Polaroid resolved into an image of a grinning child. Snap!

Wait, what was *that?*

An emaciated guy with neon-yellow hair in spikes like the plates of a dragon's back was onstage screaming into a microphone. A droning reporter said, "A reaction to the peace, flowers, and happiness movement of the hippies, so-called punk rock exploded last year and is a direct attack on the anger and confusion of modern-day Britain. And it's begun to make appearances

across the pond, too, in cities like New York and Los Angeles."
He pronounced the last two words *Loz Angel-eez*.

"No future! No future! No future for you! No future for me!"
yowled the band they were showing now. The singer spit right
into the audience, which was a roiling group of people with
freaky hair and torn-up clothes. Repelled and amazed, I couldn't
look away. The singer was acting out exactly what he felt—like
I felt!—and daring you to hate him for it. The audience was
jumping in place like they had so much raw, angry energy that it
didn't matter who was spitting on whom. The only stylistic point
of reference I had for what I was looking at was the movie *The
Man Who Fell to Earth*, which I'd seen with my mom. In it,
David Bowie played a hip, orange-haired space alien dropped
into the middle of a rural American town.

I was hungry to know more, but now we'd returned to the
set of the boring show that the segment appeared on. The host
leaned back in his swivel chair, mugging as if to say, *Would you
get a load of that!* "In London, the punk rock scene," he concluded,
then turned to his cohost. "What d'you think, Danielle? Ready
to go to a punk rock concert?"

The cohost tittered. "I think disco is wild enough for me,
Steve."

I plopped a cylinder of frozen orange-juice concentrate into a
plastic pitcher, the *thwack* of the spoon as I stirred it sounding
loud in the empty apartment. Dad always preferred to squeeze
oranges fresh by hand. He'd pour the pulpy juice over ice and
garnish the glass with a twist of peel.

The cookies in the pantry had gone soft from humidity. I
grabbed a handful anyway and took them with me on a search
for my keepsakes, just for something to do. Moving so frequently,
my family shed more belongings than we acquired, but each of

us claimed at least one cache of treasured objects. Mine was in a box I now located beneath a valise full of winter sweaters.

I set each item out on my bedroom carpet. The souvenir steer's horn from Oklahoma, the Daniel Boone cap from a trip to Knott's Berry Farm, the magic wand that reliably failed to manifest the red paper flowers that were supposed to pop out if you tapped it just right. Secreted inside that box was a smaller one in which I kept newspaper clippings of men's underwear ads. On some I'd penciled in the shadows of penises where they had been only faintly visible. There was one in particular I favored, cut from a Montgomery Ward circular, that showed a shirtless man in powder-blue briefs with darker blue ribbing, and with my finger I would follow the trail of his chest hair where it led to the mysteries of his underwear.

After I'd exhausted the possibilities of both boxes, I hunted through the closets for a certain cardboard trunk. An old hand at leaving her past behind, Mom was the least sentimental among us about belongings, but she, too, had a special trove.

She had told me the story many times. She met Dad in late 1945, during his navy days. He'd been visiting their hometown of Baltimore during a shore leave; at the time he was stationed on Treasure Island, near San Francisco. It'd been a blind date, but he'd been so instantly lovestruck that he'd proposed to her by letter the very next day, as he departed Baltimore on a slow train back to the West Coast. After struggling for weeks with the logic of marrying a man she'd basically only known for a few hours, she consented. Her sister Edie had a big hand in talking her into it. "Go, Bernice—*I* would," she'd said. As my mother readied to leave home to start her new life in California, my dad sent a blizzard of correspondence.

Ever since I'd been old enough to read, I loved to go through this bundle of letters. Written on onionskin that contained the exotic watermark PAR AVION, they held a complicated sway over me. My father had only a sixth-grade education, and his labor was evident. His avowals of love were beyond flowery, which made me feel awkward, but in these overblown lines—*"You are my darling sweetheart, I am so excited about our life together"*—I gleaned something genuine between them that comforted me. It made me a little jealous, too. I wished *I* could inspire such a show of affection from Dad.

A burst of cheering from the transistor radio outside made me startle as though guilty, and I put the bundle back in the trunk. While my mom had never minded my reading them, I suddenly realized I didn't want her to come home now to see me doing it.

I drifted into the bathroom to stare into the mirror. I looked even skinnier than usual, and there were dark circles under my eyes. My dirty-blond hair was in need of a trim. I bared my prominent front teeth, exaggerating them into rabbity protrusions. "You're so ugly," I told my reflection. The bowl of rosebud-shaped miniature soaps seemed to regard me with reproach.

IN THE MORNING I WOKE to the sound of my parents' voices buzzing through the walls, and I hurried out to the living room.

My father had forgone the La-Z-Boy into which he liked to sink, tumbler in his fist, after work. Instead he was on the sofa, his right hand gripping the armrest with white knuckles. My mother was perched on the love seat. She hated that seat, deeming it worn-looking. The expression on her face frightened me.

I knuckled sleep out of my eyes. "When'd you get back?"

He drew a breath. "I've decided to leave your mother," he announced to a spot on the carpet.

The words hung in the air.

"This has been a very hard decision to make. But I want to live alone, not . . . not in this family anymore. There are a lot of things that your mother and I need to figure out about how we're going to proceed. But . . . it's the right thing for me to do."

After the remaining awkward, halting words were exchanged and he'd left with a vague promise to see us later, Mom and I sat in silence while tears spilled down her cheeks. Suddenly I was filled with rage at her, at the way she'd sat with her hands twisting in her lap, just letting him walk out the door. "What are we going to *do*?" I demanded. "We're not going to stay here, are we?"

"I don't know," she replied faintly. "I don't know what we're going to do."

She drifted into the kitchen nook and began transferring dishes from the drying rack into the cupboards, then wiped down the countertop. She wrung out the dishrag, folded it in half, draped it over the faucet. Then she brought me a bowl of Cap'n Crunch. I ate it all, its chemical sweetness coating my mouth.

2

HOT WHEELS

My father reappeared just long enough to leave Minnesota with us. It wasn't that he'd changed his mind; it was only because my mother couldn't cope with driving alone, certainly not on interstates, they both kept telling me, as if it needed repeating. The plan was he'd escort us to my older sister Julie's place in California and then fly back, leaving us there with the family station wagon and whatever essentials we'd need to start a new life until the rest of our belongings came on a moving truck.

My mother refused to stay in St. Paul without him. But there wasn't any compelling reason to go anywhere specific either. Initially she had lobbied for Baltimore, even though she'd spent most of her waking moments trying to scrub away any trace of her past. From the few times she'd taken me to visit her sisters there, I recalled drawling accents I could barely understand, big crests of teased hair, cat-eye glasses. "Crass" was the word Mom used to describe them. Personally I found them amusing and colorful, but I'd been born in the Bay Area and I still had romantic notions about California. So I went on a campaign to talk her into going there as the better alternative, painting a picture of the ocean and the mountains, of apricot trees and sunshine.

It was the concept of being near my sister, Julie, who was twenty-two years old and shared an apartment in San Jose with a girl she'd known since elementary school, that finally persuaded her. Maybe the three of us being in the same place, Mom reasoned, would hold together what remained of our family.

THE PROSPECT OF RELOCATING was something my parents always presented as a chance to broaden our horizons and make new friends. And I was, in fact, usually at least a little bit excited to see a new house with walls that still smelled of fresh paint, to have new movie theaters to check out, to see new trees in the yard, a new library. But this was different. Dad might as well have been about to release us into outer space.

As a family we were well used to having a rootless existence; transience had always been my father's middle name. He was the adopted child of a single mother, an uneducated barfly. When he was a kid, he was hospitalized after getting hit by a car, and when he was discharged, he was shuttled directly to an orphanage with no explanation about why he was being separated from his adopted mother. He remained there for the next ten years without even a visit from her. So it wasn't surprising that he had a complicated relationship with staying put. Whenever he started to feel uncomfortable, he couldn't help but move on, trailing my mother and me in his slipstream.

The longest we'd ever stuck around in one place was my first seven years in California. I could still remember my first-grade teacher helping us plant bean seeds in containers and the thrill-

14

ing moment I saw a delicate green shoot unfurling in mine. Days after that we moved to Seattle. I secretly fretted for weeks afterward: What had happened to the vulnerable sprout without me there to water it as we'd been instructed to?

I found Seattle's moody blue-green landscape beautiful, though, and I thought it was highly cool that we lived so close to Mount Rainier, an active volcano. And while I wasn't exactly popular, I made friends. Pulling up stakes and relocating to Oklahoma in fifth grade had been a lot tougher. My schoolmates were brutal, as though personifying the harshness of the flat and arid landscape. So it was a relief when Dad got a promotion that took us to Illinois.

Something was missing, however: I saw us as an outline of a family, a sketch, and it was this outline that moved to the suburbs of Chicago into the Harvest Gold Levitt house whose color matched our car's. Still, it was a nice house, at least, and I found a few companions. Even my notoriously shy mother made friends.

But then my father was fired from his post at Federal Office Products. While Mom usually told me too much, about this she was vague. Instead she spent hours hunched over the phone weeping and whispering to her new friends. Dad evaded all my questions, redirecting me to make him an old-fashioned or teaching me how to trim and light his cigar, for which I'd be rewarded with the first puff. Once he took me to the famous Palmer House restaurant in the Loop, where "just us boys" feasted under the gilt ceilings on steak Diane and scalloped potatoes.

After this tense interlude, he'd landed the job in St. Paul. From the start my parents had characterized the Carriage House Estates as a temporary way station, but even though I'd helped by circling "Homes for Sale" ads in the paper every day, they'd never actually gone to check out any of those places. Now I knew why.

THIS TIME THERE WERE no friends to say good-bye to, no regional souvenirs to add to the keepsakes box. We just piled up the car and left.

The corn stubble and grain silos of the Midwest passed by in a blur. I sat in the back amid heaps of bedding and cookware, plus a cooler stuffed with iceberg lettuce and hamburger meat for Peewee, whose aquarium was wedged at my feet. As the miles unspooled, I ground my teeth and exhaled the requisite number of times depending on the day of the week. I spent hours staring at my father, at his thinning salt-and-pepper hair, the profile of his beard when he turned to glance at his blind spot. I wanted to get inside his mind, to understand why he was erasing us, to know whether he still loved us—or had ever loved us in the first place.

He remained noncommittal and genial, saying nothing that gave me any clues. My mother barely spoke, except to order from a menu or request a rest stop. Sometimes Dad tried to fill the silence by turning on the car radio, but it was as if every song had been crafted specially to make us feel worse. "Breaking Up Is Hard to Do," "If You Leave Me Now," "50 Ways to Leave Your Lover." I noticed that each of those fifty ways boiled down to walking away without an apology.

In Nebraska, where our motel had a western motif and a diner dominated by a wagon-wheel chandelier, the silence at the dinner table finally got to be too much for me. I asked if I could go get the road atlas from our room, to see where the next day's route would take us. I was the designated navigator, though really it was mostly a straight shot across an endless series of highways and interstates.

In his aquarium Peewee lifted his head as I let myself into the room. My father's suitcase was splayed open on the bed. To kill time I rifled through his stuff, carefully peeling away the layers: black socks, undershirts, boxers, slacks. A bottle of gin had been tucked away in one corner. The bottle looked smug to me, swaddled so tenderly in its buffer of clothing. I wanted to throw it across the room and smash it to pieces. Why was it so easy for Dad to think about leaving *us* behind, but he couldn't even go on a trip without packing his beloved gin?

As we drove through the Great Salt Lake Basin, the low gray sky above the plains states gave way to a blue I'd never seen before, a three-dimensional hue you could see deep into. A vast and dazzling expanse of sandy whiteness stretched out all around us. I rolled down the window and looked out into it, and the sick feeling I'd been carrying around lifted into a small surge of elation. We pulled over at a turnout with a view of a distant mountain range, its crags and peaks purple with shadow. Mom stayed in the car while Dad shrugged on his tweed jacket with the leather elbow patches.

We walked out of the parking lot and onto the lake bed, our shoes crunching in the salty earth. The air was so dry it hurt the inside of my nose. I read the informational plaque mounted on a cement slab, which described the ecology of the basin and the pioneer days of salt mining. "It's so strange and beautiful," I said, breathing in deeply.

I wanted my dad to agree, to put his hand on my shoulder. Instead he stood without speaking, hands on his hips, surveying the landscape like some kind of prospector. He looked so handsome framed against the azure sky.

I thought of the day he'd driven us down a long dirt road to steal tomatoes from a farm in Santa Clara, which, laughing, we'd piled into a basket in the back of the car. I thought of him pouring Gallo wine into a cut-glass decanter to make dinnertime more special, of him reading me excerpts from the Dale Carnegie books he loved. Of his deep, cackling laugh. My chest clenched with the fervent wish that the two of us could just stay here forever, him and me.

He scuffed at the salt-rimed ground. "It's a very harsh landscape. I sure wouldn't want to get stuck out here," he said finally. Then he got back into the car and turned the key in the ignition.

3

HOTEL CALIFORNIA

When my sister had left home, I'd assumed she'd taken up the thrilling life of a single girl in the big city, coming home each night to drink cocktails in a soaring glass skyscraper. So the squat 1940s apartment complex we pulled up in front of came as a shock, and with some embarrassment I realized I'd based my notions about her residence more or less on the opening-credit sequence of *The Bob Newhart Show*, conflating Bob's commute through downtown Chicago with the cosmopolitan lifestyle I imagined was Julie's.

As my father drove off to find a parking spot, I tried not to remember that today would be the last time I saw him for . . . how long? Maybe I'd never see him again. Maybe he was glad to be rid of us at last. Otherwise why leave us in the first place?

"Oh, Jim, look," said my mother, pointing to some tabby kittens that were sunbathing in the courtyard. I could tell by her strained cheer that she was freaking out about the environment. I often teased her about trying to make our house look like a magazine ad for Lysol, and this place was, well, definitely not that. I knelt to pet a kitten but drew back when I saw that its plump, fuzzy belly was squirming with fleas.

"I found it!" called my mother, knocking on the door to 12A.

I hadn't seen my sister in more than a year, and even though deep down I believed that she didn't like me, I tended to forget that between visits. I'd spent the last leg of this road trip reminiscing about how as kids we used to put on goofy voices to crack each other up—"iguana voice" was our favorite—and imagining the glamour of her life since she'd left for college—the dating, nightclubbing, and discotheques. Now, though, I was nervous.

She came out to greet us looking much older than I'd remembered, dressed in a yellow T-shirt, a leather brocade vest, and ultra-tight jeans. She had winged hair that looked as though it required much maintenance. "You made it! How was the trip?"

"It was a real endurance test," said Dad, coming up the walkway with a pair of suitcases.

Did he mean navigating the Sierra Nevada mountain pass or being in the company of Mom and me? Pushing that thought aside, I told Julie, "Once we got to Utah, it was so beautiful. Like a whole other magical world."

"Uh-huh," she said. The tone in her voice was familiar: I felt like a weird little bug that had flown directly into the zapper of her disdain. "Well, come in."

The apartment immediately brought to mind the term "crash pad." It was furnished with a sagging velveteen couch, an orange beanbag chair, a knotty pine coffee table, and plastic milk crates functioning as bookshelves. Strawberry-scented incense wafted from somewhere. In Julie's room a radio was tuned to an oldies station, and ads for car dealerships and a waterbed showroom kept cutting into the music.

Dad was already unloading our belongings and stacking them

in a corner, beneath a poster of a kitten clinging to a tree branch, captioned HANG IN THERE, BABY! Mom busied herself in the bathroom, refolding Julie's towels, which had been heaped in a chaotic pile. "Did you say hi to Peewee?" I asked my sister. The turtle snapped at the lettuce leaf I was offering him and chewed it slowly.

"I can't believe he's still alive," she said.

Did she think I was a weirdo, somehow immature, for still having him? "He's eighteen," I reminded her. "I read they can live to be forty."

She glanced toward the living room. We could hear our father calling a taxi to get to the airport. "How's Mom doing?" she asked.

"All right, I guess. She's kind of a zombie."

"I'm worried about what she's going to do. I mean, she hasn't worked since . . . well, forever. And what is Dad's *deal* anyway?"

I hesitated, surprised she was asking me; I assumed that Dad had told her everything. He always did. It often made me seethe with envy to hear them chatting on the phone. When he spoke with her, his voice would seemingly take on a relaxed and confiding tone, but in *my* company he'd clam up and become stilted. My sister had no idea how lucky she was. "I guess he just wants a new life without us," I told her. Peewee turned his head, declining another lettuce leaf.

She examined her nails, which were painted coffee brown. "I don't think he *ever* wanted to be a part of our family."

"Yeah." I felt the gulf between us widen. I was unsure how to bridge it, or even whether I wanted to try. I flipped through her stack of LPs in their milk crate. The Eagles, KC and the Sunshine Band, Santana, Jackson Browne.

"You can listen to my albums if you want," she said.

Linda Ronstadt, Bread. I thought of the guy with yellow hair on TV screaming into the microphone like he could destroy cities with the force of his anger alone. "Do you have any punk rock records?" I asked. Her laugh made me wish I hadn't.

The good-byes were over fast. Dad acted as if he were on his way to a weekend golf outing, giving casual hugs first to my sister, then me. I felt the bristles of his beard against my face and smelled his aftershave, a sharp mentholated scent, plus a faint whiff of alcohol on his breath from the night before. Or maybe he'd had a quick drink when he was unpacking the car. There was usually a small bottle in the glove compartment. "Take care of yourself, buddy."

I usually hated it when people told me to take care of myself; it felt ominous, like I was about to be abandoned to sink or swim. But he seemed to mean it, so I tried to absorb the words. To my mother he said, "I'll call in a few days."

The corners of her lips were quivering. "Are you sure you want to do this, Larry?"

Instead of replying to her, he touched my shoulder. "Take care of your mother, too, buddy." And then he was gone.

That night Julie and her roommate, Deb, doused themselves in Aviance perfume and went out to a disco on a double date. Mom and I went for a walk in the neighborhood. Although the sidewalks were strewn with fallen acacia blossoms and the air was sweet with the scent of redwoods, it seemed like we were the only two people outside. Cars whisked past us, their drivers staring straight ahead, as though we were ghosts.

WHEN JULIE AND DEB WENT off to work in the mornings, my mother would labor over the creation of a budget, fretting aloud about how we'd parcel out the monthly stipend Dad had promised while I leafed through the local newspapers, checking apartment listings. All the rentals that looked good—those with gardens and Spanish tiles—were more than the $275 a month we'd allotted. I campaigned for us to live in San Francisco, or at least Palo Alto, where I'd heard there was a high school where you could take classes in Japanese and Super 8 filmmaking. But my mom was determined to stay nearer to Julie.

We were arguing about that one evening when I noticed that the turtle had a drooping, leathery look. "Peewee seems sick!" I called.

My mom picked him up, stroking his head with her index finger. He was only faintly responsive. As she tried to tempt him with a smidgen of raw ground beef, I remembered how when I was a kid I liked to lean over his tank and inhale its funky algae aroma, how I'd let him walk around on the carpet in the sunshine. When you rubbed the underside of his chin, his eyes would squint with pleasure. I wondered if when the turtle died it would unglue my family even more.

Julie came home from work and hung her purse on a hook by the door. She spoke forcefully. "Mom? Listen, I'm sorry, but Deb and I talked about it last night, and she says you guys are cramping our style. She feels like we can't have our friends over and live the way we need to live. You guys can't stay here anymore."

Mom put the turtle down and straightened from where she was kneeling on the floor. "Julie, can we talk about this later?"

"Peewee's dying," I said accusatorily. For the first time, my sister struck me as being just as selfish as Dad.

"I'm sorry"—she persisted—"but Deb pays half the rent. You said you were looking for an apartment anyway."

"But we have nowhere to go!" Mom's voice cracked on the word "go." "Whose side are you on, Deb's or your own family's?"

"I'm sorry," Julie said, not really sounding sorry, I thought, and went to her room, closing the door behind her. Mom doubled over in the beanbag chair, sobbing. She wanted to die! How could her husband have done this to her? She hated her life! Hearing her wail and keen, I had a picture of myself adrift on a vast gray ocean of choppy waves. At that moment I felt more alone with her than I would have if I'd been by myself.

Two, I told myself, because it was a Tuesday.

4

SCHOOLHOUSE ROCK!

J im, it's time to wake up. Honey, wake up."

I opened my eyes. The quality of light coming through the bedroom window was unfamiliar, and the bed was strange. My groggy brain struggled to place itself.

Mom stood in the doorway wearing one of the outfits she put together from the small wardrobe she'd brought from St. Paul: denim skirt, polyester blouse with a Picasso-inspired print pattern, and a heavy camel-hair winter coat that seemed out of context.

Oh, right. It *was* out of context. Because this was California. And today was my first day of high school.

"Get up, honey," Mom repeated in her singsong voice. "I have to leave for work."

Get up? I'd barely slept since the day we'd gone to get me enrolled at San Carlos High.

Based on a photo I'd seen of Sequoia High in nearby Redwood City, I'd pictured my new school as looking quaint, with a bell tower and vaulted ceilings. In reality it resembled an internment camp. A dozen or so low-slung barracks made of pink cinder block radiated out in unevenly placed spokes from a cement courtyard. Cinched around the perimeter was a wall. In this unpromising environment, we'd met with Mr. Mooney, a guidance counselor with yellow teeth who'd described the student body as "a little . . . cliquish."

I'd had to look up the word afterward and had been riddled with anxiety every minute since. The prior night I'd lain awake until the sky was starting to lighten, trying to figure out what I could wear that would make me seem unweird. The bed squeaked as Mom sat beside me. "You'll do great today. Just be yourself and everything will be fine."

"Define 'fine,'" I mumbled into the pillow.

She patted my shoulder. "You're a smart and different boy who sees the world in a special way. Let that light shine through. Don't worry about what other people think. They don't really know you." She kissed me good-bye, smelling like a little too much perfume.

I could tell she wanted to stay home with me, and part of me wished she could. She'd gotten a temp job with Kelly Girl earlier that week, working as a secretary at a tool-and-die company— the first job she'd had since Julie was born. All week I'd been sitting with her at the kitchen table dictating pretend business letters aloud so she could practice her shorthand.

About halfway between San Francisco and San Jose, the sunny suburban town of San Carlos was neither particularly rich nor especially poor. On the east side of Alameda de las Pulgas, the houses had gracious, older flourishes. On the west side, the one-time ranchlands of the foothills had given way to rows of housing developments and apartment complexes like the one we'd just moved into.

My new school was on the crest of a slope, so the walk there was uphill most of the way. The eucalyptus trees lining Torino Drive dropped seed pods and fragrant leaves without providing shade. *Weird*, I thought, *the weather's like a commercial for Hi-C, but everybody is basically indoors.*

Or in their cars. The rumble of a muffler was coming up Torino Drive now. Light glinted off chrome as the sedan rolled to a crawl beside me, Led Zeppelin blasting from the open windows. I clenched with tension, having learned to fear a slowed-down approach. Bullies liked to slow their steps as they neared, to size you up. It was supposed to be intimidating, and it was.

But the teenager behind the window flashed me a smile. Maybe he was a new kid, too, needing directions. "Hey," he drawled.

As I opened my mouth to say "Hey" back at him, he tossed a can out the window. It rolled at my feet, spilling grape soda.

"Fuckin' faggot," he said with a laugh.

How could a word be so true and yet so false at the same time?

The fight-or-flight response was like falling into a river of pure adrenaline, its icy waters closing over my head. Every bone in my body trembled with certainty: *I'm about to be killed.*

The car rumbled away.

I paused to let the fear roll through me in a crescendo, then wane, like thunder, before continuing on my way, my mind working frantically. Was he headed to the same place I was? And if so, would he make tormenting me his special project? I'd never had to fight a boy with that much weight on him. He'd had the broad shoulders and thick neck of a grown man. *At least he's probably in a different grade*, I told myself as my destination came into view.

In the expanse of cement that my *New Student Handbook*

referred to as "the Multi-Use Court," students were paired off or in groups, sneaking a quick smoke. I tried to be inconspicuous, patting my pocket to check that the mimeographed sheet with my locker combination on it was still there.

I sensed at once that the ecosystem was different from the one I was used to. Back in suburban Chicago, there'd been well-defined social groups for sure, but the dividing lines between them were fluid. A jock could audition for a role in the school play without risking humiliation; a skinny loser like me could be a soda vendor at a football game and not get spit on. But here, as I watched the girls with immaculately feathered hair fawning over surfer dudes in ultra flares, the Latino guys in flannel shirts striking tough-guy poses, the black kids sporting Afros and dashikis, I sensed that the social boundaries were not to be crossed. *Cliquish*, I thought. Right. As I passed the lunch tables, a chubby kid in a baseball cap looked in my direction and asked his friend, "Who's that freak?"

This was not the California I'd been expecting.

IN TRUTH, THOUGH, we'd been lucky to find our apartment in San Carlos. There had been major challenges. My mother hadn't yet found her job as a Kelly Girl; she had no references, not even her own bank account. Without her friend Betty, whom she'd known since the 1950s, to help us, we might've ended up camping in the back of the station wagon. Betty had managed to persuade our landlord to accept a lease cosigned by Betty's husband, and not only that, she'd finagled a reduced move-in cost. Thanks to her we were safely ensconced about a two-mile walk up the slope from the center of town.

As upset as Mom was about everything, she was relieved to be somewhere that didn't blatantly advertise our poverty. It was easy for her, in San Carlos's moderate climate and manicured downtown, to pretend we were living the California dream. She decorated our apartment with a sunburst clock and framed Matisse prints from the Salvation Army. And even I had to admit that our new building was kind of cool, like a cartoon of the future with its offset rectilinear shapes and turquoise-painted balconies.

To my mind, though, San Carlos was a plastic paradise, nowheresville. Its main redeeming feature was its tantalizing proximity to San Francisco, and I constantly pestered my mother to drive us up there. We'd been once, to Fisherman's Wharf with Julie. Sure, it was a tourist trap, and the piers where the sea lions hung out barking and grunting stank like rotten fish, but it had an appealingly seedy liveliness that made me crave to explore more of the city.

Mom, however, was not interested in driving that far, certainly not on a freeway, so we remained in a tight orbit around the safety of San Carlos. Some Saturdays we'd run errands. I always asked her to take the slightly longer journey down, a winding road without sidewalks where the architecture eschewed *Brady Bunch* conformity for ramshackle wood-beamed cabins set back in the dappled shade. This hippie idyll evaporated as we pulled in to downtown San Carlos, on Laurel Street, with its identical trees pruned into gumdrop shapes. She'd park our car between the freshly painted diagonal lines, and we'd do our rounds: The Hallmark shop, for cards to send to her sisters. Foodville, a box of yellow bricks that I called the Barbie Dream Home Supermarket. Finally Woolworth's, where we'd frequently have grilled-cheese sandwiches at the lunch counter. I always found myself wandering down the toy aisle there. Model kits, chemistry sets, Uncle Milton's Fascinating Ant Farms. It was like picking a scab, calling up memories of putting together models of monsters with my dad—Dracula, the Creature from the Black Lagoon. He excelled at painting the features in very fine detail. Once, when I was much younger, he'd assembled and painted a Visible Man for me, with organs rendered in delicate, accurate detailing (is that greenish lump really what the liver looks like?). That it was a naked man had given me an extra frisson of pleasure.

IN TIME I MORE OR LESS ACCLIMATED to the routine at my new school. French with Madame Morrisette, whose wig resembled the figure skater Dorothy Hamill's famous wedge hairstyle. Algebra, social studies, gym, advanced-placement English, plus Beginning Journalism as an elective. Of those, only gym was truly painful, because Coach Woodall called me a wimp whenever I couldn't finish my ten push-ups, which was every time. But I was adept at picking up the social cues of a new environment and eager to make this one work for me.

However, either I wasn't doing it as well as usual or there just wasn't any way for an outsider to infiltrate one of the established cliques. The only person who'd shown any interest in me was a born-again Christian girl named Pam who sat next to me in social studies. Her long hair had a neat center part, and she was partial to wearing a T-shirt that read JESUS LOVES YOU. She'd asked me how it felt to have a broken family, and I'd surprised myself by answering honestly that it was a little scary. "I'll pray for you," she'd said, but we didn't have much to say after that.

So I was psyched when Greg Lee from my journalism class invited me for a bike ride. Greg was half Korean, half white, with almond-shaped eyes and glossy black hair that made the other kids call him "Eskimo Greg." Whether or not the moniker bugged him was impossible to tell. He was a burnout, the kind of kid I'd normally expect to beat me up, but there was something gentle about him, and we'd bonded over our enthusiasm for the movie *2001: A Space Odyssey*. I met him after school on an afternoon bright with California wildflowers: poppies, blue lupines, purple owl's clover.

I hadn't ridden a bike in years, and on the ten-speed he loaned me I was wobbly at first, but that soon gave way to a sensation of freedom and control. Greg pedaled fast, jumping the curbs on the wide, smooth asphalt streets of San Carlos. Our shirts billowed like sails, Greg's hair streaming behind him.

In Menlo Park he made a wide circle in the parking lot of an A&W, calling over his shoulder, "I have like a buck-fifty. You thirsty?"

We got an extra-large root beer and rode slow through the center of town, passing the cup back and forth. At one point I reached for my turn and he abruptly drew it back and sucked up the last of it with a theatrical slurping sound, but his laugh was good-natured, and in that moment I knew I'd made a friend.

Finally he coasted to a stop beside a meadow. In the near distance, the hills were cloaked in redwoods. He patted the pockets of his denim jacket. "So hey, you want to get high?"

"Sure," I said without thinking. My heart raced. Suddenly I felt like I'd crossed into some uncharted territory from which there was no turning back. It was a Wednesday, and the impulse to say *Three* aloud pressed on me slightly, but I couldn't let him hear me, so I ground my teeth three times, just in case. Hopefully I wouldn't need the protection.

My new acquaintance busied himself with rolling papers and a Baggie filled with ground buds, approaching the task with great meticulousness, as though it were a solemn ceremony. I tried not to stare. But I wanted more than anything to observe him. His jawline was sharp and manly, his lips were full, and for a second I imagined that they were pressed against mine. He licked the paper, and leaning back in the tall grass, he held the thick joint up for me to admire. I repositioned my legs to hide my burgeoning erection. The whole experience felt forbidden, and that was exciting.

Taking a deep hit, he coughed. "One cough and you're off," he announced in a scratchy voice.

I took a hit, and a swampy greenness filled my mouth. After three attempts I got the hang of it but still wasn't feeling anything. After the fourth I had just decided that maybe pot didn't work on me when I felt a sort of swipe across my consciousness. I cradled my Chicago Film Festival book bag to my chest, seeking the comfort of a familiar object. I felt like I needed to leave, except I wasn't sure anymore where I was.

Greg was lying prone in the grass. I studied his marijuana-leaf necklace and the creases in his jeans, the holes punched in his thick leather belt. My panic started to ebb. I looked at his hand, its palm open to the sky, and considered how much I wanted to hold it. I lay beside him and gazed at the changing cloudscape, imagining myself floating upward, slowly at first, then with great velocity, breathing the clouds' wet, nourishing air. It was a new feeling, as though I'd been cut free.

"How you doing?" Greg asked.

"Fantastic." The syllables popped off my lips as round and light as soap bubbles, and I laughed.

He nodded, seeming satisfied. "Do you get high a lot?"

"Actually, this is my first time."

"You seem like an old pro," he said, gazing out at the hillside. "Y'know . . ." And then he trailed off.

So much time passed that I assumed he wasn't going to finish his thought. Finally he spoke. "I've never made it with a guy," he said as he moved into a new position. "But if I did, you'd be the guy I'd make it with."

I couldn't quite believe what I'd heard. I parsed the individual words, wishing he would repeat them so I could understand their meaning better. "That's a nice thing to say," I eventually managed.

He shrugged his jacket back on. "We should probably head home."

"Cool," I said. My voice sounded weird, disembodied.

On the long ride home, my mind played a soundtrack: "Hejira," the title track of a Joni Mitchell album. I'd looked up the word, which meant "exodus" or "escape." When my family lived together, the Sony stereo had been a fixture in the living room. Now it lived on my chest of drawers, across from my bed. *Hejira* was one of the few records I owned, and I played it a lot lately. Mitchell's voice sounded smoky and world-weary as she sang that life wasn't easy, regardless of what course you chose to take. "Whether you travel the breadth of extremities, or stick to some straighter line," she sang, and I thought I understood.

5

AND THAT'S THE WAY IT IS

The phone was tucked under my mother's chin, dwarfed by giant yellow hair curlers from Woolworth's. "Larry still hasn't sent a check, Betty," she murmured. "It's the third month in a row. And I'm really worried. I don't know how I'm going to put food on the table." A pause, then, "Well, sure it *helps*. But it's not enough to support us both."

"Mom," I stage-whispered from the doorway, with a *wrap it up* gesture.

She muffled the receiver. "What is it?"

I saw the tears in her eyes, but what else was new? "The show. You promised. Come *on*."

Ignoring her put-upon sigh, I went to take my place on the living-room sofa. The show in question was a documentary that PBS was airing, called *Word Is Out*. It was supposed to address how cultural ideas about homosexuality were evolving, and ever since I'd read about it in last week's newspaper, I'd been counting down the days.

I wanted my mother to watch it with me. For all her self-effacement, she had definite opinions, and exchanging views about movies and current events—the energy crisis, the Metric Conversion Act—was a big part of how we related to each other. And needless to say, I was curious, if a bit nervous, to see if she'd recognize her son in any of it.

She nestled beside me on the couch, tucking her floral-print flannel nightgown around her legs, as the program commenced. It was mostly interviews, men and women who spoke about their struggles to be who they were. A few were granola types; others looked more straitlaced. A lot of them, I noticed, seemed to live in San Francisco.

A matronly woman with love beads draped over her drooping bosom sat surrounded by houseplants and musical instruments. "A child comes into the world," she began, "and that child is a human being, and sex research tells us that would probably be a *bisexual* human being. And yet the minute the sex is discovered, that's the time when we start to make a half person out of that baby."

"Why don't you make us some popcorn, honey?" said my mother, her face unreadable.

I hovered on the threshold between kitchen and living room, one eye on the inflating foil dome of the Jiffy Pop, the other on the TV.

The woman continued, "And every institution in society goes into full gear to see to it that girl children are brought up to be intuitive and emotional. While boy children, on the other hand, are brought up to be strong and aggressive and intellectual. And never the twain shall meet! Except, you know, when the two of them get together in the miracle of heterosexual marriage to make one whole person." She chuckled. "Well, divorce statistics, if nothing else, show us *that's* really a myth."

When I came back with the bowl, the set of my mother's mouth signified displeasure. I asked as casually as I could, "What do you think so far?"

"I think it's just sad, the way these people live. Their lives must be so hard."

"This world we live in made their lives hard," I said.

"They made the choice to be like that." Mom reached for a handful of popcorn. "What they're doing is against nature. It's not the way God intended things to be."

I felt stunned. "Since when are you so interested in God?"

"I have my beliefs."

"Maybe your beliefs need to change." The corners of my mouth burned from the salt in the Jiffy Pop.

We watched the rest of the documentary in silence.

THE SCHOOL YEAR LIMPED ON. I got an algebra test back with a red F scrawled on it, the first failing grade I'd ever gotten. Mr. Martinez had handed it to me with disapproval on his face plain as day, and I'd been filled with clammy shame.

In the past I'd never missed a chance to prove my mettle. And my ambitions had extended beyond the classroom. At five I'd sold apricots to neighbors from the tree in our yard out of a Radio Flyer wagon; at ten I was typing up a neighborhood news-letter called the *45th Street Times* for my dad to photocopy at work, with stories like "Hardwick Family Gets New Puppy" and my reviews of the latest movies and television shows. The goal had partly been my parents' attention, but my mom's responses were invariably distracted, while my dad would take my accomplishments as his cue to brag about, say, the big splash he'd made giving a presentation about a new line of filing cabinets, as if I were his competitor.

But my mother had drilled into me that society demanded excellence, so I'd excelled. Now I knew the truth, though: society was happy to throw you to the wolves. Knowing this, I felt my brain just seem to switch off sometimes. And nothing switched it off faster than algebra. So I'd missed a homework assignment or two, then spaced out on the fact that a test was coming. And when Greg Lee, my only friend, invited me to skip a class to smoke a joint with him, what was I going to do, say no?

CHRISTMAS VACATION SHOULD HAVE COME as a welcome relief from school, but it was also our first holiday as a divorced family. It came and went, with token gifts I was dispirited to recognize from the stores of downtown San Carlos, a spate of bickering with Julie, and a whole lot of television. In the absence of my father the roving gourmand, my mother seemed to stake out the frozen-food aisle of Foodville as a kind of revenge, and even our New Year's Eve dinner came in boilable pouches. At midnight she kissed my cheek and said, "Maybe this year will be a little better for all of us, honey."

"Wow. Way to dream big, Mom."

Despite my sarcasm, though, she wasn't the only one clinging to that slim hope. Everything and everybody at San Carlos High made me feel like an alien, and I was getting increasingly depressed and bored. So as the spring semester began, when I saw a flyer posted in the school library announcing a "brown-bag lecture" with a local novelist, I seized on the notion that maybe I wasn't living in a totally colorless world. I might not have recognized his name, but a real author was going to speak right here in this backwater, and that was something, wasn't it?

I brought my lunch to the library, half expecting to be ambushed and beaten up while I ate my tuna sandwich, but a dozen or so other students trickled in and took seats, and shortly a woman who looked about ten years older than my parents stepped to the podium to introduce the writer. In her tweed skirt and matching vest over a frilly purple blouse, she looked like some sort of exotic flower, the perfume of which I could smell from ten feet away. Her eyebrows were drawn on and severe, her thinning hair salon-styled into a bubble do.

"My name is Virginia O'Hagan. I am the advanced junior-level English teacher at San Carlos High School." She stated this as though she were introducing herself as a First Lady, not a teacher.

"It's been said there's a lack of intellectual life here in San Carlos. But a gathering like this one, with your fresh minds in attendance, is a testament to the fact that the life of the mind not only lives here, it thrives."

I felt jolted awake by the sound of her voice. I quelled the uncool urge to applaud, not wanting to draw attention to myself. While the guest author gave his brief and forgettable reading, I studied Mrs. O'Hagan as much as I could without being obvious. Compared to her, the writer sounded flat, a sitcom laugh track. Afterward, as Mrs. O'Hagan set to bossing the librarian around, putting the room back in order, I started stacking chairs, mustering the nerve to strike up a conversation.

"I really enjoyed the presentation," I blurted out.

She looked at me for a long moment.

"I especially appreciated what you said about the school," I added.

"You're new, aren't you?" she said finally.

I gave her a shorthand version of the recent events leading up to my being at San Carlos High, mentioning my mother and father without getting into the part about my father having so recently dumped us.

Mrs. O'Hagan fixed me with a direct look. "Your story evokes in me a passage from *The Bell Jar*. Sylvia Plath describes feeling dislocation between her father, the cold biologist, and her mother, who was a victim of her circumstances. Do *you* have feelings of dislocation toward your father?"

I was impressed by her words, but more than that, I was stunned by how she seemed to intuitively understand some of my deepest struggles. In my head I replayed the phrase "evokes in me a passage." I didn't know what "evoke" meant, but made a mental note to add it to my vocabulary. "How did you know about my problems with my dad?" I asked.

"You wear your secrets like a woman wears a piece of jewelry," she replied. "Have you read *The Bell Jar*?"

"No, but I've heard of it." I hoped that her ability to see through me didn't extend to picking up on that lie.

"Well, you must. I think it'd have a special resonance for you." With that she tossed on a suede cloak, pinning it at the neck with a brooch in the shape of a cat's head. "I've got to prepare for my next class. If you'd like to talk more, we can meet later this week, after school."

As soon as she'd left, I hurried to the card catalog to look up *The Bell Jar*. It wasn't in the collection, but I found something else by Sylvia Plath, a book of poems called *Ariel*. I leaned against a bookshelf and opened it randomly to a poem called "Lesbos."

> Viciousness in the kitchen!
> The potatoes hiss.
> It is all Hollywood, windowless,
> The fluorescent light wincing on and off like a terrible
> migraine

The words exploded in my head. I didn't know outrage could be expressed with poetry, didn't know it was possible to express violence with such precision and clarity. I checked out the book and hoped that once I'd read it, I would get the chance to talk to Mrs. O'Hagan about it.

A FEW DAYS LATER, I was getting textbooks from my locker when Greg, looking even more rumpled than usual, called my name. He leaned so close to speak to me that I could smell the Marlboro Reds and spearmint gum on his breath. "Dude, I have a favor to ask. It's a little matter involving my self-protection."

"What is it?" I asked. I liked Greg, but what was he up to?

"I need you to temporarily hold something." He opened his backpack partway to flash the contents, a large Ziploc full of fragrant pot.

"Whoa, that's a lot." Alarmed, I checked to see if anyone was observing us, but nobody was paying attention. "Are you in trouble?"

"The school narc is onto me. She has this elaborate theory that I'm a dealer."

I met his eyes. "Are you?"

"It would just be for a day," said Greg. "Maximum two."

I pictured the school narc, a thin-lipped woman with a permanent scowl. The thought of any kind of run-in with her filled me with fear. But I was flattered: Greg had lots of friends and acquaintances, yet he'd chosen me. I hid the contraband underneath a sweater in my locker, hoping the smell of weed wouldn't waft out. As I was scrambling the combination lock, Greg placed his hand on top of mine and whispered, "This means a lot to me, man."

Later I sat alone on a narrow band of grass between two of the buildings to eat the lunch my mother had packed for me: a cream cheese and chopped black olive sandwich, some Fritos, apple juice, an orange cut into quarters. Looking at these items made me feel unaccountably lonely. The giant bag of pot in my locker loomed over my thoughts.

I felt the presence of someone watching me, and the muscles of my stomach tightened.

Behind me slouched two guys in nearly identical attire—denim jackets with faux-sheepskin lining and the stringy, long hair favored by stoners. The only way to tell them apart was by the bands their faded concert tees advertised.

"Hey, homo," called the one in the Black Sabbath shirt.

So much for not drawing attention to myself. I realized with mounting fear how secluded the spot was, how out of everyone's sight. As always when this happened, I had to combat the raw certainty that I was about to be killed.

The one in the AC/DC shirt remarked conversationally, "I hear Greg Lee likes to get his Eskimo dick sucked. Are you his little dicksucker?"

"I'm guessing he'd probably rather take it up the ass," said Black Sabbath. AC/DC snickered.

I considered making a break for it but opted to stick it out, because I'd learned the hard way that running could just serve to activate a kind of predator instinct. Black Sabbath rocked back on his heels. "You know that Eskimo faggot pretty well, right? The two of you have something real sweet going on, huh?"

"Might want to think about whose dick you're sucking," advised AC/DC. "Suck the wrong dick, you can get the clap."

"Four," I murmured, for it was a Thursday. "Four, four."

"What'd you say?"

"I said 'Whatever.' Can I go now?"

"'Can I go now?' Jesus Christ, you really are a faggot," said Black Sabbath.

I started walking backward and stumbled, catching myself before I landed. Their laughter followed me across the Multi-Use Court.

6

THE SAN FRANCISCO TREAT

The Saturday paper thumped at the door.

I spread it across the kitchen table to read the movie section, my favorite part. It displayed showtimes for the whole Bay Area, including the small art-house cinemas of San Francisco that, with their foreign films, midnight movies, and "Meet the Director" screenings, seemed like the height of sophistication to me. Even their names were exotic: the Castro, the Roxie, the Strand, the Clay, the Surf.

When I saw that *Fellini Satyricon* was playing the next evening at the Strand, I was dizzy with excitement. Last year I'd checked out a book about that movie from the library, staring for hours at stills. My favorite was of two male characters fighting over a slave boy they were both using for sexual favors. It gave me a tantalizing sense of peering into a world that was sexy, bizarre, and outrageous. I'd wanted to see the movie for so long that the prospect had come to seem impossible. And now I could.

I ran to my room to check the bus timetables. The 7F ran express from San Carlos to San Francisco, making a stop along

Mission Street near the theater. That evening I did the cooking: omelets with toast. My mom always said how much she liked to eat breakfast for dinner. Normally she washed the dishes while I retreated to the TV, but this time I did that, too.

"I'm going to go see a movie in San Francisco tomorrow. I'm taking the SamTrans," I told her decisively, hanging the dish towel back on its hook. "You just need to pick me up at the bus stop down the hill afterward, okay?"

She was working an ice-cream scoop into a brick of orange sherbet from Foodville. "Honey, you can't go to San Francisco. It's dangerous."

"I'll be fine."

"There are a lot of bums in the city. And criminals. Jim, they shot sixteen people in that restaurant! Don't they have that movie in San Carlos?"

"No, they don't have that movie in San Carlos," I said, trying and failing to sound like a smart-ass. "They don't have any movies like that here. And the Golden Dragon Massacre was Chinese gangsters killing other Chinese gangsters in a Chinese restaurant in Chinatown! Does that sound like something that'll happen to me?"

But I knew she wasn't actually that far off base. It seemed like every time we watched the news, they'd reveal the existence of yet another mass murderer at large in our state, each one with his own nickname, like comic-book villains come to life. The Vampire of Sacramento, who drank his victims' blood and cannibalized their remains. The Dating Game Killer, the Trailside Killer. The Scorecard Killer picked up teenage boys, drugged them, and burned them with a cigarette lighter before throwing their dead bodies out of his car. One of the bodies they'd found had been castrated.

Changing tack, I reasoned, "I only need you to pick me up downtown. And six dollars. Or even five. You could even come with me if you want to!" I hated the way my tone had gone from resolute to childishly pleading.

The silverware drawer clattered open as she went for the spoons. "That's a lot of money."

"I'll pay it back," I begged.

"Weren't we going to go to See's tomorrow?"

Her face was guileless, but this was a gambit, I knew, to make me feel guilty. Going to the See's Candies in San Mateo had become one of our new California traditions, a continuation of our trips to the Fanny Farmers of the Midwest, and it was sacred. We'd buy a half pound of mix 'n' match, then sit in the car eating ourselves sick, laughing at our own greed, and mock squabbling over which was objectively the best flavor, the Bordeaux or the California Brittle.

I brushed a strand of hair out of my eyes with annoyance. "It's not like a regular movie. If I don't go tomorrow, I'll never get to see it."

"I still think it's too dangerous," she said with a sigh, putting the carton away. "But I can't stop you from doing what you want to do."

"Does that mean I can go?"

She turned to look at me. "I can't stop you from doing what you really want to do," she repeated. I was giddy with relief.

The next morning there was seven dollars on the kitchen counter, along with a note on her flowered stationery. It read, *"Here's money for the bus and the movie and anything else you might need. There's a sandwich in the fridge for when it's dinnertime and you're still out. I've gone out with Betty today. Back at 3 p.m. We'll go to See's next weekend. Love and kisses, Mom."*

She might not have left such a sweet note if she'd thought to ask about my latest report card, currently hidden between the pages of my journal. It shouldn't have been surprising that I'd failed algebra this semester, but it was hard to assimilate. Was this really me, the good boy? It was strangely liberating, with the thrill of rebellion about it, but I knew that Mom would freak out and lecture me about how I was going to disappoint her by ending up like her father, an alcoholic window washer with an ugly temper that often led to beatings.

I wanted to leave it all behind—San Carlos, algebra class, my clingy mom—and strike out for my newfound world.

I boarded the 7F just before the bus rolled onto the Bayshore Freeway. There were a half dozen people on it: nurses, some Mexican guys in janitors' jumpsuits, a construction worker who was completely covered in dust. It made stops in an industrial park in San Mateo and then at SFO, where I watched a plane take to the sky and tried to imagine where it was headed. Outside, fog was creeping over the hills. By the time we got into the city proper, it was gray and drizzling.

As we rolled into the Mission District, I checked the names of every street, anxious I might miss my stop. I'd forgotten to bring a map and couldn't tell how far along we were. It looked nothing like the Rice-A-Roni commercials on TV, nothing like Fisherman's Wharf. No sparkling bay or jaunty cable cars, no neatly stacked rows of "painted lady" Victorians. Many of the apartment buildings were in dire need of fresh paint, and the sidewalks were strewn with litter. I saw an old white man with a scabby face, sitting in a wheelchair having an argument with an emaciated black guy wearing a purple pimp coat. When the bus reached Eighth Street, I yanked the cord hard.

Compared to the suburban movie theaters I was used to, the

Strand on Market Street looked old and ramshackle, as though they'd just slapped a layer of garish pink paint and used carpeting over all its worn-out parts. I approached the box office and bought my ticket with some trepidation.

And then, even more gingerly, I hesitated on the stairway outside the men's room.

Like many boys, my first forays into public men's rooms entailed my mother waiting for me just outside the door. But we'd never stopped doing it that way. It wasn't something we ever discussed, so I'd never had to explain it. But if forced to articulate it to myself, I might've said that I wanted her there because public men's rooms were complicated psychological minefields. They were lawless spaces, with their graphically sexual graffiti and rank bodily smells, their veiled glances and proximity to exposed penises. It all felt like an electrified fence I wasn't ready to touch.

The men's room at the Strand was poorly lit. I certainly wasn't going to attempt to use a urinal, so I entered a stall. There was a fist-size hole cut crudely into the partition. I'd encountered those holes before, not sure of their purpose other than the notion that they were somehow sexual in nature. This time, as I fumbled to secure the latch on the door, I saw the eyes of the stranger, an elderly gentleman, in the next stall peering at me. Now I was *sure* it was sexual. But was it an invitation of some kind? A demand? Or was he just looking? My privacy felt violated, yet I was intrigued.

I met the stranger's bloodshot eyes and paused, suddenly flashing on the image of my mom watching the evening news. *The Movie Bathroom Killer! The boy's body was found in pieces in an alley behind San Francisco's Strand Theater.* Curiosity and the need to pee notwithstanding, I left, grinding my teeth seven times to dispel the demons that snapped at my heels as I hurried to the auditorium.

I chose a seat in the same row as a middle-aged hippie lady whose Janis Joplin hair and layers of corduroy and velvet gave her a safe, comfy appearance, homey as a sofa cushion. She leaned over and tipped her box of candy at me. "Want some Good & Plenty?"

I nodded and accepted a handful.

"The food they have here is poison," she said, "but I gave in. Probably the best thing you could eat is the tobacco inside the cigarettes."

Waiting for the lights to go down, I thought about the bathroom stranger's hungry, watchful gaze. It was almost as if not having Mom at her usual post had summoned him. Actually, come to think of it, she hadn't waited for me outside a bathroom since we were in St. Paul, I realized. Among all the other changes, that one, too, had happened without my input. But then the lights dimmed, and all these thoughts dimmed with them.

The opening shot of *Fellini Satyricon* was stark and beautiful, a slow pan over a wall scrawled with ancient graffiti. A beautiful half-naked young man cried angrily, "And who condemned me to be alone?"

From there it only got better. Figures in eerily garish makeup danced and wept and cackled with wild laughter amid elaborate and strange set pieces. Voices came in urgent, hushed, yet strangely staccato bursts of Italian, giving the subtitled dialogue an uncanny force and meaning. Women in gauze dresses floating to and fro on a giant swing, a shackled elephant, a Minotaur in a dark labyrinth. I was spellbound and reverent. *This is what people mean when they say they've had a religious experience*, I thought.

When the 7F pulled in to the San Carlos station later that night, my mom was waiting for me in the Dodge, curlers peeping out from beneath a kerchief.

Wishing I were speaking Italian, I told her, "It was even better than I could possibly imagine! It was like time-traveling into weird, weeeird ancient Rome. The colors in the movie were like they were from some other universe. And the music—it was old and new at the same time. And the costumes! The whole thing blew my mind."

"I really don't like driving in the dark. I just can't see well enough," she said, turning onto Torino Drive.

Usually a display of aloof coldness like this would spark an argument between us, but I let it go. I had something else now, something that was all my own, and I didn't need her approval.

The next morning I ran up the hill to school. Breathless, I paused to look ahead and took in the shining water of the bay, the faint outline of the mountains beyond. You could never have a view like this in the Midwest. If I were walking to school in Chicago now, I'd be seeing bare brown yards, leafless trees.

It was good to be here, I thought.

7

DON'T LEAVE HOME WITHOUT IT

Busing to San Francisco to see movies fast became a habit. I saw *Teorema, Death in Venice, Nashville, Last Tango in Paris, Cries and Whispers, Les Enfants Terribles, Solaris.* Each time my mom left me money and a sandwich.

On this day, I left a couple of hours earlier than usual so I could check out Polk Street. I knew that Polk Gulch, along with the Castro District, was supposedly a hub of gay life, and I wanted to see it for myself. I don't know what I was expecting—maybe some sort of homosexual utopia—but it wasn't the row of seedy-looking hot-dog stands and pizza joints that I found.

I did, though, see men who looked obviously gay. A young man in pink clogs walking a poodle, a guy in black leather chaps with a matching cap and motorcycle boots, a male couple holding hands. The couple had plaid shirts, bushy mustaches, and bandannas tucked into the back pockets of their Levi's—one yellow, one blue—which I knew was supposed to advertise sexual preferences of some kind.

As I passed them, one said to the other, "Jesus, the chickens get younger every day around here!"

"Baby chicks," his boyfriend cracked.

I poked around inside a few stores, although if they hadn't had flyers for gay nightclubs and parties littering their countertops, I wouldn't have known the difference between them and any other shop selling hardware or used clothes. Soon it'd be time to go catch my movie anyway. I sat on the steps of an apartment building to eat my brown-bag dinner.

An older guy with long stringy hair flounced down beside me. He was wearing a lavender woman's turtleneck sweater and matching slacks that had seen better days. Uneasy in his presence, I put my sandwich away half eaten, but before I could get up, he spoke to me.

"You know," he announced in an arch, womanly voice, "every man has an opinion like every man has an asshole."

I couldn't help but laugh. "I guess that's true."

He peered at me through glasses that were held together with masking tape. "You're young. Are you in high school?"

"Yeah, I'm in ninth grade."

"And do you like it?"

"Well . . . um, not so much."

He nodded sagely. "I knew I was in for a rough ninth grade when the entire student body of Hollywood High chased me down Santa Monica Boulevard after school one day."

"That sounds bad."

"Believe me, it was." His mouth hung agape, and I could see that at least half his teeth were rotten.

"I've always known that I was a woman," he (or, I supposed,

she) continued. "My mother didn't know it, and my father used to try to beat it out of me. But I always knew. I just had to grow up enough so I could be who I really was. Someday maybe I'll become a woman on the outside. But I already am inside, where it matters, you see."

I had the urge to get up and leave, but Mom had taught me that you should have manners and give everyone the time of day.

Seeing my hesitation, she said, "Maybe you'd like to come over to my place. I don't live far from here. I promise I won't rape you! We can try on dresses and makeup and have a fashion show for the pigeons on the fire escape. That's what I do sometimes. They're very kind critics!"

I smiled. "Maybe some other time?"

"Sure, anytime you like. I'm always around. You can't miss me. No one can!"

THESE TRIPS TO SAN FRANCISCO boosted my confidence, and after a few weeks, I deemed myself sophisticated enough to reapproach the worldly Mrs. O'Hagan.

When I found her classroom, its door was ajar and no one was inside; I went in, feeling as though I were breaking a rule. It was decorated with hanging plants and posters of medieval paintings and ancient cities. A miniature reproduction of *The Thinker* was presided over by towering stacks of books. One stack was topped by a tome with the intriguing title *The Masks of God*. This one I picked up and started to leaf through.

"Have you read Joseph Campbell?"

Her voice startled me. "Nope." *Nor even heard of him*, I didn't say out loud. I put the book back where I'd found it.

Mrs. O'Hagan took a sip from a steaming mug and set it

down among the clutter of her desk. I leaned in to look at the appliquéd photograph on the mug. "Are those your cats?"

"You notice things, don't you? Yes, that's my little menagerie: Coco, Princess Mikado, and Ophelia. I shower them with treats. Human children can be such a nuisance. Cats are much easier."

I laughed, sure that if I ever had children, I'd feel the same. "I had a cat named Edgar when we lived in Seattle," I said. "I named him for Edgar Allan Poe, who I thought was a magnificent writer." Tapping into my chameleon quality, I found myself automatically attempting to mimic Mrs. O'Hagan's flowery way of speaking.

In fact Edgar had been feral; I'd started putting kibble out for him on our back steps, and slowly over time he'd become a pet. But when we left for Oklahoma, I wasn't allowed to bring him along. *Now, you be a strong man and you're going to be just fine,* I'd told him, hugging him tightly. I still wondered if he was okay, but I couldn't shake the image of his body lying in a ditch somewhere.

"By the way, I saw *Fellini Satyricon,*" I told Mrs. O'Hagan. "In the city. I loved it!"

"Ah yes, *Il Maestro* Fellini! A truly original mind," she said, and I basked in the glow of this appraisal, which seemed by implication to speak well of my *own* mind. "Tell me, Jim, aside from movies, what grabs your interest? Do any of your classes engage you?"

I paused. It would be strange to tell a teacher what I thought of other teachers. As though reading my thoughts, she added, "Your opinions are safe with me. I'm a bit of an outsider here myself. Would you be so kind as to clean the chalkboard for me?"

The blackboard was covered in her precise cursive script. At the top were the words "Themes of Resurrection in Shakespeare's 'Hamlet.'" As I swept the eraser across the blackboard in broad arcs, I said, "I wish *we* were reading *Hamlet*. Mrs. Shannon is more interested in writing detention slips than in teaching plays."

"Nothing's stopping you from reading *Hamlet* whenever you like. I have an extra copy somewhere—voilà." She extricated a paperback edition from under an empty cottage-cheese container. "Have you read *The Bell Jar* yet?"

"Not yet, but I did read *Ariel*. It was excellent."

"Sylvia Plath was one of the world's great sensitive souls," pronounced Mrs. O'Hagan. "Too sensitive for this earth, probably. I saw her speak in the early sixties. You know she committed suicide?"

"Yes, it was in the author biography. She did it in 1963, just a few days after I was born. That somehow makes me feel even more linked to her."

"You're an avid reader, then."

The approval in her voice was like a salve. "I've always been."

"Do you take after your mother? Is she an avid reader?"

"To tell you the truth, she's more of an avid coupon clipper."

"Ha. I see," she said, and glanced at the clock. "Well, it's time for me to go home. Perhaps we can continue our burgeoning little friendship next week."

"I'd like that." I hesitated, wishing I could've expressed my enthusiasm for Sylvia Plath more artfully, before realizing with a jolt that I'd been so engaged in our conversation that I'd lost track of time. I'd meant to catch the 3:16 SamTrans to the city, intending to see *The Innocents* at the Strand.

Well, there was always the train. More expensive, but at least I'd get there in time to grab a seat before the lights went down.

Walking up the rattling aisle of the Southern Pacific, I passed a youngish blond man wearing wire-rimmed John Lennon–style spectacles and a bright peach-colored scarf wrapped around his neck. Something about him stood out from the usual commuter crowd. Intrigued, I took a seat in the row behind him and spent the next several miles gazing intently at the back of his neck.

I tried to recall his face, which I decided was fine-featured. Soon I'd invented a backstory for him: he was an intellectual on his way to one of the libraries at Stanford University to hunt down some obscure volume for a research project. At the precise moment I landed on that theory, he glanced behind him as if sensing my gaze.

I looked away and pulled my knees to my chest, assuming the protective position I normally favored while riding into the city. Shortly he turned and glanced at me again, and this time I didn't chicken out. I stared back, holding my breath to steady myself.

To my astonishment he rose and came to me. "Do you mind if I sit with you?"

I grinned, feeling my face flush. "Sure."

I was suddenly conscious of the black turtleneck and green painter's pants I was wearing. I'd made my mom get the pants for me at Kmart as part of a new, more artistic look that I'd been trying to cultivate in the last few weeks: they had slanted pockets on the sides, and a carpenter's loop, though probably no one who'd ever bought these pants had used it to hold a hammer.

"My name is Jean-Paul," he said, pronouncing it with a thick French accent. He seemed to be in his mid-twenties.

"I'm Jim." To have his body so close to me made me light-headed. I attempted to push down the anxiety that was rising up in me.

"And where are you going, Jim?" He smiled.

"I'm going to see a . . . a film." I'd been about to say *movie* but opted instead for its more sophisticated cousin. "*The Innocents*, at the Strand Theater." Oh, his face was mesmerizing: blue eyes and smooth, almost polished-looking skin.

"Do you live in the city?"

"No, but I go there all the time. Where do you live?"

"Near the Conservatory of Music. I study there." He explained that he was from Paris, in San Francisco to further his work as a conductor of classical music.

"I love classical music," I said, frantically racking my brain for something more to say on the subject. "My favorite piece of music is Pavane in F-sharp Minor."

"Oh, you know Fauré?"

Success! "Yes. I listen to that at night sometimes." In fact, it was the sign-off for the classical station on the radio, and I would lie on my bedroom carpet and listen to it almost every night before I went to sleep. Its slow and mournful chords made me imagine my mother as a dead princess being carried in an open coffin. Or sometimes I was the princess, alive but enduring some tragedy that had altered the course of my life forever.

"Well, Fauré is okay. But I much prefer Beethoven. That is *real* music."

My heart sank slightly. "I like Beethoven, too," I blurted. "Excuse me—" I feigned a five-breath cough into my fist. That made me marginally safer, but only marginally. The train rattled over a crossing.

I had just decided that he'd lost interest when he said, "Would you like to go to a café and have coffee with me?"

I felt as though I were entering a dream. My first thought was that I'd never actually had coffee before. I'd tasted it, but I'd never really *had* it—and certainly not in a café with a Frenchman!

Downtown, as we boarded a streetcar, he suggested we go

to a place farther up Market Street called Cafe Flore, an artists' hangout I'd read about, but as the N-Judah streetcar rolled toward the Castro District, Jean-Paul changed the plan. "Why don't we take a walk in Golden Gate Park," he suggested. "It's a beautiful day. A day in paradise."

I hadn't seen Golden Gate Park since I was a little boy. I recalled pictures in our family photo album: toddler me with chubby knees on an Easter-egg hunt. It occurred to me now, with a mix of excitement and trepidation, that I wasn't fully certain of what Jean-Paul's intentions were, though I had a pretty good idea, and hunting Easter eggs was not among them.

I'd never had sex with anyone before. Not real sex anyway. There'd been some of the usual experimenting, of course; when I was really young, a friend had dangled his penis a few inches from my face like a snake charmer before his kid sister walked in and broke the spell. And later, in Oklahoma, I'd gotten further with a certain farm-boy friend, far enough to feel as if something had really happened. But rubbing our hairless pubescent bodies against each other inside his sleeping bag suddenly seemed very far away from real, adult sex. Now that the possibility of it was so near, would I do something stupid and ruin it?

But as we hopped off the streetcar in the Upper Haight and strolled into the park, Jean-Paul seemed relaxed, chatting about how much he was enjoying San Francisco, about a hike on Mount Tamalpais he'd taken with friends from the conservatory.

I knew that if my mother could see me, she'd probably scream that I was going to end up strangled with piano wire and left for dead, but I didn't get a creepy or weird vibe from him, so I figured I'd be okay—although when my foot landed on a crack in the sidewalk, part of me was afraid that evil would seize the chance to grasp this incredible experience in its long fingers. But instead I fell into step beside Jean-Paul, telling myself I didn't need protection.

Golden Gate Park was gardenlike yet wild, with shadowy hemlocks and oversize ferns. We left an expanse of manicured lawn for a mazelike footpath that wove through rhododendron bushes covered in pink blossoms.

There he stopped and reached for my hand. The sunlight, filtered through petals and leaves, shone on his face. "You are a very beautiful young man," he said.

I felt like he was seeing a part of me that had never yet been seen. "You are, too," I breathed.

"I would like to spend some time with you."

"I would like that very, very much," I agreed. My lips were quivering. The distant sounds of other parkgoers were a million miles away.

"My apartment is close to here. But my landlady is home, so it makes me nervous to bring friends there. I think I know a place with some privacy. Come."

He led me into a bower sheltered by trees and took my face in his hands. Then he kissed me.

His lips felt lustrous and smooth. I didn't know what to do, how to respond, but it felt amazing, utterly new. It wasn't a dream. I wasn't imagining it. I was kissing a Frenchman in Golden Gate Park. We sank to our knees.

The dirt felt cold and damp. I tried to follow his lead, undoing his pants when he undid mine.

I stared in wonder for a moment at his cock. Everything about it was so different from my own: longer, more slender, and uncircumcised, which was something I'd only faintly understood, and it had a slight bend. In my mouth it was salty, a little funky, raw, slightly sickening yet pleasurable. The barnlike aroma of his pubic hair, too, was strange, even dirty, but still exciting. I worried that my teeth were grazing him. I worried that I couldn't possibly be doing it right.

Turn off your brain and just go with it, I told myself. Maybe that should be my new motto in life? Soon Jean-Paul came in my mouth. I was unsure about whether or not to swallow it, so I compromised, swallowing half and spitting out the rest.

Someone moved in the underbrush nearby. Jean-Paul stood up and briskly zipped his jeans. "There's someone coming," he said, motioning for me to get up.

Why did he care? But I rose slowly, buttoning my pants. Somewhere close by, a dog gave a volley of sharp barks; I heard the clattering wheels of a skateboard, cars honking.

As I followed Jean-Paul out of the bushes, we passed a skinny Latino guy sucking the cock of a heavyset white guy. The white guy's hand rested on the Latino guy's head as it bobbed up and down, and I noticed he wore a wedding ring. I turned to Jean-Paul, full of questions I didn't know how to ask, but he seemed to be avoiding my gaze.

We came out onto the asphalt drive that bisected the park and walked back to the street without speaking. My breath was coming fast, and I was disoriented. I wasn't sure which side of the park we'd emerged on. Evening fog was rolling in, shrouding everything in damp mist, and the temperature was dropping. Cars rushed in either direction, commuters heading for home. It was just after seven; I'd told my mother I'd be back by seven-thirty.

Would it be okay, I wondered, to ask him to accompany me to the station? Probably it'd seem too needy, but I really wanted him to.

He decided it for me. "I have a class to get to."

Could I feel any smaller than I did right now? "Can I see you again?"

"Yes, that's all right," he replied, sounding preoccupied. He gave me instructions on how to find a streetcar to get back downtown, while writing his number on a scrap of paper. Even his handwriting looked foreign.

Then he gave me a deep, long kiss. "San Francisco is the only city in the world where you can do this and it is okay," he said, and walked away, his boot heels ringing out on the pavement.

On the crowded southbound train, the only seat I could find was across from a woman in secretarial clothes who stared at me with open disapproval, as though underage gay sex was written all over my face.

In the cramped bathroom compartment, surrounded by molded steel fixtures, I looked at myself in the mirror. Jean-Paul's kiss seemed to somehow continue, as if the touch receptors in my mouth were still firing. I stuck out my tongue to see if anything looked different. I felt completely changed. Was it love I was feeling?

When I came home, my mom greeted me at the door with her head covered in the ammoniac goo required to refresh her frosted highlights. She saw her true, mousy-brown hair color as something shameful, but shelling out the extra cash to a salon was an equal sin.

"Honey, it's so late, I'm glad you're home. How was the movie?"

"It was terrific. I think Jack Clayton might be one of my new favorite directors. You would've liked it, I think."

I was surprised by how easily the lie had come.

8

SHEENA IS A PUNK ROCKER

Walking up the hill to school, I breathed deeply, filling my lungs with the clean air, enjoying its saline coolness. I was suffused with a sense of lightness and liberation; my vision felt sharper, perceiving fuller, richer colors. For the millionth time, I pulled out the scrap of paper with Jean-Paul's phone number on it. It seemed to radiate its own energy, connecting me with him.

A Ford Pinto the color of bird shit slowed down as it neared. A male voice from inside the car yelled "Cocksucker!" and then the engine gunned as the car moved on. Even though my heart was pounding and my palms were slick with sweat, instinctively I thought of Jean-Paul saying, *You are a very beautiful young man,* and instead of wanting to curl into a ball I shouted after the retreating car—once it was safely down the block—"At least I'm having sex, you fucking moron!"

Feeling newly worldly and adult, I decided to drop in on Mrs. O'Hagan at lunchtime. As I strode down the hallway, I caught my reflection in a glass case full of academic trophies, and for once I didn't completely despise what I saw.

She was bent over a student paper when I came in, red pencil flying; without pausing in her grading, she lifted an index finger in a *wait a second* gesture. I stood by the windowsill breathing in the dusty perfume of the place. There was a drooping philodendron, a few dried-out ferns. I put my finger into the foliage, crunching past desiccated undergrowth.

"Those plants need some TLC," said Mrs. O'Hagan, looking up at last. She was wearing a purple alpaca poncho, giving her the appearance of a grape-colored tepee.

I lifted the watering can that was leaving a rusty ring on the windowsill. "I could give them a drink if you'd like?"

"Yes, thank you. How are you? How is your mother?"

It was on the tip of my tongue to tell her everything about Jean-Paul, but I didn't dare. How would I even begin? *I met a guy from Paris and sucked his cock in the park*? "Mom's okay," I answered instead. "She works at her job and eats a lot of chicken breast. She keeps up with the latest in women's fashions."

Mrs. O'Hagan stacked a pile of graded papers. "You sound angry at her. Based on what you've said so far, though, she's completely devoted to you."

"Maybe." I pulled dead leaves off the philodendron and tossed them into the wastebasket. "She's very good at keeping up appearances. But she acts so helpless, just letting everything happen *to* us. It's like having a toddler in charge."

"Maybe she struggles with being the adult in the family. Maybe she'd rather be the child."

Her words swirled around in my head like bits of grit in a vacuum cleaner. They might've made cogent sense to her, but to me they were gobbledygook.

"Being a teenager is traumatizing, isn't it?" she continued. "You're learning that you can't always depend on your mother for comfort. And your mother is learning she can't always provide it either. Ultimately you have to learn to stabilize yourself."

Her words filled me with sorrow. I left the plants alone and turned to her. "But how? What am I supposed to do?"

"There's nothing you *can* do," she replied. "Be patient and remind yourself that there are all sorts of miraculous things happening that are beyond your control."

Miraculous things. Again the desire welled up to tell her about Jean-Paul. Maybe she would understand, compare me to Oscar Wilde. Surely she would be impressed by the fact that he was a classical-music conductor! In any case she probably wouldn't be repelled. Not totally anyway. "Speaking of . . . uh, things beyond your control," I began.

But the bell rang, ending the lunch hour, and Mrs. O'Hagan bade me good-bye with a briskness that, while not unkind, didn't invite further conversation.

As soon as I got home from school, I unfolded the magical scrap bearing Jean-Paul's number.

A woman answered. "Yes, who is it?" She had an accent that seemed European.

"Uh, hi, I'm calling for Jean-Paul?"

"Who is this?" she repeated.

"This is Jim, I'm a friend of his. Is he home?"

"I have to check. He does not take calls usually on this line." She sounded angry, and I worried I'd done something inappropriate. I heard the clunk of the receiver being put down.

"*Oui,* hello?"

It was thrilling to hear his voice. "Jean-Paul?" I tried to pronounce it the French way. "It's Jim. From the train the other day?"

"Oh, yes. Hello."

There was an awkward silence that I sensed was up to me to fill, so I cut to the chase. "Would you like to get together sometime?"

"I am very busy at the conservatory. There is a chance that I may become more free after one week. You can call me then."

"Oh, okay. Um . . . how did your classes go today?"

"Fine. They were fine." Another long pause. "I need to go now."

"Okay. I should be going, too," I said, as if I had somewhere to be. "I'll talk to you soon." My heart sank. It was Friday. One weekend plus five more days of school to get through, like watching an endless loop of TV reruns, before it'd be okay for me to call again. I wasn't sure how I'd endure it.

BUT AS IT TURNED OUT, another "miraculous thing" occurred. It happened Monday morning, in the form of a new student sitting at the back of Madame Morrisette's Beginning French class.

Even though she was slouched in her seat, she towered over most of the guys. She was wearing a form-fitting polka-dotted 1950s dress cinched at the waist with a wide black patent-leather belt. Her bleached-platinum hair was pulled back into a messy ponytail, her lipstick a shock of carmine red. On her lap was a glossy black purse instead of the backpack everyone else carried. Her shoes were mile-high stiletto heels. The cheerleader in the seat behind viewed her with open disgust.

I snuck as many glances her way as I could without losing my place in *Jeunes Voix, Jeunes Visages*. Her pouty mouth, her posture, her whole aura exuded boredom. She spent most of the lesson doodling in the margins of her textbook.

A punk rocker! She had to be, right? She was the only person

I'd ever seen who remotely resembled what I'd seen on that TV segment so many months prior.

She couldn't have been a more intimidating presence if she'd had DON'T FUCK WITH ME tattooed on her forehead, but the sight of somebody who appeared to be so utterly outside of, and un-interested in, the culture of San Carlos High gave me courage. Besides, wasn't I officially an outsider myself? A sexual outlaw like Jean Genet, whose existence Mrs. O'Hagan had made me aware of?

As a general rule of thumb, I dealt with strangers by modeling myself on my father, who had the natural amiability and power of blending in that mark the experienced salesman. So outside in the hallway after the bell rang, I introduced myself to this fascinating creature and asked her what school she'd transferred from.

With raised eyebrows, as if I'd done something comical, she took my extended hand and shook it, then told me her name was Helle and that she was an exchange student. Her accent made her sound like she was chewing on rocks.

"Hella? Like . . . 'hell' with an *a* at the end? Oh my God, that's so cool!" I exclaimed.

"Ya, like 'hell,'" she said, smiling wryly. "You like that, huh? But *e*, not *a*. *Helle*. In Denmark this is a very ordinary name.

"I was staying with a family in Oregon," she went on, pawing through her purse. "They loved to go to church every Sunday. They thought my name means, like, I am with the Devil. So as soon as I was just a little bit naughty, they kicked me out. Then I got sent to this fuckhole."

Students hurried past us; in their midst Helle looked like a flamingo in a flock of chickens. She was still rummaging through her handbag, which I couldn't help but peek into. It was a mess: sloppy-looking photocopied flyers, nail polish, a half pint of whiskey.

Not wanting her to disappear yet, I asked, "Do you know how to find your next class?"

"I have no fucking idea. Aha! There you are, little bastards," she said with satisfaction, producing a pack of Marlboros. "Anyhow, wherever it is, there's no way I'm going without first having a ciggy."

"Oh, you can't smoke in here, the narcs'll catch you. Go out to the field or the parking lot," I advised, glad I had something useful to tell her.

She looked down at me—as tall as I was, in her high heels she must've stood six and a half feet—and lit the cigarette that dangled between her red, red lips. Wordlessly she blew the smoke out her nose. I was awestruck by her flagrant flouting of regulations.

I asked her if she had the card with the class schedule printed on it that they gave newly enrolled students. At this she rifled through her purse again. "Jesus fucking Christ, where did I put that thing? I'm so hungover today, I can't remember a thing."

"I can probably figure it out, if you know what kind of class it is."

She pulled out a sheet of paper. "Ya, here it is. Chemistry."

"I'll walk you to the labs," I said, leading the way. Her shoes click-clacked as we went. Walking beside her filled me with pride, as though she were some sort of protective talisman. "So how long have you been in the United States?"

"Seven months. I thought America would be interesting. I had no idea it would be the most stupid place on the planet. People only, only, only talk about this bloody *Star Wars*."

I laughed. "Do you have, like, a new host family now?"

She looked as though she were smelling shit. "The wife, all she does is knit . . . what do you call them? Pot holders. And together every night, they read from the Bible instead of watching TV like normal people. I cannot get away from the Jesus lovers, for some reason. Fuck the Bible." She paused. "This offends you?"

"Nope," I said cheerfully. "Not at all. Fuck the Bible." In truth I wasn't that familiar with the Bible except as a fixture in the nightstand of every motel my family had ever slept in, but it felt wonderfully irreverent and daring to agree.

"Yo, Jim!" someone called. When I turned to see who it was, Helle wiggled her fingers in farewell and stalked off, trailing smoke, purse swinging. Well, she probably didn't care whether she ever found the chemistry labs.

"Hey, Greg."

I was glad to see his face, his familiar jean jacket with the skull-and-crossbones appliqué on the back. It'd been a while. The few times I'd let him lure me into cutting class (to learn firsthand about the finer points of pot smoking, like how to disguise its aftereffects), I'd done it in the hope that his comment about my being the hypothetical guy he'd hypothetically make it with would lead to some *actual* making it. It hadn't, and by now I could tell that it probably never would. But still, he was an ally in—as Helle had called it—this fuckhole.

"You know that girl?" he asked.

I suppressed a goofy grin. "Yeah, we're in French together."

It was a testament to Greg's sensitivity that he didn't follow this up with any of the typical apelike sexual posturing—*She looks like a freaky slut. Are you into her? Do you think she puts out?*—blah, blah, blah. It put me at ease.

I was less comfortable, though, with the sense that he had an agenda percolating under the surface. Sure enough, he shifted gears into furtive mode. "Let's go to your locker? I need, you know . . . I need it back."

His no-nonsense mood made me remember that every time I opened my locker—where we now stood—I was courting danger. "Finally," I said, trying to match his tone. "It's stinking up my stuff." As though to express impatience, I gave the locker handle three sharp taps with my left hand.

He groped under the pile of books and clothes and grabbed the goods himself; in one swift move he slid the bag into his open backpack. "You didn't tell anyone about this, did you?" he said quietly. "It could get both of us in serious trouble."

"Why would you think I'd narc you out?"

"I don't think that," he said. He looked at me, and I could feel warmth coming from him for the first time since that afternoon bike ride. It felt so long ago now.

The bell rang. Now we'd both be late to our next classes, but I didn't want our only communication to be so transactional. "Hey, is everything okay?"

He raked his hands through his hair. "Ah, it's been better."

"Can I help?"

Greg smiled. "You can help me smoke this weed."

I cut my next class, and behind the cafeteria Dumpster he taught me the correct way to use a portable bong.

9

A DAY WITHOUT ORANGE JUICE IS LIKE A DAY WITHOUT SUNSHINE

My mother's face was hovering about three inches from mine. "Good-bye, honey. I'm off to work. I hope you have a good day. I love you." She kissed my cheek.

She paused and picked up the copy of *The Bell Jar* beside my bed. "What's this you're reading?"

"A teacher recommended it. She teaches advanced English for the juniors. She's very interesting. I got it at the San Carlos Library."

"Well, that was nice of her."

I got up and pulled on a T-shirt. "It's about a girl in college who's won a fellowship at a magazine in New York. Even though everything in her life should be good, she gets horrifically depressed and tries to kill herself."

My mother reared back. "That doesn't sound like the kind of book you'd recommend to somebody you've just met."

"I think it's an excellent book. Your response evokes in me your ignorance. Also, there's toothpaste on the corners of your mouth," I said.

It had been exactly seven days since I'd called Jean-Paul and he'd told me he'd be free in a week, meaning that I was now permitted to call him. I looked at myself in the bathroom mirror, viewing with a surge of self-hatred the new patch of pimples that had developed on my chin.

I lifted the receiver, with its million miles of curlicue cord, from the wall phone in the kitchen. I was anxious, not just because I was afraid my mom might look at the phone bill and ask who I was talking to in the city, but also because I was afraid Jean-Paul wouldn't be happy to hear from me. I'd spent the night refining a mental picture: the two of us seated at a wooden dining table, sharing a platter of coq au vin, a dish I remembered from the menu at Jacques, one of the Chicago restaurants my dad had taken me to. Only in this picture, the dining table was located in a home somewhere in a leafy New England town, near a university, where Jean-Paul could teach music.

When his dour landlady answered, my voice shook, and for a moment I considered putting the receiver down. Before I could get in the requisite number of ritual exhales, she'd handed off the phone to him.

"Hi, it's Jim. I hope I'm not calling too early?"

"*Non*. My landlady and I were having *le petit déjeuner*. Eh, breakfast."

I tried to picture it. All I could conjure up was two cups of coffee. Maybe they'd be listening to classical music. Maybe there would be flowers on the table. "Has, um, has your schedule gotten any less busy?"

A pause. "Let me see. I'll be back in a minute."

I could hear some muffled conversation before he came back. "I can see you tomorrow," he whispered. "At eleven in the morning."

"Wow, okay!" Should I hang up before he changed his mind?

"You can come to where I am living," he said, and gave me his address. "Don't be late."

I TOLD MY MOTHER I was going into the city to see a Saturday matinee. It gave me a feeling of strength to tell myself that lying was simply what I must do.

It was raining, so she drove me down to the bus station, and as I was getting out of the car, she gave me her umbrella, a gigantic, see-through dome from Woolworth's. I felt idiotic holding it but took it anyway.

The ride into the city seemed to take forever, and when I got off the streetcar at Nineteenth Avenue as instructed, I discovered that I'd gotten off too soon. There were many, many blocks still to walk. Popping open the absurd, womanish umbrella, I made my way to his address, aligning my steps to avoid the cracks—entreating danger to stay away—and growing damper by the minute with rain and perspiration.

Jean-Paul met me in the dark hallway wearing nothing but underwear, and I greeted him with a rush of elation and arousal, following him into his bedroom, a cramped space with avocado-green shag carpeting.

I took off my clothes and stood before him, embarrassed by my paleness and skinniness. Taking my hands, he drew me onto the bed.

This time the sex was reciprocal, and I hadn't known I was capable of feeling that much physical pleasure. It was surprising and thrilling. Afterward, while we lay together, I gazed with contentment at the carpet, observing how the shafts of light coming through the metal blinds were falling onto its fibers. I felt high and languorous, as though I'd been smoking Greg's pot.

Finally Jean-Paul broke the silence. "Jim, you have to leave. My landlady will return soon."

The words stung. I wanted to stay there all day, possibly forever, admiring the strange bend in his cock, his greasy blond hair, the fine, sharp tip of his nose. I longed to swim around in this new kind of high all afternoon, perhaps forever. I certainly didn't want to put on my slightly damp sweater and even damper coat and head back out into the rain. But apparently I didn't have a choice.

I paused at the door. My heart felt fragile in my chest. "Can we do that again sometime soon?" My voice sounded stupid to my own ears. Weak.

"We will see. My schedule is very busy. You can call me. I have to go now."

As I was walking back down Nineteenth Avenue, looking for the streetcar stop and not really caring if I found it, I felt raindrops on my face and realized I'd left my mother's umbrella behind.

I PUT DOWN *THE BELL JAR* on the dashboard, a little bit nauseous. It wasn't easy to read in a moving car, even if said car was moving at the pace equivalent of honey being poured from a jar.

My mom was driving us to the McDonald's in Belmont. Another of our long-standing traditions was to visit a McDonald's and, once we got there, order the same reliable processed meal, which we preferred to eat in the confines of the parked car.

I stared out at the seemingly endless stream of gas stations and cheap motels. Everything in California was so spread out and oversized, so unlike the more human scale of things in the Midwest. The radio was playing a song by the Carpenters, slow and cloying.

"Can we listen to something else?"

She switched to news, which was covering a story about Patty Hearst, whose bail, the newscaster said, had been revoked, and the Supreme Court was refusing to hear her case. This made Mom tsk and pat her hair, though as always there wasn't a single hair out of place.

I wasn't clear on the details of what this Patty Hearst person had done—from watching Walter Cronkite I'd seen the photo of a teenage girl, machine gun canted at her hip, so scary she was kind of cool, but that was the extent of my knowledge. "What did she *do* that was so terrible anyway?" I asked.

Usually Mom was happy to discuss the news with me, but this time she curtailed my curiosity. "Some people are very sick," she said, and switched the radio with a click back to the syrupy music. *"Every shing-a-ling-a-ling that they're starting to sing's so fine. . . . It's yesterday once more."*

We pulled up to the drive-through window to recite our un-changing order. Two regular hamburgers, two small vanilla milk shakes, large fries to share. Wanting to stir up the stagnant atmosphere, I broached another current-events topic, this time an even touchier one, about the spokeswoman for Florida orange juice who was all over the news lately. "Did you see what's going on in Minneapolis? The gays were protesting Anita Bryant when she tried to do some kind of performance."

Foot hovering over the brake pedal, my mother let the car roll to the payment window. "It makes me embarrassed to think of people wasting their lives like that."

The cashier handed over the bag. "Your order, ma'am."

"What are you talking about?! What about that gay guy who was just elected in San Francisco?" I tried in vain to recall his name—Harvey Something Weird—but I couldn't. "Mom! Have you ever even *known* a gay person?" I demanded.

"Shh! Hand me my purse." She thanked the cashier. Once she'd gotten her change and parked, she rounded on me. "And where exactly am I supposed to have met a gay person?"

"There are lots of places you could meet gay people."

"Oh, I doubt that very much. Did they remember to put napkins in?"

I found the wad of napkins at the bottom of the milk-shake bag but didn't give her any. "It's not some crazy, weird thing. It's certainly a lot more common than you're aware of."

"Well, I don't think that's true at all. I think it's a terrible way to be, with everyone in the whole society thinking you're disturbed. That is no way to live your life. It's sad." She plucked a napkin from my grasp and spread it neatly over the lap of her belted denim jumpsuit, this season's must-have according to the magazines she obeyed. That it was the Target version, only the two of us knew.

I jabbed a straw into my milk shake. "Because most people are normal, right? The way God created them?"

"Don't mock me. It's wrong, that's all."

"There are gay people everywhere, Mom. Wake up!"

Regarding me, she took a long sip of her shake. "What you're saying makes me think that you're gay," she said at last.

My heart began to hammer. I felt like there was a bomb in my hand and I'd just lit the fuse.

"Are you? Are you gay, Jim?"

I tore a salt packet open and dumped the contents over the fries. "Even if I were, why would I tell you? You obviously wouldn't accept that information."

"Well?"

I thought of all the times, the countless hundreds upon thousands of times, that I'd carried out my private protective rituals right in front of her face without her once noticing. I bet I could spit, tap, count, grind, and exhale a dozen times in a row right this very second and she'd just keep sucking up her milk shake like she didn't see it. Because she didn't *want* to see it. She didn't want to see anything. If I were to fuck Jean-Paul right in front of her right now, she wouldn't see it! In that moment she seemed like the most willfully stupid human being who had ever walked the face of the earth.

"Why don't you just get a clue?" I muttered darkly.

"I want you to tell me the truth. This is important for me to know."

"I know one thing," I fumed. "If I *were* gay, I would be getting out of this car right now, slamming the door shut, and walking so far away that I would never have to look at your face ever again."

"That's very cruel."

"*That's* cruel? Daddy dumped us like a sack of trash and hasn't sent us one single cent. He broke his promise to help support us. I think *that's* cruel."

She fell silent. Cars pulled away, one by one, from the drive-through window and merged onto the El Camino, taillights receding into the distance.

"I know, honey, you're right," she said at last. "I just don't know what I can do about it."

I unwrapped my hamburger. "Let's just eat."

We turned back to our meal.

THE ARGUMENT LEFT ME with an anger that was as dull and persistent as a toothache, and it was a welcome distraction when I ran into Helle some days later. She'd been absent from French class twice in a row, and when I spotted her, the bell for lunch had just rung, so she must've come to school late. In her fuzzy fuchsia angora sweater and smeared eye makeup, she looked like some twisted version of a movie-musical ingenue, or a pretty transvestite.

"I've missed you in class," I said. "Have you been sick?"

"Oh my God, I've been so fucked up the last two days. To tell you the truth, I can't believe I am here right now."

I wasn't entirely sure what she meant by "fucked up," but I laughed in a way I hoped was knowing. "Well, do you want to have lunch together?"

She pinched my chin. "You're such a sweet boy! But no, I just came for—how do you say it?—attendance, so it will look like I am here. I'm going to play hooky now and go to San Francisco to see my boyfriend."

"That sounds fun." I thought of my own boyfriend in San Francisco. I wanted to tell Helle about him but thought better of it.

"Yeah. Charles is a bit of a bastard, but I like him. He just got his own apartment. Also a new supply of quaaludes."

A hulking guy who looked like he could crush a beer can against his forehead called "Freaks!" as he walked by.

"Go fuck your mother!" she replied without missing a beat,

and then continued, "If you want to come to a show sometime, it would be fun. There are good punk rock bands in San Francisco, and some clubs. You're so lucky and you don't know it, do you, little boy?"

The term "little boy" would ordinarily make my dull anger flare into rage, but something told me that hanging out with a punk rocker was going to require a thick skin, so instead I drawled, "Yeah, I'm the luckiest person I know. I'm like a fucking leprechaun with a pot of gold."

For having failed to rise to the bait, I was rewarded with a laugh. "You *are*! There is only, like, three cities in this whole country where you can see a punk show." On fingernails topped with chipped black polish, she counted, "New York, Los Angeles, San Francisco, and pfft! That's it. There's one club in San Francisco called the Pit. Oh, I love that place very much! It's so sleazy."

I'd never heard "sleazy" used as a compliment before, but it sounded cool to me, and I said so, omitting the information that I'd never been to see any kind of rock concert before in my life. In truth, part of me was still trying to wrap my mind around the blitheness with which she'd told that big bruiser to go fuck his mother.

"Charles's friend Ingo says the Dils are playing with Tuxedomoon on Friday. The lead singer of Tuxedomoon is so cute. He looks like a little Chinese drug addict. I can't wait! Unless it's a lie. Ingo loves to tell stupid lies," she added to herself.

"Can't you just get a paper and check the listing?"

This time her laugh made me blush to the roots of my hair. "Aw, you are really adorable!"

As I watched Helle leave, a cascade of questions washed over me. I didn't know what time such an event would start, but my guess was not early. Would I be able to catch the last bus back to San Carlos? How could I convince my mom to let me stay out so late, even if I lied about what I was doing? And what *would* I be doing, exactly? Would Helle's boyfriend give me quaaludes, a drug I'd read about in *Newsweek*? Would everybody be getting "fucked up"? What would I wear? That last point was especially worrisome. I had grave doubts that there was anything in my wardrobe that would make me look like I belonged at a punk rock show at a sleazy club called the Pit.

10

IT'S 9:00 P.M.
DO YOU KNOW WHERE
YOUR CHILDREN ARE?

My mother usually praised my cooking, but on that Friday evening she hardly said a word, even though I'd made her favorite chicken dish. Our conversations had been stilted since our argument in the McDonald's parking lot.

I had a momentary urge to tell her that I was going to the Pit that night. I wanted to share something with her, to resume our usual intimacy, the interruption of which was making my heart hurt. But another part of me relished the idea of keeping Helle and the punk show a secret. There was something energizing in knowing that I had another side to my life that was only mine.

While clearing the table, she said, "I'm worried about your father. It's like he's disappeared off the face of the earth."

I tossed silverware into the sink with a clatter. "For God's sake, why are you worried about *him*? He's a drunken wreck who wanted out of this family. Why don't you get a divorce and make it legal? Then he'd have to pay alimony. That's what any lucid person would do."

I was surprised at the snarl in my voice. She was still in her work clothes—an ivory polyester blouse tucked into a brown skirt, pantyhose, everything prim and perfect—which only served to further incite anger in me. I wished she would quit acting like a storefront mannequin and *do* something for once. Make my dad stop being such a dick, for instance.

"Why would I get a lawyer? He promised he'd send us three hundred dollars every month," she argued.

"And you trust him?"

Her eyes welled up. "I always trusted him, until he did what he did to us!"

"Why do you have to be so weak and helpless? Dad does whatever *he* wants," I said bitterly.

She turned her back on me and cranked on the kitchen tap. In our apartment complex, the water took forever to warm up, and sometimes it never got completely hot. "I'd like to see *you* start paying the bills around here. Are you ready for adult responsibilities, since you're suddenly acting like such an adult now?"

I wished Jean-Paul would call or, better yet, Helle. I wished I were on the bus with her right that second, on the way to the club to see the band with the Chinese singer that looked like a drug addict. I wished I had a different life. The kitchen grew thick with the smell of Dawn dish soap.

"Listen," I said, trying to soften my tone, "I need you to take me to the bus stop tonight. Okay?"

"No, not okay. It's already six. You're not staying out all night in the city."

"I'll be back around ten, ten-thirty. I'll call you when I'm catching the bus, so you know when to pick me up." The moment I said it, I realized that no matter what, there was no way I'd be home at anything like ten-thirty.

My mother clanked plates into the sink. "You can walk. I'm not going to pick you up that late."

"Fine, I'll get home by myself. I don't need you to take me." *I don't need you to hold back my life,* I thought.

I went into my room to change. The outfit I'd decided on was the product of fitful, obsessive deliberations over the course of the week, auditioning in front of the bedroom mirror as I tried to zero in on what a punk rock look might consist of. All I had to go on was what I remembered from that brief piece on television, Helle's wardrobe, and an article I'd read in the *Chronicle.*

An unknown prospect always sent me into research mode; I liked to be armed with information, and in this case I'd tried going to the record store in Palo Alto, but all I'd found was a bunch of Top 40 junk, the *Saturday Night Fever* soundtrack, and some old hippie stuff with album covers that all seemed to feature a photo of bearded guys hanging out in an overgrown country field. I'd asked the kid behind the counter if they had any punk rock records, and he'd looked at me like I was a toddler tugging on his pant leg.

"There's not really, like, *records,*" he said. Then, casting a glance at the store manager, he amended with slightly less condescension, "I mean, there's some EPs at Aquarius in the city. Imports, mostly. You could try there."

EPs? Aquarius? Imports? He might as well have been speaking Esperanto. I'd left no wiser than I'd come.

But from what I could glean, the point, as far as fashion went, was to look torn up and raw, and also maybe sexual. Rebellious, too. With the scissors from my mother's sewing kit, I cut slits into one of my plain white T-shirts. That looked cool, but not rough enough, so I ripped some masking tape into strips and stuck those over most of the shirt, creating a sort of fish-scale effect. Then, after twenty minutes of mentally filing through my limited vocabulary of punk rock, I scrawled the words "anarchy," "punk rock," and "Charlie Manson" on both sides with a large black felt-tipped pen. The whole process was absorbing and satisfying, like doing a craft project out of a *Ladies' Home Journal.*

I decided to accessorize with my mom's oversize sunglasses plus a tie I'd worn to a friend's bar mitzvah in Chicago. Finally I used the black pen to draw X's on my forearms. I looked in the mirror, striking poses. My version was more like a Halloween costume, not the real thing, but it would have to do.

Before leaving, I threw on my army-surplus trench coat so my mother wouldn't see what I had on underneath. "I'm leaving," I said, trying to look defiant.

But she already had her car keys in hand. "I'll drive you downtown."

I was secretly glad to be able to skip the long walk to the station: God only knew what kind of unwanted attention I could attract traipsing down Torino Drive alone in this getup. We rode in silence and kissed good-bye awkwardly. Her skin against my lips felt soft and old.

The San Carlos station, where both the bus and the Southern Pacific made stops, was an old train depot. It looked like it could've been a nice place once, with its chunky limestone bricks and turrets, and according to our neighbors it *had* been, before funding cuts. Its indoor waiting area was closed to the public, and its graffitied benches could be a cold and ominous place to be after dark. So it was a treat to see Helle there waiting for me.

I was afraid she might have seen me kiss my mother good-bye, but if she had, she didn't mention it. Her slick, canary-yellow pleather raincoat gave off an acid glow under the streetlight. The lopsided pigtails she'd gathered her hair into made her resemble a sort of psychotic Pippi Longstocking.

"Do I look okay?" I asked, opening my trench coat.

"Ah, hey, it's Mister Punk Rock!" she cried. "Very cute." She tapped a pack of cigarettes and offered me one. I declined, glad to hear her assessment, even though I suspected she was being kind.

On the bus I checked my reflection in the window. From the neck up, I was still my usual gay, disgusting self. I needed to take it further. But how? I should at least have bought some Dippity-do and slicked my hair back. Then I had an idea. "Helle, do you have any makeup in your purse?"

"There is never a time I do not have makeup in my purse," she replied dryly. After some digging around, she held aloft an eyeliner pencil. "Shall I do it for you?"

Lips compressed in concentration, she started drawing around my eyes. Out of my peripheral vision, I could see people staring at us. Ordinarily being watched gave me the urge to hide, to make myself invisible, but being with Helle made me feel unafraid. "What's Denmark like?" I asked.

"Hold still! It's cold in Denmark. And the men are all drunks."

"I know a little something about drunk men," I said.

She stopped for a second to give me a long look. I felt revealed, yet not exposed.

When she was finished, she held up a compact for me. The

eyeliner had transformed me into a person I barely recognized, urban and slightly frightening. I smiled.

"You like it?"

"I do!" I squinted in a sultry pout, then sang from the theme to *Mahogany*. "'Do you know where you're going to? Do you like the things that life is showing you?'"

We both cracked up.

From the bus station, we walked to her boyfriend's place in the Tenderloin. I'd never seen so many scary winos in one place in my life, and despite myself—I'd have sooner driven a spike into my eyeball than let *anyone* know about my rituals, least of all Helle—I kept watch for sidewalk cracks to avoid.

Charles opened the door to his one-room studio shirtless, in black stovepipe jeans. I pushed away the memory of Jean-Paul in the hallway in his underwear.

"Hey," he greeted us, pulling Helle to him. He was tall, pale, and as thin as a flagpole, with dyed black hair.

The apartment was a wreck. The furnishings consisted of a cable spool used as a coffee table, a mini-fridge, and a stained mattress on which was draped a sleeping bag. It smelled as though the sole window had never been opened. I was concerned that my discomfort at the squalor might show, although neither Helle nor Charles had so much as glanced in my direction since we walked in.

I sat on the floor with my back against the wall and watched a cockroach crawl into, and then out of, an empty take-out container, while they lay on the bed murmuring and drinking beer. Helle went on her hands and knees to the stereo and dropped the needle at random onto the record that was on the turntable.

"I like the Sex Pistols," she said, "they're so funny." She crawled back to the mattress, singing along.

"*'No future for you! No future for me!'*" If given the choice between confessing that I recognized the song from the punk rock thing I'd seen on TV in St. Paul and swallowing a live insect, I'd have popped that cockroach into my mouth, no question. What was I even doing there, really? And would the whole night be like this?

I considered wiping off the eyeliner and trying to find my way back to the bus station, but Charles turned to me. "So you're the famous Jim. According to Helle, you're the single person with any intelligence in that shit town you live in. How old are you?"

"Fifteen," I said.

"Want a beer?" He crouched before the tiny fridge. The top two buttons of his jeans were open, and I caught a glimpse of his pubic hair. "Or maybe you want something stronger?"

Did he mean booze? Or was he alluding to quaaludes? Or some other kind of drug? "Beer is fine," I said. I could feel my jaw working as my teeth ground out repetitions of five.

"I'm starving," Helle moaned. "Do you have anything here besides beer and pills?"

Charles tossed her a box of Hostess Ding Dongs.

"Ah, very classy," she said, tearing open the package. "Jim, would you like one of the delicious cakes our host has baked himself?" Smiling, he flipped her the bird.

Biting into the waxy, sweet coating made me feel less apart from the world I'd just left behind. Charles reached for a little packet of aluminum foil. "Time for ludes," he announced.

"Oh, yes, Daddy, Daddy, I want my candy," vamped Helle.

I was frozen, equally uncomfortable at the prospect of being offered a pill and not being offered one. I rose. "Can I use your bathroom?"

"I dunno, can you?"

Helle punched Charles's arm. "Excuse him, he's a bit of an asshole," she told me. "It's right there behind you. It is very horrible," she added as I stepped in. From behind the closed door, I heard him mumble something, to which Helle's voice countered, "What? Yes, you are a pig. A little piggy-pig!" A pause, and then she giggled.

She wasn't kidding about its being horrible. It was a windowless coffin with a rank odor like a full litter box, even though there was no cat to be seen. The toilet was lacking a seat, and the soap, which I had to take from the shower stall, was a grimy sliver. Well, the room was so gross that Charles wouldn't notice if I spit on the floor for protection.

When I stepped back into the room, they'd gone silent, lounging vacantly on the bed. Waiting, I guessed, for the drug to take effect.

Ten minutes passed, then twenty. Thirty. No words were exchanged. Unable to pierce the glassy languor they'd fallen into, I sipped my beer, wondering if we were even going out at all. Maybe the show *was* just a lie that Charles's friend had told. The greasy, foreign sensation of the makeup bugged me; I rubbed my eyes, which made them sting. I checked my pocket watch, a gift from my dad that I'd brought along, thinking it was a cool affectation, but was now embarrassed by. It was nine-thirty. "Guys? Should we be heading to the performance soon?"

Charles's gaze lit on me. "'Performance,'" he repeated. The quotation marks he hung on the word were so heavy with irony they practically clanged.

My face grew warm, but I pressed. "Yeah, at the Pit."

"Oh, right. We can go in a while. It doesn't really matter what time we get there."

Helle waved out a burning match. Her words came forth on a plume of Marlboro smoke. "No, let's go, baby. Jim's right. I want to go hear loud music. Put on a shirt and let's get out of here."

As Charles dressed, he caught my eyes lingering on the unbuttoned part of his jeans. "You like what you see?"

"Be nice, Charles," said Helle. "He's a good boy from San Carlos."

On the way out, we stopped at a liquor store, where Charles bought a pint of Southern Comfort to share and offered me a swig. It tasted like pancake syrup mixed with nail-polish remover and made my throat burn.

WHEN WE ARRIVED AT THE PIT, a few windblown, desolate blocks south of Mission Street, I silently gave thanks that, perhaps due to my protective rituals, Helle hadn't suggested we meet there, because I never would've found it myself. The unmarked entrance was in a narrow gap between two industrial buildings. I almost passed it at first, distracted by a couple of guys in black biker jackets I was pretty sure were having sex behind a parked moving van.

The few people hanging around in front were dressed in a fashion far more extreme than Helle and her boyfriend. One woman looked like a homeless mental patient in oversize ripped jeans held up by plaid suspenders. Her head was shaved, and she'd rubbed some of her dark lipstick onto her cheeks, which gave an effect more like bruising than rouge.

She caught me staring at her. "Why don't you take a fuckin' picture, it'll last longer," she snarled. Her two front teeth were missing.

Charles handed money to the bouncer, then held out his hand

to be smacked with a rubber stamp, and Helle followed. They disappeared inside, releasing a blast of cacophonous music as the door opened and closed behind them.

"Two-fifty," the bouncer grunted at me. I dug in my pocket for the correct change and got my hand stamped with red ink, an image of a shooting star. Then I stepped into the darkness.

Inside was a swarm of bodies and noise. The music was like the bone-rattling roar of a jet engine, and the air hung thick with the smells of sweat, cigarette smoke, and old spilled beer. It was so dark I didn't notice at first that Helle was waiting for me. I gripped her hand tightly, afraid to lose her. I couldn't quite believe yet that this was happening.

Nearer the "stage"—really just a space lit by a few spotlights and flanked by speakers—the crowd was even denser. As we pressed toward it, people jostled roughly against us, on purpose, it seemed. Some were doing a kind of dance, a sort of manic jumping in place, which Charles told me was called the pogo. Some guy's flailing elbow caught me right in the ribs, but instead of apologizing he screamed, "Fuck you!"

I guessed that the band playing was Helle's beloved Tuxedo-moon, because the lead singer was a slight Asian man as big as a minute. He hunched above a microphone that he gripped with both hands, his sweaty black hair falling over his face, and prowled the stage, jerking his body like a man trying to wake himself from a deep sleep.

"No tears for the creatures of the night! No tears!" he wailed in an anguished voice, over and over again. The music, with its dissonant, calliope-like synthesizer notes, reminded me of old monster movies, with a wild carnival edge to it.

"I feel so hollow I just don't understand—nothing's turned out like I planned!" howled the singer, doubling over as if punched. His ghoulish-looking bandmates played with impassive absorption, as if oblivious to the primal agony that was thrashing in their midst.

Squeezed next to me, Helle and Charles were equally oblivious, eyes shut, bodies swaying. Helle looked so intoxicated that it crossed my mind I might not be able to count on her for anything—a condition not unfamiliar to me from having lived with my father.

Realizing that I was still carrying the bottle of Southern Comfort, I took a swig. Someone bumped me hard, knocking the bottle's sticky mouth against my teeth, and I felt blood on my lower lip. The band launched into a spooky melody that I gradually realized was a bizarre rendition of a Cole Porter song my mom used to listen to. They'd slowed it down to a narcotized, droning incantation. I closed my eyes against a wave of dizziness, feeling as if the floor were undulating.

When I opened them again, the song was concluding in a burst of feedback, and Helle and Charles were gone.

Panic jolted through my body. As the crowd by the stage loosened a bit, I tried to get my bearings, but there was no sign of the people I'd come with. I sat on an amplifier, disoriented and drenched in sweat in my trench coat, and scanned the club, counting by fives under my breath and hoping I didn't look like a little kid who'd gotten lost at the fair.

Everyone seemed older and more put-together than me. Feeling a little silly in my craft-project outfit, I checked out the parade of carefully constructed looks. A woman in a jumpsuit with a geometric print that made her resemble a living Constructivist propaganda poster was lighting her cigarette off the cigarette of a woman with pink hair, zombie-black lipstick, and liquid eyeliner that extended all the way to her temples; her torn dress, trailing a raggedy hem of taffeta, made her look like a debutante who'd just been assaulted in a dark alley.

I watched a black girl in a tartan skirt and Converse tennis shoes skip up to a group of girls and laugh. They seemed closer to my age. The Southern Comfort was starting to go down easier. The taut wires that had been holding my skeleton together for so long slackened somewhat. The band started playing again, not so much music as a corrosive progression of electronic noises, loud enough that it felt like a solid mass I could lean on. It vibrated through my body. For the first time since I'd smoked pot with Greg in the meadow, I felt a sense of letting go, of fully occupying the moment. And, blissfully, of not really caring about much of anything.

Then I realized that someone was watching me: a handsome guy, with full lips and short, curly hair. When I met his eyes, he smiled. In another time and place, I might have immediately been gripped by an anxiety attack. But here, enveloped in a warm blanket of booze and sound, it was as if my frequent social terror had been knocked away, and I smiled back.

He sat beside me on the amplifier and asked me something that, although he was inches away, I couldn't make out over the volume of the band.

He leaned even closer, his breath hot in my ear. "YOU LIKE TUXEDOMOON?" he bellowed in a deep, southern-accented voice. "THERE'S SOMETHING SPECIAL ABOUT THE MUSIC THEY MAKE!"

"REALLY SPECIAL!" I agreed.

He offered me a bottle of whiskey from his jacket. I took a

pull and, coughing, handed it back. "YOU'RE VERY BEAU-TIFUL!" he said.

"YOU'RE MORE BEAUTIFUL THAN ME!" It was like trying to communicate in the funnel of a tornado. He smiled again, although I wasn't sure if he'd actually heard me. I placed my hand on his. It was very warm.

"I LIVE IN AN ARTISTS' COLLECTIVE!" He jerked his chin toward the singer writhing onstage. "WINSTON COMES FOR DINNER SOMETIMES! YOU SHOULD COME OVER!" He pulled a folded-up flyer for a punk rock show from his jeans pocket, tore off a corner of it, and wrote down an address and directions for how to reach it. Below that he wrote his name: Calvin.

Calvin and I gazed at each other. The thought of my boyfriend swam up through the thick, sweet haze of drunkenness. Was Jean-Paul the jealous type? Was this considered cheating on him?

I flashed on my mental picture of eating coq au vin together in the countryside. It struck me now as a childish fancy. Boyfriend? He wasn't even returning my calls! I leaned in and kissed Calvin, right there in the middle of everything and everybody.

He pulled away.

Oh no. Had I read the signals wrong, done something stupid? Unsure of what to make of the situation, I shouted into his ear that I needed to find my friend. "I'M IN SCHOOL WITH HER," I added irrelevantly, and stumbled away.

Once I got up, the booze hit me like a train. The room was pullulating with strangers and I couldn't find Helle anywhere. Finally I went to look outside. The night was quiet, silent, a lunar surface. I saw her and Charles in the alleyway, making out. Helle was barefoot, her feet naked among the glittering bits of glass and grit. Her trademark black stilettos lay discarded nearby.

I rushed to her. "Helle, I met somebody!"

"That's good," she said, almost in slow motion. Lipstick was smudged all over her chin. "But I'm a little busy now."

"Why'd you guys leave?"

"There were too many people stepping on my shoes."

Charles blinked, expressionless. "You gonna stay for the Dils?" he slurred. I realized I had no idea what time it was. I checked my watch, unable to grasp the implications of "11:40." Briefly I reveled in the possibility that maybe I didn't have to think about it. But then I remembered with a lurch that the last bus for San Carlos left at midnight. Where was the Pit in relation to the bus stop?

"I've got to get home!"

"Bye-bye, kiddo," sang Helle.

I started walking fast past one unfamiliar street name after another. Even the sight of a couple of guys who were *definitely* having sex at the end of an alleyway didn't divert me from my panic. Just as I was considering the prospect of having to spend the night huddled in a doorway, I got to Mission Street. On instinct I turned left and broke into a jog, lungs burning, sweat streaming down my back.

Panting in sets of five, I steered my numb feet to skirt the sidewalk cracks. Finally I could make out a clutch of people at the SamTrans stop, and then the lights of the approaching 7F.

On the ride home, I was hungry and nauseous, and my ears rang so badly it was frightening. But I also felt as though an escape hatch had been opened and I'd tasted the freedom outside.

At the station in San Carlos, I called home from a pay phone and woke my mother. Ten minutes later her car pulled up.

"It's after one in the morning! Where have you been?"

I looked down at my hands. "At a concert."

"Have you been drinking? Don't lie, I can smell it."

"A little." I sighed, resting my head against the cool glass of the window.

"Are you wearing *makeup*?"

But by then I was falling asleep.

11

JUST WHEN YOU THOUGHT IT WAS SAFE TO GO BACK IN THE WATER

I got up at the usual time, went through my usual morning rituals, and headed off to school, but everything had changed.

It wasn't that I had any less anxiety about starting another day at San Carlos High. But I had the curious sensation that it was happening to somebody else, someone I was watching from a distance. There he went, sloping along Melendy Drive with a Chicago Film Festival book bag over his shoulder, a skinny fifteen-year-old in a striped rugby shirt. It seemed impossible that he was the same person who'd kissed a strange man in a punk rock club. The faint red shape of a shooting star on the back of my hand was the only proof.

As the manicured pastel landscape scrolled by, a montage of impressions replayed in my mind: the smell of gum on Helle's breath as she outlined my eyes in makeup, the bouncer's grimy hands, the admonition DON'T BELIEVE WHAT YOUR MOTHER TOLD YOU on the bathroom wall, the woman in the freaky geometric Russian jumpsuit, the sardonic way that black girl had skipped up to her friends with her hands clasped behind her back, like a wide-eyed child in a 1950s movie. The way Calvin gazed at me after we kissed, a look that seemed to say yes and no simultaneously.

I was eager to swap stories with Helle and hurried to French class. But when the bell rang, her seat was still empty. The school year was almost over, and she'd barely shown up for any of it.

Feeling dejected, I ate my lunch on a bench close enough to a trio of chattering girls to eavesdrop on their conversation, something about a party they'd gone to over the weekend. They were all feathered hairdos and lip-gloss-slathered mouths, and I pictured them at some football player's house, maybe pushing whoever was the lowest on their social totem pole into the swimming pool before passing out drunk. Compared to Helle, they appeared to be made out of interchangeable plastic parts, as though extruded onto a factory conveyor belt.

I tried to picture them in punk rock regalia, but I couldn't; it was like they were missing some essential ingredient. They were just too satisfied with normality. In the parallel world I'd discovered, where to be a freak was to be interesting, no matter what you looked like or how you dressed, these girls and their kind would be hopelessly uncool.

One of them noticed me staring and flashed me a look before turning back to her friends. "Fags like him make me want to puke," she informed them.

THE FIRST DAY OF SUMMER VACATION found me on the bus to San Francisco, taking Calvin up on his invitation to visit the artists' collective.

Just a few blocks away from the Pit, the building didn't look like the sort of place where anyone would, or even could, live. The windows were bricked up, and the sign on the front reading BAY PIPE AND TUBING hung by screws so rusty it looked poised to come crashing down. According to Calvin's note, I was supposed to look for "Shazam Productions" on the third floor. Shazam was a strangely childlike, comic-book name for an arts collective, I thought.

But then, after I was buzzed in, I entered the vast and gloomy warehouse and perceived the irony in the name, its gee-whiz amazement. In my mind I heard Helle's deadpan, husky voice pronounce "Shazam," and I almost laughed aloud. I clanked along a catwalk. Below, disused machines hulked like relics.

On the mezzanine between the second and third floors, a haggard blond woman dressed in pallbearer black was scribbling something in a sketchbook, and I stopped to ask her if I was in the right place. She rolled her eyes and snapped shut the sketchbook, then hurried past me down the staircase like the White Rabbit.

At the sole doorway on the third floor, Calvin answered my hesitant knock, smiling. "Oh, I'm so glad you made it!"

He led me into a space that was subdivided by drywall partitions into a warren of small rooms. Pot smoke drifted toward the ceiling beams. "You want to peek at the rooms?"

I did. There were about a dozen windowless boxes, most with a hippie vibe, with mattresses on the floor and a smell of sweaty bed linens. One had fabric draped from the ceiling so it would resemble a desert tent. Others were spare, the building materials undisguised by the bare bulbs dangling overhead—which explained the fabric-draped ceiling. "This one's mine," Calvin said, opening the door to one of these starker rooms. Its only decoration was a framed line drawing of a sailor nude from the waist down. "I share with Frederica. My homage to Cocteau," he said, meaning the drawing.

But I didn't respond, too busy trying to wrap my head around the question of whether it was possible for Calvin to share a room with a girl and *not* be her boyfriend. Maybe they weren't exclusive? It seemed like a pretty bohemian setup here, after all.

The kitchen was decorated with hanging plants and featured a rough-hewn dining table with a big earthenware bowl as its centerpiece. The fridge was plastered with flyers for concerts and art shows, plus a poster of Anita Bryant getting a pie smashed into her face. A guy wearing eyeliner and a kaffiyeh was chopping a heap of herbs, and a girl in industrial coveralls spattered with paint was taking a loaf of bread from the oven. Music was filling the space, wailing saxophones and lyrics recited like an incantation.

"This is Jim," Calvin announced, and they nodded hello. "We're having a pheasant tagine," he told me.

"What's pheasant tagine?" I asked, immediately regretting the unsophisticated question.

"It's a Middle Eastern stew. Howard's request. D'you want a glass of wine?" He installed me on a stool beside Eyeliner Guy. "Back in a minute. I just need to call Howard."

I sipped my wine, hoping that one of the cooks would speak to me. They didn't, instead talking between themselves about some kind of gay protest they'd been part of or were going to be part of—they spoke in a dense jargon I couldn't comprehend. "So," I ventured finally, "what are we listening to?"

"Pere Ubu," said Coveralls Girl, tearing lettuce into a salad bowl. I heard the unspoken addendum, *Obviously*.

"It's cool," I said. Without acknowledging me, Coveralls Girl said to Eyeliner Guy, "Calvin's in for a bummer phone call. Howard's been in a foul mood today."

Eyeliner Guy swept the herbs into a bubbling pot. "Yeah, well, he's waiting to approve the final cut."

I perked up on hearing the words "final cut"—Howard must be a filmmaker, which was an exciting thought. I wondered if it could actually be Howard Chaney, whose short, experimental film adaptation of a German play I had seen at a local cinema. When Calvin returned, he asked me to help set the table, and while we did that, he asked me about my background. For the first time, I gave the uncensored version, not leaving out the part where the alcoholic dad ditches his family.

The woman I'd passed on the mezzanine came in and kissed Calvin on the lips, sending a stab of jealousy through me. "Jim, this is Frederica," said Calvin.

You share a bed with that bitch? I thought, dismayed.

She gave me an unmistakably pitying look, then glanced at Calvin. He busied himself with setting down cutlery. "Nice to meet you, Jim," Frederica said without enthusiasm.

Fuck you very much, I replied in my mind, but I was unsettled. What was up with looking sorry for me? And what *was* their relationship?

Luckily, at dinnertime Calvin sat between us. There ended up being more than a dozen guests. Everyone was dressed in either black from head to toe, like Frederica, or else in bright clashing colors, making it look as if a flock of crows had settled down to eat with a flock of parrots. There were platters of salads, stew in pottery bowls, and lumpy loaves of homemade bread.

It was all delicious, but I felt small and inadequate. Frederica exerted a gravitational pull on Calvin's interest, for one thing. Plus, I couldn't follow the conversation, which mostly centered on something called semiotics.

When an older man with pale, papery skin and an immaculately trimmed salt-and-pepper goatee took a seat at the head of the table, the dynamic shifted perceptibly; Coveralls Girl, who'd been speaking in a Donald Duck voice for comic effect, turned abruptly professorial.

"I've been reading the de Saussure lectures," she told the man, who I knew must be Howard. "You were right—Lacan *is* a pale imitator."

Howard deigned to accept a glass of wine from a parrot. "Eh. De Saussure and Lacan don't hold a great deal of interest for me anymore."

Looking cowed, Coveralls Girl sawed at one of the loaves and put a slice on a plate that was passed from hand to hand until it reached the great man.

"Here's the thing," Howard went on. "What I've come to understand is, neither of them grasps that film is the only language that has any claim on being *true*."

This sent murmurs down the table, as if everyone had to assimilate that Howard had changed his opinion on the topic. Calvin said, "Speaking of films, that scene in your latest when all the lights go out? So bleak and far out!"

Howard chuckled, buttering his bread. "Well, that's nice of you to say. My fear is the critics'll say it's derivative of Bergman."

Oh my God, it *was* Howard Chaney! I knew exactly what scene Calvin was talking about—it was the play adaptation I'd so admired. But what could I say about it that wouldn't sound fawning or, worse, stupid? All I could seize on was the Bergman reference, and before I could stop myself, I blurted, "I recently saw *Hour of the Wolf* at the Strand."

Silence hung over the table as Howard rested his gaze on me, chewing. "You don't look old enough for Bergman." He seemed inexplicably pleased by this. "Aren't you more excited about, say, *Grease?*"

Laughter ensued, and I felt myself flush. "No, I like him. I think *Persona* is my favorite."

"Really," Howard said indulgently. "And how long have you been such an avid cinephile?"

"Ever since I can remember. I'm hoping to go to film school someday, maybe become a director."

Frederica drove a corkscrew hard into a bottle of wine. She might as well have had a sign around her neck declaring that she wished I weren't there. Calvin shot her a glance that said to be cool. *That's right, bitch, be cool,* I thought, but I was starting to grind my teeth.

"Oh, don't be a pill, Freddie. We're the torchbearers of the avant-garde! It's our *job* to encourage creative young people. Especially if they come in such a pretty package," said Howard. At this a few people smirked, apparently finding his lechery charming.

I looked to Calvin for help. He smiled back. The expression "cat that swallowed the canary" came to mind.

After dinner the parrots and crows broke into factions, preparing for after-hours clubgoing. I was glad to see Frederica among them, lacing up a pair of thigh-high boots. Meanwhile, Calvin directed me to assist with washing the dishes, then excused himself to the bathroom down the hall.

As soon as he was out of earshot, Frederica accosted me at the sink. "Jim. Hey. There's a party at our friend Max's. Want to go?"

Was she drunk? I set a bowl in the dish rack. "Are you and Calvin going?"

"No. I'm going to the EndUp. But some of the others are going to Max's. A couple of them are closer to your age."

Oh, I get it. Foist me off with the kiddies so I'll stay away from Calvin. Sorry, but nope. "That's nice, thanks. But I'm fine here."

Her eyes searched my face with that same pitying look; then she seemed to come to some conclusion, and her face closed and became cold again. "Okay. Bye, Jim. Take care of yourself, please."

Howard sauntered into the kitchen, rubbing his potbelly with satisfaction. I saw contempt on Frederica's face as she passed him.

"That was delicious, I'm stuffed." He groaned. Then, "What's this? Calvin's turned our new friend into a scullery maid!"

"I don't mind," I said.

"Don't mind what?" Calvin asked as he returned, drying his hands on his jeans.

"Calvin, Jim's a guest," chided Howard. "*Eraserhead*'s playing at the Roxie—why don't you take him? Expand his filmic horizons! He can crash here tonight. We've certainly got the space."

"I'd love that," I said. By which I meant going out alone with Calvin, especially to see that underground movie, which I'd heard about and which sounded fantastically strange. The "crash here tonight" part I was less excited about. There was something about being in this place, even in the presence of the great Howard Chaney, that was making me think of the witch's gingerbread house in the fairy tale.

Still, I didn't want to be a baby.

The night was damp, dulling the sound of our footsteps as we walked to the Mission District. "Cigarette?" Calvin offered.

"Oh, I don't smoke, thanks." But, after watching him light one with a series of fluid, sexy movements, I changed my mind and asked for one. The smoke scoured my throat and made me dizzy.

Compared to *Eraserhead* the Bergman film looked like *The Sound of Music*. It was the story of a lonely freak living in a postapocalyptic world in a fantasy relationship with a miniature woman who lives inside his radiator. But being close to Calvin again, breathing his scent, sipping from the bottle of Jim Beam he kept passing me, was exhilarating. I put my hand on his thigh, but while he didn't push it away, he didn't reciprocate either. The taste of the cigarette persisted, mingling with the aftereffects of the rich, oily dinner and the increasingly sickening and grotesque images on-screen, and when we took a cab back to the collective, we had to have the driver pull over so I could vomit. Thankfully, Calvin was nice about it, quipping, "No worries, that's most people's response."

When we came in, Howard was in the kitchen, sitting on a stool with his legs crossed, reading. He'd changed into a silk robe so short I could see his scrotum peeking out. "Have fun, my pretties?" he greeted us.

"Going to get cigs, be right back," Calvin told me, and the lock clanked into its tumbler as the door closed behind him.

"Wait," I said, too late.

Howard put his book down. "He'll be back. Meanwhile, what's your verdict? Scarier than *Jaws 2,* am I right?"

He meant to be playful, I could tell, but I was uncomfortable. "Yeah, that was pretty much a total mindfuck on every level." *Especially the part about being with Calvin.*

"Care for a drop?" He waggled a wine bottle.

The idea of more alcohol made my gorge rise again. "Oh, thanks but no, I have to go. My mom's going to be freaked out if I don't come home tonight."

"Suit yourself." Howard shrugged. "I doubt the buses are running, though. Feel free to come back if you get into trouble."

He was right about the buses, and I had to wait until sunrise on a bench outside the Transbay Terminal, grinding my teeth and trying not to fall asleep so I wouldn't get mugged. But I was glad to be outside, the dank chill of a San Francisco summer night beating back the hangover.

And for once I was glad to be alone with my thoughts. I kept thinking about how I used to moon over that film still from *Fellini Satyricon,* the two men fighting over the young boy slave.

A cute guy just tried to pimp me out to a distinguished filmmaker. If I put it to myself that way, it was sexy and glamorous. And it meant I was attractive. Yet it *hadn't* been a turn-on. I would've expected it to feel like being desired, but it made me feel more like a prop. For the dozenth time, I played back the evening's events.

With a jolt I remembered the look on Frederica's face as she'd walked past Howard. The way she'd rebuffed me from the start. The attempt to get me to leave after dinner. Of course, I wouldn't be the first boy brought before Howard to curry favor with him, would I? It probably happened all the time. And her own boyfriend (or whatever Calvin was) had done it right in front of her. Yes, she'd been disgusted, but she'd been trying to push me out of there for my *own* sake, not hers.

A bus rumbled to life in a parking bay and rolled up to the boarding area. Stiff with cold, I rose to meet it. Its doors opened, beckoning me home.

PART II

12

WESSONALITY

had showered and dressed, and now I was pacing around my bedroom, restless and discomfited, repeating my compulsive rituals with increasing urgency.

"Jim, you can't be late for the first day of school!" my mother called.

"Yeah, coming!"

I tried to home in on what I was feeling, exactly. It was like watching a movie with the sound just a bit out of synch with the image, a barely perceptible disconnect. Abruptly I tore off my flared Lee jeans and striped jersey. I needed to be wearing clothes that matched how I *felt*—that was the problem!

"Better hurry! I'm leaving for work now! I love you, honey!" I heard the front door click shut.

I pulled on the Levi's with holes in the knees that my mom had tried several times to throw away, plus a black turtleneck sweater. From the kitchen I got a bottle of Wesson vegetable oil and massaged a little into my hair. I tried to comb it back and flat like Dracula's, but every time I had it just so, it would spring up again. Still, I was sanguine about my look, even with its imperfections. To my mind I wasn't so much dressing as trying to make a statement. And what better time to make one than on the first day of my sophomore year?

I walked up the hill to school with a confident step, but as soon as I reached the campus, there was a subtle shift in the air. It was as if the entire student body had been paying attention to my inner monologue as I'd gotten dressed. Everywhere I turned, whispers followed.

Ew, what is he wearing?

So weird.

Omigod, is today Halloween?

During the lunch hour, I tried to locate my friends. Greg was nowhere to be found, including in his favored hideouts for a lunchtime toke. That was puzzling, because as endlessly clever as he was at coming up with ways to get out of class early, his parents were strict about his attendance, and it was unlike him to rack up an absence on the first day of school.

And even though I knew Helle's exchange program had ended by now, I found myself still looking for her. Over summer vacation we'd gone to a couple of punk shows together; at the last one, she'd had a gnarly-looking bruise on her cheek. When I'd asked about it, she'd cut the discussion short with "You know Charles is a brat." After that she'd barely been in touch. Without her presence San Carlos High reverted instantly to a faded Kodak snapshot of cinder blocks and sunburned lawn.

My itinerant childhood had trained me to be good at taking in stride the way connections came and went—or at least to convince myself that I was good at it. "There's always someone new to meet around the corner" was my motto. The truth was, though, that being rootless is not liberating but tiring, and I felt just as sad as anyone else when a friend faded away. And without Helle especially, I was aware of being the only outward manifestation of freakiness at San Carlos High.

Plus, if she was really gone, what would happen to my connection to the punk rock scene? I was on chatting terms with some of the people I saw at shows, but I didn't really know anybody. By fourth period my confidence was flagging. The oil in my hair was feeling simply greasy, and I was perspiring in my black turtleneck as the afternoon sun burned off the morning fog.

As I walked down the steps after the final bell, a blond guy wearing a faded Farrah Fawcett tee shouted, "Fucking fruit!" He and his friends laughed. I started walking faster.

LATER, I HAD A SLEEPWALKING EPISODE. It was the first I'd had in a long while, and it was coupled, as it always had been, with a certain recurring nightmare. There's no beginning to the dream: it begins in the middle, as though on a continuous loop.

I am being pursued by a man with a knife. I can't see him, but sense him behind me as I stumble, panting with terror, through a dark, rambling, unfamiliar house. I hide, motionless and silent, knowing that it is futile: he will find me, and he will kill me.

This nightmare had been causing me to sleepwalk on and off since I was about six. At one time it had been so much a part of my daily life that I'd been hesitant to sleep at someone else's house. The dream of scrambling for a hiding place would overlap with reality, and in the morning I'd be found asleep inside a closet, ensconced behind the hanging clothes. Often I would have worked myself into a corner, unable to move forward, like a windup toy bumping its head into the wall.

That night, I walked in my sleep to the kitchen and closed

myself into the utility closet, crouching beside the mop bucket and the broom. My mom appeared in her nightgown and woke me gently. Groggy and feeling exposed, I grumbled as she led me back to bed and kissed my forehead. There I fell back to sleep quickly, but the next day I woke with a sense of foreboding, haunted by the spectral blade that was still in my mind's eye, poised to sever.

HELLE SURFACED ONCE MORE, near the end of that month, on a Friday evening when a Pacific storm was hurling eucalyptus pods against the windowpanes and sending trash cans rattling down Torino Drive.

"Hey, kiddo," she greeted me on the phone, as though no time had elapsed since we'd last met.

"Hey! Where've you been?"

"Eh. Things are a little complicated right now. My visa expired. It's a month already since I'm supposed to go back."

"Oh, shit. Can your parents go to the consulate or something?" When she didn't respond, I asked, "Is everything okay with Charles?"

I heard the long exhale of a cigarette. "Charles is Charles." Apparently I was supposed to stop asking questions. "Listen, the Germs are playing the Mabuhay tomorrow night, did you hear?"

"Oh, cool." Somebody I'd met at a show had told me about the Mabuhay Gardens, a Filipino restaurant by day and a punk rock club by night. The Mabuhay had started running small display ads in the *Chronicle*'s Pink Section, the Sunday entertainment portion of the paper. I'd been following the ads with almost religious zeal, acquainting myself with the jigsaw puzzle of punk band names that played in the city: the Mutants, Crime, the Flesh Eaters, the Bags, the Nuns, X, the Suburban Lawns, Middle Class, the Zeros, the Screamers. And yes, the Germs. "Are you guys going to go?" I asked her.

"Ya, we'll try to make it." The implication in her tone was that they probably wouldn't.

WELL, WITH OR WITHOUT THEM, I was going. I'd have to plot out an outfit, but my options were thin, given my still boring wardrobe. I was used to clothes that came in shrink-wrapped packages from Sears or J. C. Penney, but I knew I wouldn't be able to concoct the right look at those kinds of places. So after my mother and I did our Saturday rounds at Foodville and Woolworth's, I asked her to take me to the local Salvation Army. I knew she thought that shopping at a thrift store for occasional housewares was fine, but clothes were another story. The idea made her contort with embarrassment, made her feel I was undoing the image she strove so hard to project—a projection at which she was so successful that most people who met her thought she was rich.

Unless, of course, I was there to spoil the effect, like now. She stood in the men's-clothing aisle with her arms crossed while I went through the sweater selection, moving through them fast, one after the other, like I was browsing albums in a record store.

"That looks like something a bum would wear," she pronounced as I pulled an antifreeze-green sweater on over my shirt. When Julie and I had been little, Mom had dressed us to look like catalog models. When I was two years old, I'd had a matching jacket and bow tie. "I raised you to have class. And look at this."

I turned this way and that. "Does it fit?"

"People would stop picking on you if you'd stand up straight and stop wearing things like that. You might as well have a sign hanging over you that says 'Hit me.'"

"Oh, okay, so if I had feathered hair and bell-bottoms, everyone would love me."

"Don't be sarcastic. Be whoever you want to be on the inside. But people don't have to see it on the outside."

I rolled my eyes. "I'm going to pretend you didn't just say that."

"Honey, that sweater's *dirty*. Someone else has worn it. And it looks like it's for a woman."

"I know that someone else has worn it—this is secondhand clothing. It doesn't matter if it's a man's or a woman's. Just tell me if it fits."

"Turn around," she sighed. "Yes. It fits."

THE MABUHAY GARDENS WAS IN NORTH BEACH, a part of San Francisco unfamiliar to me. Midway through the ride on the 30-Stockton bus, I worked up the courage to ask the driver if he crossed Broadway. He nodded curtly, and I wondered if he didn't like the look of my thrift-store clothes. The black wool pants I'd found to go with the sweater were itchy and had a musky smell.

I got off the bus just past Chinatown and walked up Broadway, a seedy stretch of strip clubs, porn theaters, and souvenir shops with a rowdy, rough energy that I found intimidating. For the first time in my forays to the city, I had the uneasy feeling that the invisible cord that connected me to my home and to my mom could snap, propelling me into some dark urban oblivion— lost, hungry, cold, and smelling like black Salvation Army pants. Even the glimpse I got of men cruising, which usually excited me, just felt sordid and menacing. The sidewalk was crazed with cracks; I couldn't possibly avoid all of them, which made me even more uneasy. I alternated grinding my teeth and exhaling in sets of Saturday's power number of six.

Outside the Mabuhay Gardens was a scrum of exotic-looking people; inside the club was a jumble of faded tiki kitsch, leatherette booths, and threadbare carpet. I snaked my way through the crowd toward the bar. No Helle. I did see some faces I recognized from the Pit, though. I spotted the woman who'd been wearing a crazy Constructivist-looking jumpsuit at the Tuxedomoon show, who tonight was dressed in even stranger garb: vibrant blue jodhpurs, jacket and tie, with hair dyed to match.

I also saw the black girl with the ironic schoolgirl shtick. As I neared the bar, I heard her saying, ". . . campy, salacious tart!"

"Hi," I said, sidling up to her. "I remember seeing you at the Tuxedomoon show."

"Well, hello," she replied, turning from the bartender she'd been talking to. I'd admired her style, but hadn't realized how stunning she was, with slender, elegant limbs and striking green eyes. I inadvertently gasped.

"Would you care for a drink?" she continued. She opened her purse, revealing a bottle of cheap booze. "A lady should always be prepared!"

"Absolutely." The vodka had a harsh, fiery taste.

"I know, I know," she said, watching me cough, "but until I become the kept woman of some landed-gentry type, it'll have to do."

She seemed to have a mind like a gyroscope, spinning at a velocity above and beyond the rest of us. I wanted to know everything about her, but instead I just asked her name. It was, she said, Blackie O—which had to be the coolest name I'd ever heard in my life.

"I like your name. Mine's Jim." The single syllable seemed to land on the floor like a bag filled with rocks. I made a mental note that I needed to devise another, one that was glittering and ironic, one that would embody the new person I felt myself becoming.

I wrote my phone number for her on the back of a pamphlet that a Jesus freak had been handing out on the bus. It had an extra-gruesome illustration of the crucifix on the front.

"Nice details on the flesh wounds," Blackie O said admiringly, tucking it into her purse. "Well, I have to find my friend now." She tilted her head and batted her eyelashes flirtatiously. "I'll see you around sometime, Jimmy."

I'd been called a handful of nicknames during my life, all of which had felt alien to who I was. When I was small, my sister would sing a made-up song with annoying frequency that went, *Jimbo, Jimbo, whatcha going to do-eeyo? Jimbo, Jimbo, where you gonna go-eeyo? You're going down the lane to see your little girlie-yo!* The name Jimmy was only slightly better, but somehow coming from Blackie O it had a sardonic twist, in that way she apparently had of making things sound breathless and disingenuous at the same time as she was roasting them.

The band was late, and the audience heckled the empty stage. Since the bartender didn't appear to be carding anyone, I ordered a plastic cup of beer and gulped it down, and then another, masking my anxiety about catching the last bus home. I didn't want to repeat the frightened footrace to Mission Street.

But when the Germs finally started performing, it was immediately clear that they were worth the wait. The lead singer, Darby Crash, had a demonic charisma, stalking around the stage like a drunken cat. My eardrums felt like they were being strip-mined. Some guy doing a jerky, spasmodic dance slammed into me hard, sloshing beer from the cup all down the front of my sweater. Experimentally, I bumped him back, and found myself knocked nearly off my feet by the force of his body returning the blow. But he gave me a wild grin, and instead of feeling injured or insulted, I felt some kind of strange animal kinship. I threw my empty cup to the floor and did the pogo, jumping up and down, up and down, higher and higher each time.

13

BREAKER, BREAKER, OVER AND OUT

I plopped down on the sofa to watch *The Mike Douglas Show*, where some balding, sweaty comedian who seemed drunk was doing a bit about space aliens, something to do with *Close Encounters of the Third Kind*. The studio audience's laughter reminded me of frozen TV dinners, fully artificial. Then the comedian pulled a Princess Leia wig over his sweaty bald head, and the audience whooped and cackled.

I thought of Helle when we'd first met, the exasperated and unintentionally funny way she'd said, "People talk only, only, only about this bloody *Star Wars*." It made me smile to myself, but then I felt sad. She'd never shown up that night at the Mabuhay Gardens. When I'd called the number at her host family's house, a woman had said that they were "no longer taking messages for her," leaving me to work out the implications on my own. I supposed she'd gone back to Denmark, a million miles away.

I was grateful when the phone rang and even more grateful that it was Greg Lee. But the news was not good.

"Dude, I'm at fuckin' juvie, in Redwood City," he said. I knew he was referring to the much-dreaded juvenile hall, a sort of jail for minors.

"Shit! What happened?"

I heard a deep male voice say something unintelligible but unmistakably commanding. Greg answered it, sounding meek, saying, "I'll be off in a sec, okay?" Then to me he said, "Sorry, Jim. There's only one pay phone. Short version, I got busted. They're supposed to transfer me to some kind of halfway house after a couple of months."

"Oh, fuck. Can't your mom and dad get you out?"

Greg was quiet for a moment. "I don't think they even *want* me to come home," he said finally. "It's probably easier for them this way. It smells like socks in here," he added sadly.

"Please deposit ten cents for the next three minutes," said a brisk recorded voice.

"Shit," muttered Greg, "hang on." I heard the pip of a dime being put in the phone's slot.

"Can I come see you? Maybe bring you some books or magazines or something?"

"Uh, no visitors allowed."

"Jesus, Greg. Is there *anything* I can do?"

He was quiet again. I could hear more male cursing in the background, a burst of harsh laughter. Something crackled over a PA. "No," he said finally. "I'm basically fucked."

When I went back to the couch, my mind was racing. *The Mike Douglas Show* had given way to an ad for Final Net hair spray. No longer, I realized, did I have anyone to go on a bike ride with, to listen to records with, to smoke pot with, to go to a show with. It was official: I had no friends at San Carlos High.

The theme music for a *Starsky & Hutch* rerun floated out of the TV set. I took the faded scrap of paper that bore Jean-Paul's phone number out of my wallet.

The mean European landlady answered. "Jean-Paul is gone," she told me.

"Do you know when he'll be back?"

"I said he is gone. He does not live here anymore."

A cold and empty feeling washed over me. "Did he say where he was going? Do you have his new number?"

"No," she said, and hung up.

AT SCHOOL I SAT in my usual plot of grass in between two buildings, picking at my lunch. My solitude felt like a balloon blown to the bursting point, stretched thin. I'd paid a visit to Mrs. O'Hagan, but she'd been preoccupied with administrative matters, and it was clear she was only tolerating my presence.

Morosely crunching barbecue potato chips, I imagined what she might say if she knew I had to appease the invisible dynamo of chaos inside me with secret rituals, that the whole time I'd lingered at her desk I was grinding my teeth in twos because it was Tuesday. *Jim has a complex psychological character,* I pictured her saying. *Often the most sensitive minds are those most difficult for ordinary people to understand.*

Yes, Mrs. O'Hagan could probably grasp the complicated structure of my mind. If she didn't have to spend so much of her time dealing with teacher business, she'd probably be delighted to talk to me about some book she was reading, even if I *was* neurotic. At least I knew who Sylvia Plath was.

Walking home from school in a funk, I watched my elongated shadow walking alongside me. The shape of my hair, flopping against my shoulders as I moved, struck me as hopelessly suburban, deflating my image of myself as a counterculture clubgoer. I paused at a crosswalk, considering. Why not change that at least? I made an about-face and headed downtown to the barbershop.

As I sat at Rich's Cuts for Men waiting for my turn, I studied the rows of black-and-white photos of 1950s hair models. There was one in particular that caught my fancy, a kind of streamlined military cut, neatly parted, longish on top and buzzed on the sides and back. I imagined myself at the Pit, doing the pogo in torn-up black clothes and eyeliner, with a haircut that was straight out of an army training film from the fifties. It struck me as an amusing visual joke, ironic in the way that "Shazam Productions" was ironic.

While Rich plied his scissors, I watched with alarm and anticipation as large clumps of my hair fell to the floor. It was an extreme cut, I realized, nervous and excited. I'd made at least a temporary commitment, and I wasn't turning back.

MRS. O'HAGAN MUST HAVE PICKED UP on my loneliness—my mooching around her classroom at lunchtimes was likely the giveaway—because she invited me and my mother to her house in Palo Alto for dinner.

When I emerged from my room that Saturday evening, ready to go, my mother gaped with incredulous horror.

"You're wearing *that* to your *teacher's* house?"

"I am." I'd chosen my clothes for this event as carefully as I'd choose it for going to a club: a white T-shirt on which I'd written *"Dead Kennedys"* in front and *"Holiday in Cambodia"* on the back with a Sharpie. The Dead Kennedys were a new punk band I'd heard about, and "Holiday in Cambodia" was one of their signature songs. To top off the look, I'd smudged my mom's dark-brown brow pencil around my eyes so they looked bruised.

"Virginia"—for Mrs. O'Hagan had given me permission to call her by her first name—"likes me for who I actually am," I informed her. "She's not a slave to conformity. She doesn't need me to pretend I'm some *Brady Bunch* robot."

Mom twitched the car keys nervously. She was wearing one of her work scarves tied into an ascot, her newest bit of fashion flair. "It doesn't make you a robot to show some *respect*."

"Well, it's respectful to show up on time, so let's go."

"Oh my Lord. Call her Mrs. O'Hagan, at *least*," she pleaded.

Palo Alto, for me, represented something a bit more exalted than San Carlos. To my mind it was a cultured place, where people had volumes of Chaucer and Dostoyevsky filling their bookshelves, instead of dime-store mystery novels and casserole cookbooks. As we wended our way along surface streets through Redwood City, Atherton, and Menlo Park, I felt a surge of pressure. If we succeeded in impressing Mrs. O'Hagan, maybe she'd believe that I came from an interesting family and that I showed promise. If we failed, she might see me as just another suburban loser with zero future.

I switched the tremolo voices on the radio—*"'Cause we're livin' in a world of fools, breakin' us down!"*—to a classical station, which was playing a string quartet, and turned it up, hoping its refinement would somehow get inside us.

Mrs. O'Hagan greeted us in a silk caftan brocaded with

swallows in flight. After shaking my mother's hand, she rested her gaze on my eye makeup for a moment before she turned rather briskly, saying, "Please, come in."

The inside of her house was even more wonderful than I'd pictured. There were books everywhere: lining the built-in shelves, in thoughtful stacks on coffee tables, piled crudely in the corners. There was a lacquered Japanese folding screen and a chandelier. Taking our coats, she led us to the living room, where a Siamese cat appeared and made a little trilling sound until I picked it up.

"His Royal Highness Coco," remarked Mrs. O'Hagan. "He only lets special people pick him up! Now, what can I get you two to drink? There's cranberry juice, Perrier, or Chablis. Or, best of all, we can have spritzers—Chablis and Perrier together. It's how they drink wine in the Côte d'Azur in the summertime."

"Isn't that festive," my mother said cautiously. I could tell she disapproved of Mrs. O'Hagan's offering me wine, but apparently she wasn't brave enough to object.

Mrs. O'Hagan turned to me. "Jim, come join me in the kitchen. We'll fix something nice for all of us. Mrs. Oseland, won't you make yourself comfortable?"

The kitchen was surprisingly messy, piled with more books, comatose houseplants, and a clutter of half-empty liquor bottles that reminded me of Dad. "Get me the Perrier from the fridge, please," she directed me.

The refrigerator had the intense odor of overripe bananas and looked like it had only ever had items added to it, never removed. I found the Perrier wedged behind a jar of cocktail olives.

As she made the spritzers, Mrs. O'Hagan said, "Do me one

favor, Jim. Just relax and have a good time. All right? Now, be a dear and bring the crudités."

I followed her out and placed the platter on the coffee table, admiring its artistry. There were julienned carrots and celery, radishes carved into rose shapes. "Here's to making new friends," toasted Mrs. O'Hagan. We clinked glasses. My mom placed hers down without taking a sip.

"The vegetables are so pretty I almost don't want to disturb them," I said.

"My first husband, Herschel, taught me you begin a meal with your eyes. We traveled in France after the war," Mrs. O'Hagan continued. "We must've dined in a hundred bistros serving crudité plates like this."

Addressing my mother, she went on, "We were there hoping to lose our 'American-ness.' Even though France was in bad shape after the war, everyone was still so gracious." She gave us a coy smile. To my eyes she seemed in that moment like some otherworldly goddess, not quite human.

"I've never been," my mother replied, and hesitated before plucking a rose-shaped radish from the platter. I shot her a pleading look. Couldn't she at least *pretend* we weren't completely uncosmopolitan?

"Well, you simply must go," said Mrs. O'Hagan. "This fall I'll be in Paris with a former student. We're going to explore the parts of the Louvre that people usually ignore."

I was envious of the travel that she was about to embark on. Wasn't there some way she could take me with her?

She turned to me. Her smile faded as her gaze lit on my T-shirt. "Tell me, Jim," she asked, straightening in her chair, "why are the words 'Dead Kennedys' written on your shirt?"

"It's a band. 'Holiday in Cambodia' is one of their songs."

"I see." Something chilly crept into her tone. "And can you tell me, please, what could conceivably be amusing about the Kennedy assassinations?"

My mother's face reddened. "Mrs. O'Hagan, I'm sorry. I knew I shouldn't have let him leave the house in that thing."

The evening was sliding out of my control like an airplane skidding off a runway. "It's not to make *fun* of it," I entreated. "They sing about political stuff, like how bad it is in Cambodia, with Pol Pot. It's important! I mean, people are getting killed, and it's not like anyone's singing about it on the *radio*."

"Duly noted," said Mrs. O'Hagan without warmth. "Would you help me bring out the main course?"

She'd made chicken breast rolled up and stuffed with ham and butter, along with wild rice and asparagus. It was delicious, but I was so upset I could barely get it down. My mouth was dry, chewing the food in repetitions of six. My mom picked at her plate with polite determination.

"So tell me, Mrs. Oseland, how is it being a single mother?" asked Mrs. O'Hagan.

I knew that my mom would resent the question. Could this evening go any more wrong?

"I manage," replied my mother.

"At least you're in California. There are a lot of women in the same boat here. You have a good job, I hope?"

"Well, I'm just a Kelly Girl. Where I work changes all the time."

"I see. Maybe one of the places you're working will offer you a full-time position. Do you have health insurance?"

I could tell that my mom was growing increasingly disturbed by these intimate queries. *I'm very private*, she liked to repeat, as though it were a mantra rather than a character trait. "Well, no, we don't have insurance right now. My husband dropped us from his policy." As she said this, I noticed that tears were welling in the corners of her eyes, and I suddenly wished my dad were here so I could punch him in the face.

"Well, that's not a good situation." Mrs. O'Hagan sighed. "But you're smart. And you've got real poise. I'm sure an employer will come to see your worth and value."

"Oh, I don't know about having any worth or value. I'm just little old me."

I stared down at the greasy blots and trails on my plate.

Mrs. O'Hagan bit the tip of an asparagus spear. "At least you have Jim. He's a special young man."

"Yes, he's always been different."

I rolled my eyes, but relief coursed through me. Mrs. O'Hagan was smiling again, although there was something about the smile that kept me from relaxing entirely.

"He has a restless intellect," she continued, setting down her fork. "Though I'm afraid to say that because of that he has a tendency to seize on misguided notions."

Six, I thought, not liking where this was going.

"Having the bad taste to advertise for such a musical group as Dead Kennedys, for instance. But more to the point, I find that bright young people often believe that they know how the world works. When in *fact*," she said, speaking with cold emphasis, as though she really wanted me to hear every word, "they're ignorant. And, in their ignorance, mistake their solipsism for reality."

On the drive home, my mother and I sat without speaking. I stared with unseeing eyes at the traffic lights on Alameda de las Pulgas, a name Mrs. O'Hagan had once told me was Spanish for "grove of the fleas."

When we finally got home, I went directly to my room, slamming the door behind me, and screamed into my pillow, *"Fuck you, you fucking cunt!"*

I screamed and wept, and then, guts churning with misery and chicken Kiev, I masturbated, thinking about Calvin kissing me at the Pit. I could hear my mother turning on the TV in the other room, the theme music blatting over the sounds of her readying for bed. *"And love won't hurt anymore—it's an open smile on a friendly shore!"*

Now I felt drained and hollow. In the bathroom I smoked a fat roach, blowing the smoke into the fan vent. Then I took the disposable razor from the medicine cabinet. I stared at my reflection: long limbs, pale skin, brown eyes. So normal. So fucking boring. I scraped the blade across one of my eyebrows.

It looked strange. I swiped the excess hair off onto my jeans and did it again, more closely, then shaved the other brow. Above my eyes was now naked, puffy skin, slightly scratched and bloody. I liked it.

I suddenly felt a jolt of power. Maybe it wasn't impossible for me to escape my suffocating life. Maybe I could live in a loft in New York City, with an artist boyfriend. We would go to dinner parties and galleries. I could be witty and urbane. Fuck Mrs. O'Hagan. Fuck Helle. Fuck all of them. I, James Oseland, could be a citizen of the world!

No. That person wasn't going to be anything special. Because that person wasn't me.

James was a nonentity, as was Jim. I liked Jimmy better—for a while I'd been sort of embarrassed to be associated with our peanut-farmer president, who wasn't much respected—but it had an edge to it that was both friendly and tough. And ever since Blackie O had called me Jimmy, it had felt more comfortable, like a broken-in pair of jeans.

Oseland, on the other hand, was irredeemable: it represented the false notion of a family unit. It was a remnant serving no useful purpose and would be better off removed.

Flushing the end of the roach, I ran through some possibilities in my mind. Jimmy Boredom. Jimmy Blah. Jimmy Disgust. Jimmy Misery. Jimmy Nausea. Jimmy Breakdown. Jimmy Suburbia. None of these seemed quite right.

I thought of Blackie O, how that moniker simultaneously skewered the notion of being prim and ladylike while embodying it, mirroring her true essence. What was *my* true essence?

Anxiety. Self-hatred. Depression. Obsession. Manic compulsion.

Neurosis.

It was as if a perfect chord had been played on a guitar. It was like the best song I'd ever heard, and the lyrics went, *"This is who I am, not who you want me to be. This is me, the totally fucked-up product of a totally fucked-up world."*

I met my gaze in the mirror. "Jimmy Neurosis," I said, and laughed with pure delight.

14

ONLY HER HAIRDRESSER KNOWS FOR SURE

As the holiday season approached, with its Hallmark-card air of happy families and its chatter about who was being invited to whose house for Thanksgiving dinner, I was more aware than ever that I no longer had any friends.

Luckily, I could take refuge in music. I'd make pilgrimages to Aquarius Records in the Castro and spend my allowance on whatever punk rock music they had in stock. My record collection, which until now had been, with the exception of Joni Mitchell, mostly movie soundtracks, began to expand to include an EP by Tuxedomoon and a 45 by the Dils (one song on each side, a rip-off at the price, but still). I bought a 45 by the Offs called "Johnny Too Bad" for the cover art, which I found compelling, a grainy black-and-white photo of a guy having a gun pointed into his mouth. Devo released a lushly produced full-length album called *Q: Are We Not Men? A: We Are Devo!* which I played until the needle wore its grooves down.

The leftover jellied cranberry sauce and turkey breast ("Why cook the whole bird when there's only two of us?" my mother had argued) was sitting in its Tupperware container when the news exploded with the announcement that Harvey Milk, the first openly gay elected official in California, had been murdered, along with the mayor of San Francisco.

The guy who shot them was some prick they used to work with, a square-jawed model of normality who looked like a G.I. Joe doll. Governor Jerry Brown had ordered the flags to be hung at half-mast, and even President Carter made a special address to express his dismay. I'd never dreamed I'd hear the word "gay" on TV every night of the week, but there it was.

I longed to have someone to talk about it with, and I tried with my mother, but it made both of us tense. So it came as a relief when Blackie O called to ask if I wanted to go see a punk show in the city with her. I couldn't believe she'd even remembered me, let alone held on to my phone number, and yet here she was inviting me to see the Mutants! I wasn't about to launch into a discussion of the assassination of Harvey Milk with her, but so what? I'd be out with a cool girl at an infamous nightspot, which was good enough.

We'd be going to a place called the Deaf Club, and it was located, she told me, "in the filthy heart of the Mission. It's a very amusing place, as long as you don't mind that the price of admission includes getting scabies."

She was reluctant to let me come to her house in Berkeley, convinced that it wouldn't be convenient and we should just meet at the club, but, anxious at having to find it by myself, I pestered her about it.

She sighed. "The last time I brought somebody from punk rock home, it was Biafra from the Dead Kennedys."

"You mean Jello Biafra?"

"Only poseurs call him Jello. He got a bloody nose and bled all over the bathroom. My mom didn't take too kindly to that, and I think there's not a day that goes by that she doesn't bring it up."

"I'll be on my best behavior. I won't bleed. It'll be fun," I cajoled. "We can have a drink and listen to records first to get in the mood."

"Oh, goody, I do love a sock hop," she deadpanned, but finally relented.

Later that evening I stood on the welcome mat of a small, two-level home in North Berkeley, hoping my clothing would pass muster for a night at the Deaf Club. When the door swung open, a woman in her forties with a close-shorn, Black Power–style Afro was giving me an appraising look, cinching the belt on her housecoat.

I introduced myself with my most polite, grown-up-approved demeanor.

"Nice to meet you. You may call me Joyce. Charlene," she called, "your friend Jimmy is here."

Charlene?

"Come on in. We're just finishing our supper. Have you eaten?" The southern cadence of her voice—she was, I learned, from Georgia—sounded alien in this environment. She seemed fierce yet soft, and I wished I could be enveloped by her maternal energy.

In an alcove that served as a dining room, Blackie O was seated at a two-person table bearing the remains of dinner: fish, salad, corn bread. "Charlene, pull up a chair for your guest," Joyce admonished, and Blackie O, obediently fetching a chair from the living room, flashed me an embarrassed smile.

From my seat I had a view of almost everything on the first floor, and I scoped out the details, trying not to be obvious about it. There was a pot of ivy on top of the TV console, and there were lots of framed black-and-white family photos all over the place. They had the same beige Trimline wall phone on the threshold of the kitchen as we did at home, and I realized that when Blackie O and I had talked about going to the show tonight, we'd been mirror images of each other. It was amazing to me that someone as scintillating as Blackie O could come from somewhere as ordinary as this. Maybe there was more hope for me than I'd thought!

Joyce handed me a dish of corn bread topped with a generous pat of butter. "So where are you kids off to tonight?"

"We're going to see a band in the city. The Mutants," Blackie O told her. Gone was the sarcastic, Dorothy Parker–esque tone I was familiar with, replaced with a restrained, softer voice.

"The Mutants? What kind of name is that?" Joyce poured herself iced tea from a pitcher. "That sounds like something from a horror movie. Don't you agree, Jimmy?"

"That's sort of what I like about it," I ventured, hoping to neither alienate my brand-new friend nor incite her mother's irritation.

Joyce continued, "All of those rock bands you like have the worst names, Charlene. Mutants! Weirdos! Suicide! I just don't think that's right. We all have enough problems in our lives these days. Why would you want to mock people who try to kill themselves? I don't think that's funny at all."

Blackie O briefly looked as though she was at a loss for words but recovered quickly enough. "Mother, it's just creative expression. Punk rock is a way of being ironic, so you can feel better about how horrific the world is."

Joyce sipped her iced tea. "Well, the world might be terrible, but there's no need to add to that by making fun of the disadvantaged."

"Me and Jimmy should really get going," said Blackie O. "We're meeting Annie, and we shouldn't keep her waiting."

"And go you will, young lady, just as soon as you've cleared this table."

Blackie O rose at once and began carrying plates to the sink. To defuse the tension, I asked Joyce what she did for a living, and her mood seemed to lighten as she explained that she was a social worker, helping families get the social services they needed. I was impressed by how humanitarian that sounded. "That seems like a way to make your life really matter," I said.

There was pride in her expression, but Joyce snorted. "It's a way to keep yourself scraping and scrambling to stay caught up with your mortgage, that's for sure."

On the way to the bus stop, Blackie O rustled a pint of vodka out of her clutch purse and took a slug before passing it to me. "My mother means well," she said, wiping her lips with a vintage handkerchief. "She's just a tad overbearing."

"I think she's kind of cool," I said. *Charlene.*

"HEY." She jabbed me in the ribs hard enough to knock the breath out of me, sloshing liquor down my shirt. "NO."

"Ow! Okay, okay." Giggling, I threw my hands up in surrender as she raised her pocketbook to hit me again. "Really. I get it."

She gave me a sideways look, just to be sure, but it was warm. "Seriously, my mother has a finely tuned skill for knowing exactly how to get under my skin at any given moment. It's like a party trick."

"My mom drives me insane, too. I wish she'd just let go and

stop trying to control me." Saying this aloud to Blackie O made me feel that I wasn't so alone.

"Oh, Joyce wrote the book on control. Maybe your mom has signed up for the free lectures that she's been giving at the Emeryville Holiday Inn? 'How to Destroy Your Teenager's Individuality in Ten Easy Steps'?"

At the Transbay Terminal, her friend was waiting, a scrawny figure about our age in a green sequined dress and red cowboy boots. She was tall and lanky like me, with a high forehead and an upturned nose.

"This is my friend Annie A Go Go. Annie, this is—"

"Jimmy Neurosis," I supplied, shaking her hand.

Blackie O grinned. "I like, I *like*!"

Sitting beside them on the bus, being included in their scene, made me feel like I was somebody. Annie told a convoluted tale of an after-party she'd been to, concluding with, "Anyway, I think he likes me. I mean, he didn't actually *say* he likes me, but he gave me that *look*. Do I sound crazy to you guys? You're looking at me like I'm crazy."

Blackie O explained, "Annie's very high-strung. Her mom works for Werner Erhard, so she thinks every conversation is an est training seminar."

Annie looked sad, and I made a mental note to find out what an "est training seminar" was.

A large guy who looked like a prison escapee boarded at the next stop. He had a gigantic boom box and sat across the aisle, glowering at us. "I refer to this as the rape-and-pillage bus," Blackie O remarked, loud enough for him to hear.

I laughed at her audacity. The demure girl from dinner was long gone, swept away by geographical distance and vodka. "So, Annie, where do you live?"

"The Haight, but I barely stay at home anymore."

"A girl always on the go-go, our Annie," added Blackie O. "Wherever there's a sofa to crash on or a blow job to be given."

Annie shoved her playfully. "Jealous!"

"No, *you're* jealous, because unlike me you don't live in Berkeley," Blackie O said. "The historical home of bra burners, tired old leftists, and other sundry losers who refuse to accept the fact that the 1960s ended almost a decade ago."

I laughed again, in love with the way she used language. It was a jewel-encrusted alternative to the way my family used it, as if words had a price and they were deeply concerned about overspending. The scary guy was still glaring at us, his contempt coming at us in a clear wave. Normally I'd have been frightened, but being with these girls made me feel invincible. "I live in San Carlos," I told them, "down the peninsula. It's about as interesting as a roll of paper towels."

"Oh, Berkeley's fine if you enjoy the smell of human urine," said Blackie O. "They should give tours of People's Park to show the dark side of humanity." She raised a finger in the air. "I have seen the enemy, and it is wearing patchouli and flashing the peace sign."

"Are you in school, Blackie O?" I asked. I couldn't imagine her in school, but neither could I imagine Joyce allowing anything otherwise.

"If you could call it that. Berkeley High is little more than a millhouse for the pothead sons and daughters of Berkeley liberal intellectuals and ghetto denizens."

"I hate San Carlos High. Sometimes I think that carrying a spray bottle of hydrochloric acid might be the best answer." I was trying to sound clever, but as soon as I uttered the words, they sounded flat and unfunny.

The Deaf Club was on a depressed stretch of Valencia Street peppered with burrito joints and pawnshops. As it turned out, the club's name was devoid of irony: located up a flight of rickety wooden stairs, it was actually a club for the hearing-impaired residents of the neighborhood. It had a stench that was equal parts public restroom and ashtray, with low ceilings and a forlorn bar where a few inebriated deaf men roosted on the barstools, watching the scene before them like spectators at a sporting event.

Yet there was an energy to the place that struck me as being focused and pure. Virtually every surface of the men's room, including the toilet, was covered in graffiti; among the more memorable was one that read CONFORMITY IS DEFORMITY. The Mutants were already onstage when we came in, messing with their amps and swigging from beer bottles. I thought they were beautifully weird; the lead singers were a short, whip-skinny guy in a tight-fitting suit and two women with hair teased out to within an inch of its life.

Blackie O introduced me to her friends in the crowd, whose faces I dimly recognized; I was starting to understand that certain people were fixtures on the scene. Ginger Coyote was a drag queen with blue hair in Kabuki makeup. Jennifer Blowdryer was a scowling but fiercely smart and funny blonde. Mary Menace's iconoclastic look I recognized at once; she'd been the one in the weird jumpsuit and later the electric-blue jodhpurs.

Mary Menace had a wealthier air than the rest of us, and tonight she stood out in a baffling outfit that she explained to me as being "sort of New Wave, but filtered through the TV show *Bewitched*." She seemed earnest and kind in a way that reminded me of my mother, but the Mutants' thick, buzzing guitar chords coalesced into a song about—from what I could make out of the lyrics—a lover who was devouring her romantic partner. It was so loud that conversation was impossible.

I drifted away from Mary Menace and moved in closer to the music, to that place of complete sonic engulfment, shut my eyes, and let it fill me up. The crowd around me thrashed violently, like piranhas in a feeding frenzy.

As the Mutants launched into another maelstrom of sound, I noticed a sincere-looking older guy in a 1950s bowling shirt standing aloof from the scrimmage of bodies. He had pouty lips, a rockabilly hairdo that climaxed in a swirl on the top of his head, and eyelids that drooped at the corners like a bloodhound's. Our eyes met, and my heart began to pound, but then someone slammed into me and I hit the floor. This set off a chain reaction, and seconds later I was pinned under a pile of sweaty, laughing, groaning people. Once I'd extricated myself, I hunted through the crowd until I found him again.

This time I was more savvy. I led him by the hand into the men's room, not forgetting to lock the door behind us. I'd learned enough from Jean-Paul to unzip the man's jeans with confidence and sink to my knees. This time, feeling loosened and playful, my clothes already disheveled by slamming up against a dozen strangers, I cared much less about doing it incorrectly.

Intoxicated on Blackie O's discount hooch, cheap beer, and the high of a sexual encounter with a handsome stranger, I missed the bus back and ended up having a rollicking breakfast in the dead of night at Zim's Coffee Shop with Blackie O and Annie A Go Go, then went to Annie's place, a cute Victorian near the intersection of Haight and Ashbury.

We tiptoed, drunk as lords, up a flight of stairs into her

bedroom. It was a classic teenage flophouse, with clothes strewn everywhere and an unmade bed. Annie put a tape in the tape player, twangy, creepy rock-and-roll.

I sprawled on a jumble of knitted afghans and tiny blankets that had obviously been stolen from an airplane. I snatched the cassette box off the floor where she'd tossed it: *The Cramps Live at Napa State Mental Hospital.* "What the fuck," I laughed. "What *is* this?"

"It's a psychobilly classic," she said cheerfully. Blackie O knelt by the mirror propped against the closet door, carefully wiping off what appeared to be five pounds of eye makeup. She never took any drugs, she didn't even smoke weed, so even at the end of a long night she was always ten times more composed than the rest of us.

"Won't it wake up your folks?"

"They're away at Esalen this week."

I lay back on her bed in a boozy glow. "What's Esalen?"

"It's basically a giant hot tub in Big Sur where you go to find yourself."

Blackie O laughed knowingly, and for a moment I felt like a hick. I watched Annie exchange her sequined dress, which she dropped onto the floor, for a kimono with a coffee stain on the sleeve, and I admired her defiantly unnatural tresses—an aggressively artificial orange hue.

"How in the hell do you get your hair that amazing color?" I wondered.

"That's between me and my hairdresser, darling," she said. "No, actually, hang on . . ." From under a clump of shoes, purses, and jackets, she produced a box of Roux dye with a label that looked unchanged since the fifties, an artless, silhouetted photo of a model with a Zsa Zsa Gabor bouffant. The color was called Flame.

"Oh my God, *I* want to have Flame hair!" I realized that I was slurring my words.

"Well, I've got a bottle, sweetheart, and you've got the hair. Let's do it," she said, applying a lighter to a bong.

"No time like the present," agreed Blackie O. Her eyes were ringed now like a raccoon's.

The bathroom, too, was in a state of disarray, with jars of makeup on every surface and splotches of what must be hair dye on the towels. As instructed, I stripped down to my underwear. Perched on the edge of the tub, I felt self-conscious in my whiter-than-white skin, gooseflesh coming up on my arms.

With professional briskness, Blackie O draped paper towels over my shoulders while Annie A Go Go, donning Rubbermaid kitchen gloves, stirred dye in a cereal bowl. "I feel like I'm going to have some kind of surgical procedure," I said as Annie slapped a wad of cold, viscous dye onto my head. It smelled eye-wateringly acrid, like something that might leak from a car engine, and it burned my scalp. "Oh, it stings, it stings!"

"That's how you know it's working," advised Annie, massaging it in. "And so what if you have brain tumors from this stuff in twenty years? None of us are going to be alive then anyway. Here, have a hit." *God, I love her,* I thought, sucking up smoke from the bong.

At sunrise they left me to shower it off. I was queasy from the fumes and the hangover, but I also felt happy, watching the deep orange dye spinning down the drain. With one of Annie's damp towels cinched around my waist, I checked out my reflection. My hair was straight out of *Willy Wonka & the Chocolate Factory*.

Though it didn't come out looking exactly the way it did on the box and though splotches of orange stained my forehead and neck, the overall effect was phenomenal. I looked like somebody else entirely, and I loved it.

In the bedroom Annie and Blackie O were asleep under the snarl of mismatched blankets. "Ta-da," I whispered to the silent room.

When I got home later, my mother took one look at me and burst into tears.

15

WHO LOVES YA, BABY?

I mustered my courage and invited Blackie O to hang out, just the two of us. To my delight she suggested we spend the day roaming around San Francisco, which immediately got me spinning a fantasy in which I ran into the handsome guy I'd had sex with at the Deaf Club. I realized it was an absurd notion, but I couldn't banish it from my mind, and I confessed as much to Blackie O as we strode the city pavement in our shabby finery.

To my relief she didn't scoff. Instead she pronounced, "Stranger things have happened," and opened the door to a little shop marked SH'BOOM. This was a tiny establishment that catered to the punk rock crowd, the only one of its kind, where she knew the shopkeeper, Margie, a friendly and effusive, chain-smoking ex-hippie.

At the shows we went to, there was a lot of verbal hippie bashing, but according to Blackie O, Margie wasn't the only hippie who'd traded in Birkenstocks for the glamour rags of a punk rocker. Seeing me eye a pair of black vinyl boots with toes that came to a sharp point, Margie urged, "Oh, the wicked-elf shoes! Go ahead, try them on."

They did look like something an evil fairy would wear, and I wanted them badly. They were so tight that my feet felt bound.

"Welcome to the tyranny of womanhood," intoned Blackie O. "May you ache endlessly and find a good man."

I posed at the mirror, admiring their weirdness. Shortly I was pouncing upon a spectacularly garish pair of skintight, peg-legged, neon-green jeans. Everything about them was wrong in the most appealing way, and I knew at once that they would disturb my mother deeply. I walked out of Sh'boom having spent all of the cash I'd saved up for Christmas presents.

After that we walked up Market Street toward the Castro. "I'm taking you to Cafe Flore," she told me. "You'll love it. It's where all sorts of trouble gets hatched."

"I almost went there once," I mused, "but I ended up giving a French guy a blow job in the park instead." At this she threw her head back and guffawed.

From the outside Cafe Flore resembled a steamy greenhouse, its glass panes enclosing a scrappy garden of potted plants. Inside, it was a crowded mass of people in black leather jackets and wild hair colors, like a punk show with cappuccino standing in for a loud, wailing band. There was loud, hyperactive electronic music playing. On Blackie O's advice I ordered a steamed milk with orgeat syrup, which sounded exotic and tasted like almonds and roses.

We were carrying our drinks to a table when I saw him, sitting alone at a table in the corner reading a book. Those pouty lips! That hangdog air! Those tight black jeans!

"Oh my God, it's *him*," I whispered. "It's the guy from the Deaf Club!"

She took a slurp off the top of her overfull cappuccino. "You're fucking kidding."

"I'm fucking not!"

"Why are you still yakking at *me*, then? Go talk to him!"

Trying to look cool, I made my way through the scrum of leather- and black-clad strangers to his table. He looked so cute and radiant it made me want to weep.

Smiling up at me, he put down his book, a paperback with a stark black-and-white cover. *Tristes Tropiques,* by Claude Lévi-Strauss. It looked important, and like a not particularly easy read. "I remember *you!*" he exclaimed. "Sit down. What's your name? I guess I should've asked!"

We both laughed. "Jim. But everybody calls me Jimmy. Jimmy Neurosis. Everybody has so many names these days. I guess that's all the rage."

"Stephen Schaub," he said, extending his hand.

I blushed, feeling silly to be shaking hands after I'd had his cock in my mouth in the dirty men's room of a nightclub.

"Would you like a drink, Jimmy?"

I glanced over at Blackie O. She was watching, and, smiling wryly, she gave me a shooing *go for it* gesture, then batted her eyelashes. "Sure. I mean . . ." I said. Then I remembered I had only enough money left for bus fare. "No, I'm okay."

"I'll get you a glass of wine. That's what I'm having. Hang on a sec."

"Okay." Trying to ignore the fear that something was going to rapidly go wrong, I surreptitiously ground my teeth seven times. Watching Stephen lean over the counter to give the barista his order (*Man,* I thought, *he is so sexy*), I realized I hadn't done any protective rituals for at least . . . twenty-four hours? More? Come to think of it, I'd been pretty nervous about meeting Blackie O today, yet I hadn't done anything compulsive. Could it be possible I was changing more than just my image?

Here was Stephen, setting a glass of red wine on the table before me. "Do you go to the Deaf Club a lot?" I asked.

"That was my first time. I have to admit, I expected more from the bands. I thought they all sounded like juvenile anarchists. But I liked meeting you."

"Aren't I a juvenile anarchist, too?"

"Well, yeah, but you're cuter," said Stephen.

I smiled shyly. "Where are you from? You don't sound Californian, exactly."

"I live in Manhattan. But I'm staying here until at least mid-December. When I go back, I'll be taking over a loft space and building it out."

Mid-December wasn't that far away from now, I thought with disappointment. But . . . a loft in Manhattan! He had my fantasy life! "I went to New York once when I was a kid. I always dreamed of returning."

I glanced over at Blackie O, worried she'd be angry that I'd basically bailed on her. I was in luck, though, for it looked like she'd run into people she knew. Three young women about my age were crammed in with her around the little table, faces bright with gossipy laughter. I gulped the rest of the wine and caught a buzz, which further eased my nerves.

When Stephen asked me more about myself, I was self-conscious, since the details of my life could fit on the head of a pin, whereas his could seemingly fill a few Olympic-size swimming pools. But my tipsiness and his presence calmed me.

"I'm an artist," he told me, bringing another round of red wine to the table. "I'm starting a street-art series that documents the takeover of the Battery Park City landfill in Manhattan. For ages it's been one of the few places in the city where you could get some peace and quiet. The developers plan to put up a bunch of luxury apartment buildings there. They dream of turning Manhattan into a shopping mall."

I didn't fully understand what he was talking about, but I loved the sound of it. He seemed to disdain the status quo, which appealed to me. "What do you mean by 'street art'?"

"I make flyers about corporate greed. I spend half my life in a Xerox store. The other half I'm a landscape designer for rich people's rooftop gardens. Oh, and I moonlight at a bathhouse, mopping jizz off the floor!"

I was starting to get genuinely drunk. And turned on. His knee pressed mine beneath the table. When I twined my leg around his, he looked at me suggestively. "Do you want to come see my flyers?" he suggested.

"I most certainly do. I've got to tell my friend, though."

When I weaved my way over to Blackie O, she introduced the three young women as the Pop Tarts, whom she described to me, sotto voce, as trust-fund punks. All of their hairstyles were like works of abstract art, gelled and spiked into impossibly cute angles and colors.

"I'm, uh . . . He's inviting me to his house," I said, unable to control a grin.

Blackie O narrowed her eyes at me. Through the wine and adrenaline that was buzzing through my veins, I perceived a flicker of what might have been disappointment or resignation in her face. But it vanished as quickly as it had appeared, and she dismissed me with an indulgent kiss on the cheek. "I told you, didn't I? All *kinds* of trouble. Don't do anything I wouldn't enjoy!"

STEPHEN'S APARTMENT WAS a mazelike railroad flat. When we came in, his roommate, a freckled, red-haired, middle-aged man wearing nothing but a T-shirt, was in the kitchen slicing an avocado onto a piece of toast. He introduced himself as Rusty, and I gathered all of my powers of concentration to look at his face rather than his pubic hair.

"You must be hungry. Let me get you something to eat," said Stephen, setting down a bowl and three plates. "It's pesto pasta. A lot of garlic, but I think you'll like it."

I stared at the bowl before me. The pasta was mossy green and alien, but also beautiful, and it had an intoxicatingly delicious aroma. The three of us sat to eat.

"So where did you meet him?" Rusty asked Stephen, as though I weren't there.

"Cafe Flore. It's such a scene there sometimes."

Smirking, Rusty twirled pasta onto his fork. "So I guess it was Chicken Hawk Night?"

"There were a few teenagers in attendance," Stephen replied dryly.

To change the subject, I asked Rusty what he did for a living.

"Bathhouse," he said. "An even raunchier one than Stephen works at. I tend to get more involved with the clientele, too. I make it my goal to suck off a minimum of three men per shift."

Stephen's bedroom wasn't much bigger than the bathroom stall we'd had sex in. The walls were papered with a collage of flyers for punk rock shows, and the sole source of light was a single lightbulb that he'd covered with the type of chintz floral scarf my mother favored to keep her hairdo neat while she did the housecleaning. I flashed on the image of her sitting in San Carlos wondering where I was, and I asked Stephen if I could use his phone.

It was in the adjacent room, a more orderly space decorated with reproductions of posters from the Russian Revolution. On the coffee table sat an enormous upright pink dildo.

"I'm probably not coming home tonight. If you don't hear from me, I'll call you first thing in the morning," I told my mother. I picked up the dildo and brought it to my nose: it smelled faintly of soap. I couldn't imagine such a large object ever going into my ass. "Relax, Mom, I'm with Blackie O. Her mom's taking us to see . . ." I considered the dildo. *Revenge of the Pink Panther.* I'll be fine, I promise."

When I returned, Stephen was in his bed, smoking a joint, which he passed to me. Music played on a small turntable. I'd never heard anything like it. There was a joyous clarity to it, but it was spartan, just a few chords played over and over again until they abruptly shifted into another few chords.

"Listening to this makes me feel like I'm moving through a field of knee-high grass," I said dreamily. "The grass is no longer green. It's brown and brittle and brushing up against my jeans. The sky is blue. You can see forever."

"It's Philip Glass," Stephen told me, then thought for a minute. "To me it sounds like being stuck inside an isosceles triangle."

After we'd listened to the A-side in silence, he beckoned me close. The warmth of his body felt so delicious, like sunlight falling on my face in the wintertime. I was so relaxed I dozed off, and the next thing I knew, we were under the covers, naked, our legs entwined, and Stephen was sound asleep, snoring. I gazed at his shapely nose, his small mouth, his well-defined Adam's apple, and watched his chest rise and fall. Then I drifted off again.

I woke up in the morning to the sensation of Stephen's mouth on my cock. For a moment I felt exposed. Why hadn't he just woken me? But that feeling quickly gave way to arousal, and I surrendered to pleasure. He slid his fingers up my ass, a new sensation I didn't particularly enjoy, but because they were Stephen's fingers, it was vaguely thrilling. When he kissed me, all my emotional complications felt like they were dropping away, leaving me in a kind of positive emptiness. I was acutely conscious that I was absolutely letting go.

16

GOOD NIGHT, JOHN-BOY

The day Stephen was due to come visit me in San Carlos, I got to the bus stop downtown a half hour early to wait for him. When at last the 7F rolled in, I hugged him tightly and kissed his lips, immediately sensing his discomfort at the public display. I wondered if where he came from it wouldn't be acceptable. Well, it wasn't here either.

I started the tour by showing him my lucky bench, where I waited on days I went into the city, with its scratchiti carved into the slats—JOAN JETT FROM THE RUNAWAYS WUZ HERE— that always made me feel less alone. "How did that get there?" I asked rhetorically. As we strolled through downtown, I narrated the highlights like a campy tour guide. "This is Woolworth's, purveyors of the finest aspirin, pantyhose, and cancer-causing substances in San Carlos. The library, where the world's largest collection of romance novels is housed. Should you be in need of a Crock-Pot cookbook, there's the used-book store. Oh my God," I groaned in conclusion, "it's sooooo suburban! Please forgive me."

"No, no, don't worry about it, I love it! It's like some surreal dream of perfection. *The Stepford Wives*, but with century plants and palm trees."

"I'm glad you see it that way. That's lost on me."

When we came into the apartment, I was suddenly and vibrantly aware of how absurdly country-cute everything looked. The plaid sofa, the wicker cornucopia centerpiece spilling gourds onto the dining-room table, left over from Thanksgiving. I poured us glasses of Ocean Spray, and when I put my glass down and kissed him, his tongue was cool and tasted slightly bitter from the juice. I led him to my bedroom.

I watched his face, trying to gauge his reaction to my room. The movie posters of my earlier teen years had given way to flyers for punk rock shows. Scotch-taped to the walls were Polaroids that Blackie O and I had taken of each other (the one I liked best was of me in a lurid red sweater, wielding a butcher knife and smiling demonically), and for the past few months I'd been writing on the walls with marker, inspired by the exuberant graffiti I'd see at the clubs I was going to. TEENAGE PERVERTS. WORK, WORK, WORK FOR THE REST OF YOUR LIFE AND LOOK WHAT YOU GET!

I couldn't read his expression. Wanting badly to share something of myself, I led him to my bedroom window, which overlooked the tawny, puma-colored hills, their flanks dotted with oak trees. "This is my favorite part of the house. I sit here and stare for hours on end."

He gazed out. A red-tailed hawk was wheeling high above the dry grass. "I can see why. It's gorgeous."

"*You're* gorgeous," I said, reaching for him. This time I was much more aggressive than usual, even dominant.

As we sank to the bed, he whispered, "Do you want to fuck me?"

I hesitated. I'd always thought of anal sex as the gay version of heterosexual fucking, and why on earth would I want my sexual practices to echo the straight world's? But when he rolled over onto his stomach, I perceived it as less a suggestion than a request, and I assumed I was obliged to see it through.

I spit into my hand, rubbed the saliva onto my cock, and aimed it at what I thought was the right place but was met with unyielding skin. It took a few tries, and I only managed to penetrate about an inch, but Stephen sighed with pleasure. "Go deeper," he said.

It felt good to fuck him, though I struggled for a moment with the distinct aroma of ass. Still, urged on by his moans, I came. He rolled me over and probed me deeply with his tongue, which felt amazing and luxurious; afterward, when we kissed, I could taste the inside of my body, which was a trip, as though I were somehow devouring my own dark self.

We lay on the floor for what seemed like an eternity. Stephen was the first to break the silence. "How old are you, Jimmy? And tell the truth," he added, not unkindly.

I was quiet for a moment, concerned that answering would risk spoiling a good thing. "Fifteen." After a long pause, I asked, "How about you? Fifteen and a half?"

He smiled. "No, I'll be thirty-eight next month."

"Oh, an older man. I like that. Somehow I feel that inside you're not so old."

"You may be right about that," he said quietly, "except I could get arrested for statutory rape." We laughed. I kissed his shoulder. We were both starting to doze off.

I was jarred awake by the sound of the front door opening. Adrenaline shot through me. "Fuck. My mom's home early."

She was in the kitchen, unpacking a bag of groceries, when

we approached a few minutes later. "Mom, I want you to meet somebody. This is Stephen."

She set down a box of Hamburger Helper to shake his hand. With her huge sunglasses and her hair in tight pin curls, she resembled, I thought, an owl. "Oh, hello, very nice to meet you. Have you known Jim a long time?"

He shifted uneasily. "No, just a couple of weeks."

"Oh, that's nice," she said. There was a loaded silence. "Can I offer you anything—tea, coffee?"

"Be right back," I said, scurrying into my room to make sure there was nothing too revealing still visible. After throwing a blanket over a large wet blob on the bed and quickly washing my face, I returned to find them sitting in the living room. *Oh God.*

"Well, the art I make isn't like the kind you see in a museum," he was telling her. "It's more conceptual. It's designed to be displayed in public places. The point is to encourage people to think about things with a new perspective."

She nodded. "Oh, that sounds *very* interesting. I'd like to see some of that."

I hated it when she spoke this way, believing it was insincere. How could she be that oblivious to what we'd been up to? Was she simply incapable of overriding her Polite Housewife setting to stop everything and say, *For God's sake, I'm not an idiot, you both stink of sex?* Or maybe she really *was* interested. I couldn't possibly know for sure. Either way, I wished she would be this nice to *me.*

"Mom, are you wearing *Anita Bryant* glasses?" The outspoken, antigay spokeswoman for Florida orange juice had her own line now of oversize frames, just like those my mother was wearing.

"What? No."

Casting an oblique glance my way, Stephen asked about her job.

"It's so boring compared to what you do," she demurred. "I push paper and answer the phone all day long and sit in a cubicle that I call the fishbowl."

I could see that he was warming up to her, so I thought it best not to disrupt their flow again. But when there was a break in their conversation, I seized the opportunity to escort him back to my room.

"Your mom seems like a very nice lady."

I made a face. "I don't think you're getting the complete picture. But I guess she is nice. She's just very misguided."

"Mothers are mothers. There's not much you can do about it."

I wanted to know about *his* mother, but I was getting sick of talking about family. I kissed him to change the subject.

WITH MY SOPHOMORE YEAR at its midpoint, I began to get overwhelmed by the concept of my future. *Just focus on each moment as it occurs,* I told myself, trudging up the hill to face the school day.

A Trans Am full of teenagers pulled up alongside me. *Oh, what now?*

In the backseat a girl wearing a tube top rolled down the window and called, "Weirdos suck dick!"

An egg hit my shoulder, gooey yellow yolk oozing down the sleeve of my jacket. "Why don't you go back to Faggotland, you stupid fucking Martian!"

The Trans Am tore off up the hill, probably toward the school parking lot, as I stood on the sidewalk clenching my fists with fear and rage.

I didn't want to earn yet another citation for tardiness, but I also knew that things would only get worse if I showed up for class covered in egg yolk. So I went home, not so much humiliated as furious. I *liked* how I looked, I *liked* my clothes. More to the point, I had the right to wear what I wanted. I had every right to not have a fucking egg thrown at me.

Fuck all the small-minded motherfuckers. I selected a clean jacket and then, determined to be even more provocative, switched out the pants I was wearing for a pair of tight-fitting, forest-green polyester women's capri pants that I'd bought for a buck at the Goodwill.

I came in late to homeroom, where everyone twittered and cackled as I went to my seat.

The day dragged on. During classes spitballs pelted the back of my head; in the hallways people catcalled. It boggled my mind to think how much energy was being expended in my direction. If even a small percentage of it could be directed toward something useful, society would be a better place! But instead San Carlos High School collectively seemed much more interested in pooling its efforts to let me know that it disapproved of my wardrobe choices. *What a fucking idiotic world.*

This was a perfect example of why computer-generated attendance notifications sent to our address were becoming an almost daily occurrence. I'd been intercepting them and then shoving them to the bottom of the kitchen trash. My last report card, too, had been catastrophic: four F's, a C, and a D. I'd made the conscious decision to stop caring, and it was surprising how easily shame had fallen away. A sort of blankness had wafted in to replace it. Was this freedom?

By the time I got home from school, my swaggering fury had dwindled to misery. I called Stephen, but the line just rang. I tried again and again, returning in between tries to chain-smoke in my roost by the window, blowing smoke out in triple puffs. The magic hour grew dim, darkened to blue dusk. "Three, three, three," I murmured. Even my secret rituals were beginning to feel monotonous, imprisoning.

I passed my mother on my way to the front door. She was on the phone with Julie, yammering about skin care. Seeing me putting on my evil-fairy shoes, Mom mouthed, *Where are you going?*

"Out." Simmering with fury, I headed downtown, letting my anger carry me up the long blocks.

Stationery store, pet store, grocery store, barbershop. Like the landscape of a child's train set, I thought. And I was the train, forced to go around the same track in an endless, dull fucking loop forever.

As I passed the station, though, I heard someone call out in a strangely androgynous voice. It was the person I'd met months before on Polk Street. Same dirty lavender turtleneck and slacks, despite the warm evening, and the glasses had an extra layer of masking tape holding them together. When she approached, I had to breathe through my mouth, the funk of her unwashed body was so intense.

"Young man! I haven't seen you in forever. I went away for a while."

"Yeah, hi. Where've you been?"

"They locked me up in the happy place." She did a theatrical twirl.

"The happy place?"

"Otherwise known as Agnews State Hospital. If you like being wrestled to the ground by two burly men and violently tied into a straitjacket, it's the vacation for you!" For emphasis her index finger landed in the center of my chest.

I offered a cigarette, which she accepted eagerly. "Shit. How long have you been out?" I asked.

"Oh, a little while. Enough to reconnect with all my special places and people. Except for you, darling. I've missed you. You look different. You've been transformed by a guardian godmother from on high. Look at your hair! Your pants! Your shoes! I love it. You're fabulous now! That makes me happy."

I smiled but felt awkward at this outpouring. Passersby were staring. "The semester's almost over. I can't wait. I'm flunking anyway."

"Oh, you're going to be fine. You're a courageous boy—I mean, sister—and you'll make it through to the other side, just like me. And you're going to celebrate the beauty of life on this magical planet that we live on."

Just like you? I hoped not. But I did wish this person well, and I gave her the five dollars in my pocket, plus the rest of my cigarettes, before we hugged good-bye.

Walking home, I kept thinking of the name Agnews State Hospital. It had dislodged a long-buried memory, but of what?

When I got back, my mother was in her customary spot on the sofa, watching *The Waltons*. I came in and turned the volume knob to low.

"Hey, I'm watching that!"

"I know." I sat beside her. "But listen, what do the words 'Agnews State Hospital' mean to you?"

She gave me a long look. "Why do you ask?"

"I just heard it mentioned, and it jogged my memory, but I don't remember anything specific."

"I don't want to talk about it."

"Talk about *what?*"

"Your father and that place," she said. "It makes me too upset."

I certainly wasn't about to let it go at that.

After some pointless straightening of already straight magazines on the coffee table, she said with reluctance, "That's where Daddy was . . . institutionalized. He'd had too much stress, and he was drinking. Honestly, honey, I don't want to remember it. You were only about four anyway."

"Hold on a second. Dad was . . ." Confused sensations tumbled over me. My father was put in a loony bin? Little shards of memory started to come together in a way that made me feel unsteady. I suppressed the urge to grind my teeth. "Mom, I want to know more about this. I *should* know more about it."

For a moment she covered her face. Then she put down her hands, took a breath, and said, "He admitted himself. It started out okay. But then they wouldn't let him go. They kept him there. We had no way of paying for anything. There were bill collectors calling at all hours." She paused. "I can't think about this. Why did you have to bring it up?"

"Because it's important!"

"Well, it's too painful for me. Now, can you please just let me watch my show." She got up and turned the knob, and a commercial exploded with noise. *"Kool-Aid brand soft drink, made with pure sugar! You loved it as a kid—you trust it as a mother!"*

I was so overwhelmed I couldn't move. I wanted to sweep the magazines off the coffee table, smash all the idiotic tchotchkes on the shelves, put my foot through the TV screen. Why couldn't she be stronger for me? Why did she have to hide from everything real? It felt as though the Molotov cocktail inside of me was transforming into a neutron bomb, an anger with limitless proportions, a pure, clean rage that could propel me far from here.

I leaped up, standing between her and the set. "Fine. Watch the fucking *Waltons*. But you should know, I can't stand going to school anymore."

"Quit blocking the TV. You have to go to school or you won't get into college."

I put my hands on my hips, not budging. "I am not spending any more time in this place where I am harassed every day and am learning nothing! *You* didn't go to college!"

"Only because I didn't have a choice. Now, would you move away, please."

Ever since I could remember, she'd guarded facts about her family history with the ferocity of a bear guarding its cubs, but I did know she'd gone to a semester at Johns Hopkins with the goal of becoming a pharmacist, and I did know that the money had run out, leaving her to take some dead-end job or another. Still, I was so enraged I taunted her. "Are you sure it wasn't because you were too dumb?"

She unfolded her arms and looked heavenward. "I can't take this."

"Well, you're just going to have to." I paced around the living room like an animal in a zoo. "Isn't that what parenthood is? I didn't ask to be born into this nightmare. You and Dad created this. So what are you going to do about it now?"

"Oh God, please. Would you just be quiet?"

In a mocking falsetto, I parroted, "'Would you just be quiet? Would you just lower your voice?' You make me sick!" I paused, breathing hard. "You don't get it. I'm quitting school."

"No!" she cried. "*You* don't get it! You don't know how hard I've worked to get away from . . . I sacrificed so much! I'm not going to stand by and let you throw your future away! You're going to end up just like my—"

"I'm not your pathetic drunk father! I'm not my *own* pathetic drunk father! I'm my own person!" I stopped pacing to glare at her. "And I'm quitting school. It's a sick, stupid waste of time. I'm done. End of story."

I left her to the television and stalked away to try Stephen's phone again.

This time he picked up.

"It's me. Do you feel like a visitor tonight?"

"If you're the visitor, sure."

I packed an overnight bag, intending to walk back downtown.

"When will you be coming home?" my mother called over the sound of John-Boy and Jim-Bob and Mary Ellen cozying up for the night.

I stuffed a jacket into my backpack. "I have no idea."

17

BE ALL THAT YOU CAN BE

W hen, during pillow talk, I shared with Stephen my intention to drop out, I felt delirious and free. I was unsure about what would come next but took comfort in the certainty that there needed to be some radical change before the plot of my life could advance.

"There's a usefulness to school." He frowned. "You won't be able to get into college without a high-school diploma. Unless it's somehow different in California, but I doubt it is."

Stung, I rolled over and gazed at the now-familiar flyers for shows long past on his wall. I wished we could always be having sex, that he could somehow always be inside me and me inside him. All that night I lay awake, watching him snore.

In the morning he treated me to brunch at a gay restaurant in the Castro. I had eggs Benedict and a mimosa, which made me feel like an adult, but a nameless sorrow was gathering in my chest. When he left for work, I hung around near the restaurant, feeling at loose ends.

I stood gazing at the display window of a shop selling campy knickknacks. A row of Gay Bob dolls gazed back, with their vacant blue eyes and their plaid shirts and peroxide-blond hair. COME OUT OF THE CLOSET WITH GAY BOB. CLOTHING CATALOGUE INSIDE, read the copy on the box.

"Hey, you're cute," someone murmured. A real-life version of Gay Bob had sidled up to me, minus the plaid but with the addition of a handlebar mustache. "D'you want to go to my place, look at skin mags? I've got poppers and a weight machine."

"Not now, thanks."

He moved away without another word. I sat on a bus bench staring at the traffic, the people driving this way and that with mysterious purpose. A sense of emptiness threatened to engulf me completely, and I found myself thinking that death would be easier than trying to figure out what to do with my life.

WHEN I GOT BACK TO SAN CARLOS, my mom suggested, as a peace offering, that we go on a nature walk: she'd read an article about a county park nestled deep in the redwoods. In my mind I heard Blackie O reminding me that the Trailside Killer was still out there somewhere lurking in the bushes, but I appreciated my mom's effort to take control and make everything okay, so I refrained from mentioning it.

The trailhead was crowded with other families taking Sunday hikes. "It's nice," I said, "but I wish there wasn't anyone else here. I hate these people."

"Why? They're just out for a nice walk, like we are. Ignore them. They don't really matter."

"That's easy for you to say."

"Just hold your head up high like you belong," she told me.

"Oh, yes, I am a proud member of the Oseland family," I said jokingly. "Perhaps you have heard of them?"

The air was cool and clean and smelled of California bay laurel and damp earth. As we went along, the trail began to empty of other people. We rounded a switchback that led into a grove of redwoods, where sunlight gilded the tops of the trees.

"It's almost like you can feel the energy of these trees," I said. "Like they know something we don't know."

She smiled up at the redwoods. "That's a nice thought. The beauty of nature always makes you feel better."

I crushed a bay leaf between my fingers to release its fragrance. "Did you ever imagine that your life was going to turn out this way?"

"Not in my wildest dreams, honey," she replied. "I wanted more than anything in the world for us to just be together, as a family, in a nice house somewhere."

We fell into a meditative silence. Tiny clouds scudded overhead; a red-winged blackbird chirped and took flight. "I wanted your father to love us," she said at length. "I just don't understand why he couldn't."

"Are you depressed?" I asked.

"I don't believe in that word."

I studied her face as she gazed at a dell of maidenhair ferns. She squinted her eyes, baring her teeth and exaggerating the wrinkles in her face. Then she tied her scarf into a babushka and continued along the trail.

On the way home, we had a serious conversation about the logistics of my dropping out. Neither of us really knew what it entailed, and there was limited information in the student handbook. There was really only one teacher I trusted to discuss it with, but the wound of her rejection still felt as raw and vivid as a dog bite.

For hours that evening, I hovered by the phone. Still, I desperately needed to speak with someone who was worldly yet also in touch with the realities of high school.

When Mrs. O'Hagan answered the phone, my pulse was pounding in my veins and my mouth was dry. "It's Jimmy Neuro—uh, Oseland. Is this an okay time to talk?"

"I wouldn't have picked up the call if it weren't," she said in a matter-of-fact way.

"I need your advice. I want to leave San Carlos High."

"I take it you don't mean that you want to transfer. You want to drop out. Is that it?"

I twisted the curlicue of phone cord around my index finger. *Four, four, four, four.* "What do you think of that?"

"It's of no consequence what I think," she said tartly, "if you've already made up your mind."

"Well, if I *hadn't* made up my mind, what would you say then?"

"I don't want to play psychological games with you. If you're serious about it, I can advise you on next steps. If you're still exploring the idea, we can discuss it."

"I have to leave." My voice cracked, and I cleared my throat forcefully. "It feels like high school was created specifically to destroy every shred of creativity that exists in me. I literally feel like I'm going to die if I don't go."

"Well, that's a dramatic way of putting it. Sometimes things feel much worse than they really are. Especially when you're going through a vulnerable time." She sighed. "I've been a high-school teacher for more years than I care to remember. To be frank, I rather hoped you'd go beyond what I've achieved in my life. Dropping out nearly guarantees you won't. But who knows, maybe you'll be an exception."

"So what are you telling me?"

"I'm telling you that you have to make up your own mind. I can't do that for you."

"I think I've made it up. What do I have to do next?"

She instructed me to go to speak with the school's guidance counselor, Mr. Mooney, with my mother present if possible, and suggested the most ideal times to schedule that appointment. "Now, if you'll pardon me, Jim," she said, "I've got to feed the cats."

I REMEMBERED MR. MOONEY and his jowly face from the day I'd first enrolled at San Carlos High, but he didn't seem to remember me. He spoke in a low monotone. "Are you absolutely positive that this is what you want to do," he stated, the question forgoing an interrogative lilt for an abrupt full stop. "Do you truly understand the permanent consequences."

I swallowed and glanced at my mother. She looked ashen, as though I were being wheeled on a gurney into an operating room.

On the one hand, I thought, I'd come to the decision in the heat of the moment. On the other hand, high school was poisoning me. "I do," I told Mr. Mooney.

After the meeting my mom took us to San Mateo for lunch at Heidi's Pies. I struggled to find my appetite while she crunched away at her chicken salad on toast. The crunching sounded deafening, and I wanted to swat the sandwich out of her hand. Beads of sweat ran down the sides of my face like misplaced tears.

She took a sip of Sanka and replaced the cup onto the saucer with a clink. "Well, honey, you have certainly set yourself up for failure," she announced. "You already have every disadvantage in the world. You're poor, and you're . . . you're not like other people. And now you've gone and done *this* to yourself."

I gave up trying to eat and crumpled my napkin onto my plate. "Why are you so scared of being alive?"

"I'm not. But life isn't fair, and you have to protect yourself."

I scoffed.

"Jim, I know that things haven't been so easy for you, so far, like . . ." She gazed at her coffee cup as if she wished it would finish her sentence for her. "Daddy's drinking problem was bad, I know that. And now he's . . . he's not around, and I don't have much money. I just . . . I want something better for you. What are you going to *do* now? How are you going to make your way in the world?"

"What do *you* really know of the world, beyond being a secretary and a mother?"

"You're a brat," she said, and signaled for the check.

18

MAKING OUR DREAMS COME TRUE

Mr. Mooney had advised me to take the California High School Proficiency Exam, so I'd be able to leave with the equivalent of a high-school diploma. Testing was held the first week of December at a community center in a nearby town.

That morning a handful of other teenagers and I filed into a room furnished with chairs so absurdly small they must have been donated by a grade school. Our bags were checked for materials that might lead to cheating, like pocket calculators, and the proctor, laying each test facedown on our desks, made solemn announcements about the importance of completing every question, of finishing on time, and of not glancing at anyone else's test, all of which underscored the anxiety I'd felt in the days leading up to this.

However, once we were allowed to turn the sheets over and

begin, I had to smack my hand over my mouth to suppress a
raucous guffaw.

Which sequence of numerals contains all even numbers?

a) 1, 3, 8
b) 2, 4, 6
c) 3, 6, 9

I snuck a look at the pages that followed. Yes, it was nearly
all like that, multiple-choice questions on basic math and English that a third-grader could have answered blindfolded, the
intellectual equivalent of the tiny chairs. If I'd been looking for
proof that staying in high school was a colossal waste of time,
here it was.

When I got home, my mother suggested that we drive up to
Belmont on one of our McDonald's runs to celebrate. Considering her feelings on the subject of my dropping out, it was a sweet
gesture, but what I really craved was a taste of my life to come.
So I caught the next bus to the city, to meet up with a new acquaintance.

I'd first met Theresa at the Temple Beautiful, a punk club in
an unused synagogue on Geary Boulevard. I thought its location
was very cool; it was a few doors from the former headquarters
of Jim Jones's Peoples Temple. Jones had recently led his followers
in Guyana to commit gruesome mass suicide. Death by grape
drink laced with cyanide, 642 adults, 276 children. The parents
made their kids consume the beverage first, then drank it themselves. Great.

Although Theresa, too, lived in a boring, complacent suburb—
Pleasant Hill, which sounded like something out of *Leave It to*

Beaver—she was in a band called the Situations, and she had that Kim Novak–gone-bad look I admired, with platinum-blond hair piled in a pouf atop her head like a sumptuous meringue. Also intriguing was the fact that she was dating Biafra, the lead singer of the Dead Kennedys.

We met at Cafe Flore and waited for her boyfriend. "So where in Pleasant Hill," I asked, pronouncing the name with ironic cheer, "do you go to school?"

"I dropped out last year." Shuddering dramatically at the thought, she dragged on her cigarette, blowing smoke out her nostrils in a perfect V-shaped jet that would have put Helle to shame. "High school is like concentration camp for teenagers. I'll take the next train out, thank you very much."

I laughed. "No kidding. There were times when I actually thought I was going to die." I was impressed that she'd beaten me to dropping out.

"Oh, no, don't do that. School is seriously not worth dying for."

When Biafra arrived, I was starstruck; I'd only ever seen him performing onstage or from a distance. With his full lips and curly eyelashes, he was sexy and slightly feminine. As we chatted, I could tell from the way he was looking at Theresa that he was in love with her.

We ambled together down Market Street toward Geary, where Biafra wanted to visit a Christian supply store, in search of a crucifix to wear as a necklace. "I want to take it to a jeweler to hang it upside down," he said, kicking a rusted hubcap off the sidewalk into the gutter. "I think the world needs a little more Antichrist." Theresa slung an affectionate arm around his shoulder.

On one hand it made so much sense, felt so right, to be in this city, hanging out with these people. On the other, I saw myself as less substantial than they were. They seemed solidly occupying their selves, while I was still kind of hovering at the edges of mine.

I realized I was starting to grind my teeth, and I forced myself to stop. "I really want you guys to meet my boyfriend, Stephen. I think you'd like him," I said.

It made me feel embarrassed to say the word "boyfriend," but it also gave me a little burst of confidence. "He's from New York," I told them, "and he's doing this art project where he makes flyers protesting the development of Battery Park City. I mean, I guess the way I'm describing that, it doesn't sound so interesting. But his work is totally political," I added, for Biafra's benefit.

"Cool," he said. Such a simple word, but what it *didn't* say spoke volumes. It didn't say, *You're a fucking stupid fag.*

At the Daughters of St. Paul Bookstore, Theresa and I wandered around admiring the decoupage illustrations of Christ, Virgin Mary prayers, and trading cards of the saints, while the taciturn woman at the counter removed crucifixes from their little plastic bags for Biafra's scrutiny.

"Ma'am, can I ask you a question?" he said, examining a silver rosary. "Why do you believe in all this stuff? The candles and cards—all this."

"For me it's not stuff. These things remind me that there's a higher power controlling everything that happens. That gives me peace."

"With all due respect, that sounds like something from Aesop's fables," he said. "What proof do you have that there's any truth to it?"

"I don't need proof," she answered. "I know it in my heart."

After he'd picked out a crucifix featuring an especially skinny and morose-looking Messiah, we explored the Tenderloin for a bit. Vietnamese cafés had lately been springing up next to the seedy liquor stores and derelict motels, and Theresa wanted to try eating at one, so we got bánh mì sandwiches.

In the unforgiving light of the café, Biafra and Theresa appeared like some postmodern Catherine and Heathcliff, haggard and glamorous. I was struck by the way her crimson lipstick was echoed by the red of the altar mounted to the wall above, where twin red candles framed a tangerine. Incense smoke mingled with the plumes from their cigarettes.

Set off by these stark, colorful details, the two of them looked like the very model of cool. But there was more than that to it. As Biafra leaned across the table to explain to me how the whole Vietnam War had been—from start to finish, including its decades-long incarnations involving the French, other Southeast Asian nations, and our own—an imperialist charade, I had the sense that I was witnessing a fleeting moment that encapsulated something larger.

It seemed like a waste to let it just pass without marking its significance. I wished I could take a picture at least.

THAT NIGHT, ALONE IN MY BEDROOM, I unearthed the camera my dad had given me for my thirteenth birthday as a change from the stationery sets and embossed fountain pens—obvious office-supply giveaways—that I usually got from him.

The camera was in one of my boxes of souvenirs. I'd never used it; in fact, I only remembered having been surprised by its not being, say, a ream of colored paper, which is the kind of thing Dad normally put under the Christmas tree.

He had assured me that he'd help me master taking photos, but he never seemed to be home long enough for that to happen, and I'd given up after one frustrating attempt. Now I picked it up—it felt like a brick in my hand—and slung the strap around my neck. It was a weighty, bare-bones Canon with f-stops and apertures that were a fully mysterious language to me. I popped the film slot open. Empty.

Peering through the viewfinder, I directed the camera toward the window seat. Framed by the glass rectangle, the familiar sight of my habitual resting place, with its overflowing ashtray and off-kilter curtain, took on a poignant and dislocated quality. It seemed freighted with meaning, like an urgent message I couldn't decode.

19

SHARE THE MOMENT...
SHARE LIFE

When I told Blackie O I'd dropped out of school, she gasped. "Well, *that's* news!"

"I know. It makes me both scared and happy. Scared-happy. Scappy."

"Anxieted, perhaps? Full of anticinervousation?"

I laughed. "Yes, I'm uncomforthrilled."

Now that I was free of San Carlos High, I'd persuaded Blackie O to play hooky that day and hop on the bus to the city with me. When we arrived, we first made a stop at a Jack in the Box for a vanilla milk shake, to which we added a generous slug of liquor. Then, passing the gloopy concoction back and forth, we shambled through North Beach to the infamous Condor Club, where Blondean, a stripper we knew from the punk scene who also went by the moniker Fuchsia Shock, had invited us to come see her act.

Blondean made a splash whenever she turned up at a punk

rock show. She had the over-the-top theatrical presentation of a drag queen, with—needless to say—massive blond hair, which she paired with skintight leopardette outfits, always punctuated by absurdly high stilettos. In the sixties, she'd lived in Timothy Leary's so-called acid house in upstate New York, and now, a sucker for any countercultural moment, she'd found her way onto the periphery of punk rock.

The Condor, dim, cool, and stinking of spilled beer, was sparsely populated with businessmen and couples who looked conspicuously like tourists. As Blackie O and I tried to fend off the cocktail waitress, the tired strains of "Stayin' Alive" began to thump offstage, and a middle-aged woman came on and performed a desultory striptease, sagging against the pole as though she didn't have the strength to stand unassisted. One of her shoes seemed to be held together with Scotch tape. To hesitant applause she sauntered offstage, forgetting to retrieve her discarded bikini bottom. Blackie O and I stifled giggles.

Then the lights dimmed and the frantic drumming of surf music filled the club. Over a twanging guitar, a female voice averred that a "woody shine was dazzling to the soul," and San Onofre was the goal. It was a familiar voice, a television voice, I thought, bright and processed as Velveeta.

A single spotlight came up, illuminating Blondean in a taffeta dress. As she strutted around the stage in her towering heels, the cheery, Disneyland voice narrated the tale of a surfing party that arrived at the beach to find a gang of skin divers squatting on the sand. "They were on our coast that we loved the most, with their suits and their spears and their air. 'Twas a rumble fight to the girls' delight, and bloody was many a nose."

As Blondean pranced out of the dress to reveal a spangled silver

G-string and matching tasseled pasties, I leaned into Blackie O. "What the fuck are we listening to? Is that Annette Funicello?"

"It is indeed," she said. Onstage, Blondean shimmied, causing the silver tassels to twirl faster and faster. "Somewhere out there the Mickey Mouse Club is shitting its collective pants."

As the former Mouseketeer's bizarre tale of surfer–versus–skin diver gang warfare unfolded on the soundtrack, Blondean reversed boob direction and the tassels spun counterclockwise. Then, to whoops and applause, she made the two spin in opposite directions at the same time. We were spellbound. "Blondean is God," I whispered, and Blackie O nodded slowly, wide-eyed.

We'd been invited to the dressing room afterward, so we clomped downstairs to a messy basement room crowded with strippers in various states of undress and relaxation. Blondean took our hands and said warmly, "It's wonderful to have you here."

"Thank you for inviting us! You were extraordinary," I gushed.

"You're the personification of female glamour," Blackie O added. "Every woman should see you as an example of how to put her best foot forward."

"That's sweet of you to say. Come! Sit, sit!" We watched, rapt, as, ensconced in a creaking metal chair, she began to touch up her makeup in one of the many dressing-table mirrors.

My hand snuck into the bag over my shoulder. Inside was the Canon, which I'd begun to bring with me whenever I went somewhere promising. My dad had been wrong about its being a piece of cake to figure out, but I had to admit he might've been onto something in giving it to me.

"So how did you come into this profession?" Blackie O wanted to know.

"Once upon a time in New York, I was a go-go dancer in the Village." She swiped blue shadow over her eyelids. "I danced in a cage—it was *very* sixties. Then one thing led to another. It was an organic process."

I drew out the camera. "Um, would you mind if I . . . ?"

"Go ahead, darling. It's not like I have anything left to hide!"

"Hey, boy. Don't be pointing that thing in *my* direction," admonished a stripper who was rubbing Jergens Lotion into her thighs. It was the one with the forgotten bikini bottom; her shoe with its taped heel lay on the floor nearby. I felt my face turn red, because it was as if she'd read my mind; I'd been wondering if I could snap a picture of her deftly enough to capture the bruise marks in the crooks of her arms.

"Don't worry, these are cool kiddos," Blondean assured her, and the stripper went back to her lotion.

Coming from Blondean, being seen as kids wasn't embarrassing. It felt protective and considerate. Cautiously I raised the Canon. "How does it feel to have so many people out there loving you?" I asked.

"Love is a fantastic thing, even if it's just some horny old guy in a seersucker suit," replied Blondean, applying lipstick. I clicked the shutter once, twice, as she smushed her lips together, blotted, and turned to me. "Don't you think so?"

"Love kind of freaks me out," I confessed. *Click* went the shutter. It was easy to be honest with the lens between us. "It seems like something that's always at risk of falling apart."

Blondean laughed. "That's what keeps it interesting." I could see swooshes of pubic hair protruding from around her G-string, but for some reason it didn't bother me. It seemed unremarkable, a homey detail. *Click, click.* I could feel the rest of the world falling away. *This is the life*, I thought. Dropping out was the smartest thing I'd ever done.

IN MY TEENAGE ESTIMATION, San Carlos was the epitome of banality, and I began to use my now-endless supply of leisure time to make forays downtown with my camera to try to capture its static quality on film. It was cathartic, I discovered, to focus a lens on the faded wares of the stationery store and the Art Deco–style neon sign of the town's signature bar, the Carlos Club. Still, having little to do with my days except take pictures of the barbershop, listen to records, buy secondhand clothes, and gorge on chocolate with my mother, I began to embrace any excuse to get back to the city. When I'd found out there was going to be a huge party at the Mutants' loft, I was on the first bus out.

20

COME ON DOWN!

Annie A Go Go was in possession of that teenager's holy grail, a fake ID. The moment she emerged from Terminal Liquors, which we all agreed was a great name for a liquor store, I cracked open the bottle of vodka and started sucking it down. I wanted to get drunk, and I wanted to do it *fast*.

Annie, Blackie O, and me linked arms and skipped around the corner, singing, "'Weee're off to see the Wiz-aaard! The wonderful Wizard of Oz!'"

"If you only had a brain," Blackie O remarked to me sadly. Annie snorted and snatched the bottle out of my hand.

We heard the party before we reached the loft. Guests were teeming around the building as though it were the scene of a disaster. Mary Menace greeted us on the staircase with a wave of her cigarette.

"You've outdone yourself tonight," I told her. Even an uninebriated person would have found her a sight to see, but to my drunken eyes she looked like some kind of sinister circus act.

Her dress was two gigantic triangles of green felt, set at odd angles to her body. The conical object on her head was probably a hat. She was carrying a pink alligator purse.

"Oh, thank you!" She did a little pirouette. "I was up all night sewing." Her plastered-on makeup seemed to draw attention to the fact that underneath it her face looked drawn and pale.

Blackie O gave me a wink as she and Annie A Go Go were swept into the crowd and up the stairs. "It's possible I went mad at some point," remarked Mary Menace conversationally. Her pupils were huge, her eyes darting from one point on my face to another with unsettling speed. "Do I look completely mad?"

"Mad is good," I advised her, and allowed the human wave to carry me into the party.

The loft was mobbed and daunting. It didn't feel so much like a celebration as a pileup on the freeway. I was already too drunk, swimming through jangled, delayed reactions. Yet when someone handed me a joint, I took it and chased it with gin straight from the bottle. I heard someone say, "This place is so crowded it'll be a miracle if the cops don't shut it down." I was so out of it that the idea seemed abstract and almost quaint, like an old film reel of cops rushing up the stairs in fast motion and herding everyone into a paddy wagon.

Nothing was quite tracking. My esophagus felt scalded by the raw alcohol. I imagined I was a lit Bunsen burner, the heat of a forceful blue flame pushing up into my mouth. A blanket of cigarette smoke mingled with the smell of hair spray and sweat, alcohol and perfume. Over drunken shouts and shrieking laughter, the sound system was playing the Los Angeles band X at full decibels. The chords stormed my ears, wailing out a scene of horror that made me feel queasy: *Beside the bed he found clumps of hair. . . . She wasn't what you'd call living really, but she was still awake!"*

Air, I needed air. Pushing my way toward what I thought was a window, I saw something fall in slow motion into the milling crush of bodies, two green triangles that sank from view.

"I want some of whatever *she* took," somebody said.

"Excuse me. Pardon me," I gasped, struggling to squeeze through the bodies. Now there was a different tone to the hubbub, distinct voices taking shape in the thick, smoky air.

"Shit, man, she's passed out."

"Oh my God, she's *dead*?"

"She's just wasted."

"Someone should call a fuckin' ambulance."

I'd never seen a dead person before. I remembered a picture I'd come across in *Life* magazine when I was very young, a photo of an American soldier in Vietnam covered in mud and blood. His arm was extended as if reaching for something he could almost, but not quite, grasp. That couldn't be what was happening to Mary. The hair rose on the back of my neck, and my sweat went cold. Where were my friends? I ground my teeth four times, but maybe it should have been five. What the fuck day was it, even?

I found the girls wedged under the stairwell with the Pop Tarts, convulsing with screeching laugher. Annie's head lolled on her neck; she had spit bubbles in the corner of her mouth. Even Blackie O's usual composure was marred; she had a smeared, damp look.

"We gotta go," I slurred urgently, clutching the wall. The floor seemed to buckle under my feet. Lights wheeled around my head. "Please. Guys. This isn't a good place. I can't . . ." The whole building was starting to swing like a pendulum. Getting out became mandatory. I staggered away, with the girls stumbling after.

Outside, Annie knelt in the gutter and vomited copiously. I lay on the pavement, struggling to breathe, able to see a pile of dog shit right beside me but unable to roll away from it. Blackie O huddled on the curb with her head in her hands, groaning at the earsplitting shriek of approaching sirens.

A Muni bus materialized in front of us, and we climbed aboard. I turned back and saw the swirling red lights of an ambulance lighting up the street like a carnival midway.

I WOKE UP ON ANNIE'S BEDROOM CARPET, feeling sick and hopeless.

Sprawled on the bed, the girls snored as sonorously as a couple of old winos, on pillowcases splotchy with hair dye. My jacket smelled of smoke and somebody's puke. *"Went home,"* I scrawled on the blank side of a bus transfer and wedged it into the dressing-table mirror.

Since I was already close to Golden Gate Park, I decided I'd go there, hoping the greenery, even before dawn, would be soothing. I walked until, coming upon rhododendrons in full bloom, I realized I must be near the clearing where Jean-Paul had taken me—*In more ways than one,* I thought. *Or even two.* When I found it, I masturbated, aware that there were almost certainly men's eyes watching from the surrounding bushes.

Afterward I lay down in the dirt and slept again until dusk, comforted by the smell of earth and dead leaves. Then, knuckling grit from my eyes, I groped my way out of the park and ended up spilling forth somewhere in the Sunset District. I found a pay phone, plunked in a dime, and dialed Stephen's number. There was no answer.

I called my mother, and she picked up on the third ring. When I heard her voice, a lump tightened my throat.

It's not that I'm grateful, I told myself, scrubbing at an irrational tear. *It's just that I'm fucking hungover.*

21

IT TAKES A LICKING
AND KEEPS ON TICKING

C hilly marine mist was blowing in from the bay, and I leaned against Stephen for warmth as we walked toward the bustle of North Beach. His sharkskin jacket shimmered in the glow of the streetlights.

"When you were my age, did you get along with your mom?" I asked, trembling with cold.

"Well, she worked in a department store. She wasn't around much."

"Sometimes when I'm with my mom, I feel like I'm being choked."

We turned onto the steep incline of Kearny Street. "Growing up is painful no matter what—and then it's finished," said Stephen. While the words weren't comforting, his voice was. I took his hand.

A Cadillac Eldorado, a barge the width of the whole street, rumbled toward us up the hill. From inside came the strains of Journey's "Lights," an anthem-rock ode to San Francisco that was in constant rotation on the radio that year. Whenever Blackie O heard its sentimental chorus begin—*"When the lights go down in the cit-aay, and the sun shines on the bay-aay!"*—she'd whip out her lighter and wave the flame over her head in parody of a worshipful concertgoer.

As it neared, the Eldorado slowed down, and instinctively I let go of Stephen's hand.

"Pansy fucking cocksuckers!"

Stephen whirled around and shouted, "Ah, go back to Jersey!" He'd gotten his epithets mixed up, but it didn't matter. In an instant, he'd broken the rules that could save your life: look down, keep moving, and whatever you do, don't talk back—at least when they are in earshot.

The car came to a stop, and the doors flew open. Six young men poured out. I felt a sense of free fall, as if I'd stepped off a ledge twenty stories high.

"What the *fuck* did you say?" yelled the driver, a teenager in a checkered shirt. Without waiting for an answer, he shoved Stephen to the ground, and two of the others closed in on him. The other three came for me.

I lost sight of my boyfriend as a fist the size of a boulder drew back, looming in my vision, and spun me with the force of its impact. When the heaviest one's foot landed in my ribs, I bent double; he grabbed me around the waist as though to comfort me and hurled me headfirst toward a wall. White stucco flew at my face, a starburst of pain exploding behind my eyes with a sickening thud.

I thrashed in his grip like a fish on a line, and he smashed my head against the wall again. I was conscious of a horrible sound ringing out in the narrow street. It sounded like raw meat was being pounded with a hammer. I knew it must be punches raining down on Stephen's flesh.

"Please!" I gasped. Blood poured into my eyes as I crumpled to the pavement. Then Stephen screamed, a horrible animal sound that made me scream, too. This seemed to give my attacker a burst of superhuman strength; he hauled me up by the hair and smashed my head once more against the wall. My vision darkened and fuzzed.

It was, I knew, the end. *I should tell my mother I love her. Why don't I ever tell her?*

A voice called from nearby, "Hey! Stop! What's going on?"

The guy killing me paused at his task. Through a scrim of blood, I could make out the dark figure of a man standing across the street, beside him the smaller, darker figure of his dog.

Everything stopped as quickly as it had begun. Released, I collapsed. I heard the slap of sneakers on pavement and the squeal of tires as the Eldorado tore up Kearny Street.

As I struggled to rise to my knees, the man leaned over Stephen. His Scottie dog hung back warily. "Sir? Do you need help?"

Stephen did not stir. The only sound was my own jagged breathing.

When at last my boyfriend sat up, I went faint with relief. His face was the color of putty. His sharkskin jacket lay in the street; his shirt had been torn open. "No. We'll be okay." His voice was thick and his breathing labored, but he spoke with a strange composure.

"Well, if you're sure," the stranger said doubtfully.

Stephen nodded and, wincing with the effort, swiped at his nose. Gore was worming its way toward his lips.

My vision returning in swirling molecules of color, I rose unsteadily and went to him. People in their cars were slowing to gape, then continuing past. With agonized slowness we walked south toward the lights of Broadway, arms linked to steady ourselves.

A few people were milling around outside the Mabuhay Gardens. From across the street, I recognized Lawless. She was the toothless, shaven-pated, crazy-looking person who'd snarled at me at my first-ever punk show, but I knew now that she was a friend of Stephen's, and I felt a momentary rush of relief. By her expression I could tell she knew what had happened. Probably the very same thing had happened to her, probably more than once. Swiftly she tossed her cigarette to the gutter and, exchanging some words with the bouncer, led us inside.

Across the Mabuhay's kitschy carpeted dining room we went, past the bar and the crowds jockeying for position near the stage, to the ladies' room. I sat on a toilet seat in a stall that was missing its door, and Stephen slumped against the sink. With the lucid, self-possessed quality of a nurse, Lawless wet a wad of toilet paper under the faucet. "So what happened?"

Because of her missing front teeth, Lawless had a wet lisp, and her face had the look of a Kewpie doll that had been punched. Still, I was awed by her competence as I tried, through puffy eyes, to focus my gaze on her combat boots, tracking their progress from paper-towel dispenser to sink to me. "We were on Kearny," I croaked. "These guys came out of a car."

She nodded sagely, wiping the blood and goop from my face with a sure hand. "Saturday nights are bad," she said. "That's when all the assholes come into the city looking for fun. Wash your hands. You need to clean out those scrapes."

I sat on the floor and watched her minister to Stephen. My favorite pants had torn, and through the hole I could see that my knee was raw, bits of gravel embedded in the flesh.

"Wait here," said Lawless, and the bathroom door swung in her wake.

Stephen and I stared at each other wordlessly. The right side of his face was grotesquely swollen. Onstage, we heard the first band launching into their set. It sounded like a dump truck full of drum kits being unloaded onto a cement floor.

A girl wearing bondage pants and black electrical tape wound around her skinny torso in lieu of a shirt stepped inside, then froze. "Whoa. Are you guys, like, hurt?" She paused, contemplating what to say next. "It's okay, I'll just come back." I was desperate for a cigarette, but the vending machines seemed a million pain-filled miles away.

Lawless returned at last and handed each of us a quaalude. "All right, here you go. These'll make it all go away."

"How much do we owe you?" asked Stephen. Waving the question away, Lawless escorted us back through the club and out to the street. I didn't want to leave her, unwilling to let go of the feeling of safety in her presence.

There was a yellow cab idling nearby, and we clambered in, Stephen grunting in pain, before the driver could get a good look at us and change his mind. Stephen gave him his address, and as the taxi pulled away, the first wave of that warm, milk-bath feeling from the quaaludes started to wash over me. Outside were the twinkling lights and hurrying crowds of Saturday night in North Beach.

The driver glanced at us in the rearview mirror. He cleared his throat and, perhaps to combat the charged silence, switched on the radio. The song came on midchorus: *"When the lights go down in the cit-aay, and the sun shines on the bay-aay!"*

Stephen laughed mirthlessly. "Gotta be fucking kidding me."

In the darkness I met his gaze and gave him a crooked smile. It made my lip split, and fresh, warm blood coursed down my chin.

At his place we got into bed with all our clothes on. Stephen leaned over to kiss me. "Let's go to the ocean tomorrow," he said quietly.

"I'd like that," I murmured as sleep overtook me.

"WHAT HAPPENED TO YOU?" gasped my mother when I came in the next morning.

I hung my jacket by the door. The muscles of my arm felt flayed. "I got beaten up."

She sighed. "I had a feeling this might happen."

I didn't have the energy to fight about it. And I knew that hearing any form of the words "I told you so" would cause a rift between us that, unlike my physical injuries, would never heal.

As soon as I'd bathed and put on clean clothes, I called Stephen. He'd gone to the ER, and it turned out he had three broken ribs and a broken wrist. In minutes I was back on the bus to his place. After what we'd been through, I had an urgent desire to be close to him.

I'd barely walked through the door when we fell into bed. We had to be careful and slow because of his injuries, so the sex felt especially intimate, and afterward we lay together for a long time, my head on his chest, breathing in the comforting smell of his cooling sweat and the Indian herbal soap from the health-food store that he liked to buy because he thought regular supermarket soap was evil. When we kissed, I could feel his split lip. Finally he broke the silence to ask me how I was feeling.

"I'm okay, as long as I don't think too much," I replied. "I guess I'm getting better at training myself not to dwell on how messed up things are. How about you?"

"Pretty terrible. At least they didn't break my writing hand. I guess I should be grateful for that anyway." He paused. "There's something I need to tell you, though."

My guts clenched. He wanted to break up but didn't have the heart to do it over the phone, right? He probably blamed me for what had happened to us. Or maybe he wanted to tell me he'd been sleeping with somebody else.

"It's time for me to go back to New York. I have a flight for next Thursday."

I knew it had been coming, but I still felt like I'd been sucker punched. A parade of memories started to march through my mind, of all the times my father had disappeared. Only the trappings were different. A geyser of self-hatred boiled up inside me. I was stupid and worthless, and the more I tried just to breathe and not consider how stupid and worthless I was, the more true it seemed. I wanted to die right then and there.

"I'm sorry. I did warn you I'd probably leave in December. The loft I've been waiting to build has been vacated, so it's time. But also . . ."

He sighed and, seeming to be searching for the words, nuzzled the top of my head with his lips, a tender gesture that only deepened my despair.

"Also, San Francisco's not what I expected. I mean, it's great in some ways—you especially. But I thought it'd be easier to be gay here. Safer. But really, compared to New York it's just kind of . . . provincial. Brutal, actually." He paused. "I'm finished."

It took all my strength to find my voice. I realized I was grinding my teeth. "I really wish you wouldn't," I managed. "But I don't suppose I can talk you out of it."

"No," he said, sounding sad. "You can't."

I tried to imagine my life without Stephen to anchor it. *Don't cry*, I told myself. "I guess I thought that somehow once I dropped out of school, our relationship would get deeper. I wasn't expecting you to just . . . leave."

"I'm sorry, Jimmy."

I pushed my face into the pillow, forcing down the sobs that wanted to come out. I felt them trapped in my stomach.

He massaged my shoulders, but I was tense under his touch. I lifted my head to face him. "Maybe . . . I can come visit you in New York?"

"Sure, if you can get your mom to agree to it. You'd be most welcome."

"Oh, my mom can go fuck herself," I said. He didn't respond to this. I hoisted my backpack off the bedroom floor and rummaged through it. "I wrote some poems," I said, my voice shaking, and brandished a few loose sheets of paper at him. "I was going to ask you to read them. You might as well take them today, I guess."

"Thanks." He reached over me to get his reading glasses.

I was aghast. "Wait, you're going to read them *now*?"

"Of course, why not?"

I didn't want to say, *Because you might think they stink*, so I stalked to the window and lit a cigarette, gazing down on the backyard. It was weedy and untended and looked long forgotten.

New York City. It seemed so distant, yet maybe, just maybe, I *could* go there. Thinking about it brought a new rush of anxiety.

"Hey, these are good," said Stephen from the bed.

I turned. "You're not just saying that?"

"No, I mean it in all sincerity. They're unhappy, but good. Someday you should meet my poet friend Anya. She knows Andy Warhol personally. And she really knows her stuff, poetry-wise."

"Really? You'd introduce me to your poet friend?"

He smiled up at me. "Just as soon as you come visit."

22

SOMETIMES YOU FEEL LIKE A NUT, SOMETIMES YOU DON'T

I t felt like no sooner had Stephen broached the topic of leaving than we were meeting at the airport to say good-bye.

Waiting at the gate, I could see him approaching from a distance. His hair was freshly dyed poppy red, and he stood out like a wildflower among the sea of drab people at the terminal. We held each other tightly for a very long time. I could feel hostile gazes on us, but they didn't matter. I buried my nose into the nape of his neck and inhaled deeply, trying to etch his scent into my memory. A boarding line formed at the gate.

"Thank you for everything you've done," I told him. "Thank you for turning me on to Philip Glass. And for reading my poems. And for everything."

"You're a good guy," he said. "Don't let anybody ever tell you otherwise."

"I love you," I whispered in his ear. It was the first time I'd ever said it to anyone.

"I love you, too," he whispered back.

I followed him down the walkway with my gaze until he disappeared from view. Then I watched the plane taxi up the runway and take to the sky.

I BEGGED MY MOTHER to drive us to the seashore. Being in nature together always made our connection with each other easier, and I yearned to be cradled in that space. While at first she was reluctant to scrap her plan to do her usual weekend routine, she must have sensed my desperation, because she reaffixed her shopping list to its place under the lemon-shaped refrigerator magnet and drove us to Pebble Beach, a craggy Pacific inlet with pebbles instead of sand and a few picnic tables.

The honeycombed rock formations there created tide pools filled with life: purple and orange starfish, bristling green anemones, silvery fish darting in and out of waving fronds of kelp, miniature crabs and snails.

I eased myself down to lie on my stomach, my whole midsection still sore to the touch and livid with bruises, and gazed at the teeming underwater world. The stone was cold and wet, yet I took some comfort in its solidity. Waves came crashing in at forceful intervals, spattering me with spray. The beach was empty except for the distant figure of my mother in silhouette, hunched against the wind with head bent, hunting for seashells.

Though the surf was rough at the shore, out on the horizon it was a smooth, straight line. I pictured the kelp forests beneath the turbulent ocean surface. They were down there, I thought, swaying in some rhythm all their own. Feeling as fragile and inert as a pane of glass, I imagined what it would be like to step off the rock shelf into the water. First my pant legs would soak through, and then I would plunge in, sending up an insignificant splash. I would swim out farther and farther, until my limbs were too cold to keep moving. Then I would sink into the deep darkness, and everything would finally just stop.

It sounded wonderful. I lay there, calm and numb inside, wishing I were brave enough to do it.

That evening my sister, Julie, was due to come over for dinner with her new boyfriend, Mark. While my mother bustled around tidying and fluffing up throw pillows, I smoked in my bedroom in my underwear, applying one layer after another of thick black eyeliner. *That's right, straighten up,* I thought in an uppity voice. *It's so important that everything be straight, isn't it?*

The numb, dissociated calm I'd felt at the tide pools had dissipated, giving way to an edgy, twitchy, simmering irritation. Why was it that Julie could bring her boyfriend over for "family dinner" without a second thought, when *my* boyfriend and I couldn't even walk down the fucking street without getting nearly killed? What was the point in perpetuating the bullshit lie that Julie and Mark even occupied the same *world* as Stephen and I?

I pulled back to admire my handiwork in the mirror. My face was splendidly ugly, like something from *The Cabinet of Dr. Caligari*. I laughed, a broken cackle.

I heard them come in, the sound of their greetings rising over the sound of the TV, but I stayed where I was, wanting to hole up until they'd gone home.

After a few halfhearted visits during our first months in San Carlos, Julie had pretty much dropped out of my life. She and my mom still spent hours every week yakking on the phone, but I sensed that to Julie's mind I was finally old enough to simply ignore. Well, if that was good enough for her, it was good enough for me. I popped a couple of uppers. They left a chalky taste in my mouth, but I was glad for the rush of energy they imparted, although they also made the cooking odors coming from the other side of the door smell overpowering, almost repulsive.

Finally there was a knock. My sister stood before me in a fluffy white cardigan. "Oh my God, eye makeup?" she said with a sigh. When I didn't respond, she said, "Dinner's ready. Can you put some pants on and come say hi to Mark?"

"I'm not hungry."

"Jim, you need dinner. You're way too skinny."

And you're way too much of a bitch. Behind her I could see her boyfriend in the living room. Blond and typical. A Ken doll. I closed the door in her face. *Have fun in your Barbie Dreamhouse with its pink bedroom and plastic food.*

When eventually I went out, feeling like an alien intruder, they were seated at the dining-room table. With clammy skin and a heartbeat revving from the amphetamines, I stood paralyzed and silent at the threshold.

"Why don't you come sit down, honey," my mother said in her most appeasing singsong.

Why did she always call me "honey"? I wasn't sweet. Mechanically I sat, hyperaware of the black Naugahyde on the faux-Spanish chair sticking to my thighs and of the light glinting off the glassware. The only sounds were the clink of cutlery and my mother's lip smacking, which grated on my raw nerves. An attempt to swallow a mouthful of stuffed bell pepper failed. I gulped water.

"Isn't this delicious?" Julie asked generally, trying to be upbeat. "They're Mark's mom's recipe."

"Yup," he said, his voice affectless. *Plastic-doll voice.*

Julie beamed. "Your mom's such a good cook."

"Yes, they're delicious," my mother agreed.

I'm going to lose my mind, I thought.

Julie and Mark started to chatter brightly about a sailboat trip in Napa they were planning for the spring, how they would stop at a local winery first and choose a bottle to bring on the boat. Julie turned to me. "Maybe you'd like to join us. It'd be fun for you."

They resumed the conversation about the imaginary boating excursion in Napa. The notion that they would ever in a million years invite me to come along was so transparently bullshit that it was hard not to laugh in their faces. "Maybe. That might be nice." *I'd prefer to take a bath in Windex.*

"Please try to have some more," my mother urged, nodding at my mostly uneaten dinner.

"I can't." It was taking all the control I possessed to sit still. I couldn't do it. I rose, feeling Mark's eyes on me, and moved into the living room, where the TV was showing *The Wonderful World of Disney* with the sound off.

I changed the channel to *60 Minutes.* Harry Reasoner, the anchorman, was looking serious under a grainy superimposed photograph of Jim Jones, the leader of the Peoples Temple. The media were still talking about the tragedy in Jonestown a long time later.

"Where I come from, you're not allowed to leave the table until you've finished what's on your plate," I heard Mark say.

"Where I come from, you can do what you fucking want," I retorted.

If the tension that resulted had had a sound, it would have been that buzzing squeal a radio makes as it drifts off-station.

My mom started clearing the table. Julie and Mark spoke in hushed tones. My heart was flapping around my chest like a moth trapped in a screen door, and my breath was coming in shudders. Two amphetamines on an empty stomach, I realized, was maybe not a brilliant idea.

"Would everybody like dessert?" called my mother.

"Yum, that would be wonderful, Mrs. Oseland," said Mark.

My mother peeped around the doorway. "Jim, dessert?"

"Right now I'd rather eat my own vomit," I muttered.

Mark charged into the living room. "What did you just say to her?" he demanded, looming over me.

The speed at which he'd moved terrified me, but I was also consumed with rage. "What difference does it make to you? Who *are* you?" Ken Doll needed to get his plastic, denim self the fuck away from me. When I stood up and moved past him to go to my bedroom, he tried to grab me and missed.

I slammed the door to my room behind me and shouted to no one, fumbling for my pack of cigarettes. "What the fuck is this monster doing in my house? Get it out!"

Mark threw open the door to my room. "*What* did you say?"

"Get it out. He's one of them. He's the enemy. Get him out!" I shrieked, losing all semblance of control.

He seized me by the shoulders and twisted my arm behind me. I thought of being beaten up with Stephen. "Apologize. No son should talk to his mother like that."

The veins in my neck were throbbing. *"Fuck yourself, mother-fucker!"*

"Apologize—*now!*" he roared.

My mother and sister came running in while I cried, "Get him off me!"

"Leave him alone, Mark," said Julie urgently. "Put him down."

He did not release me. "Say you're sorry," he repeated. "You need to learn some manners."

My mother was crying. I let out a long scream, and Mark loosened his grip. Breaking away, I lunged out of my room and into the kitchen. There I spotted the butcher knife on the cutting board, its blade still flecked with tomato seeds, and my fingers closed around its handle.

My mother dashed in. "What are you doing, Jim? Put that down!"

"I'm going to fucking kill myself, you dumb fucking cunt!" I screamed, holding the blade above my wrist. I was hyperventilating, a metallic taste flooding my mouth. "Get the fuck away from me!" Flourishing the knife at the three of them, I retreated slowly toward my room.

Inside, I held the door closed with my back and pushed the blade into my flesh, hoping it would instantaneously draw blood. It didn't. Out in the hall, my mother's voice was pleading.

I pushed the blade in harder. The shock of seeing blood caught me off guard, and Julie forced open the door, shouting my name. I let out another scream that disintegrated into sobbing.

Gently my sister took the knife from my hand, set it carefully on the floor, and guided me to the bathroom sink. There she turned on the tap and drew my wrist under the flow of cool water.

My mother came in to take over, washing the wound with soap, patting it dry. As she secured a square of gauze with a pair of Band-Aids, she said softly, "Don't you ever do that again."

I heard the front door close. When we emerged from the bathroom, Julie and Mark were gone.

23

YOU'RE SOAKING IN IT

Through the punk-scene grapevine, word reached me that Mary Menace had died at the Mutants' loft party. Rumors differed concerning what exactly she'd overdosed on, but all agreed that she was already dead by the time the paramedics arrived. Repelled by the glibness with which everyone, including Blackie O, took this information, I descended into a bottomless well of depression.

As the bruises from the beating faded from purple to green to yellow, my daily life became a whirling kaleidoscope of going to shows, getting fucked up, and fucking. Unwilling to go through the trouble of trying to talk to Stephen on the pay phone near his loft and finding out he didn't love me back, I began to pick up homeless guys on El Camino and take them to our apartment for a quick screw while my mother was at work, their unwashed bodies leaving a raunchy smell in my bedroom and on my own skin. It was my attitude of visibly not giving a shit that made me feel different when I was at shows. Gone was the shy, awkward boy, to be replaced by someone with sharper edges.

It might have been this demeanor that got me invited back-stage at the Deaf Club by the front man for the Offs, Don Vinil, who, rumor had it, was gay. As I followed him through the door, a tiny, scrappy black woman with an unkempt natural put her hand on my chest and gave me a death stare, growling, "You can't go in there, motherfucker."

"It's cool, he's with me," Don told her, and introduced her. Mad Dog, she was called. "Completely lives up to her name," he remarked, leading me backstage. Which was, funnily, basically exactly as dumpy as the main room, but even smaller. Knots of scenesters stood chatting and casting appraising glances from their protective circle. Their aura of cool-kid entitlement re-minded me uncomfortably of San Carlos High. It made me want to return to the front of the house and mingle with the regular showgoers.

Still, though, I couldn't help but feel singled out, chosen. So after the band played, I piled with the rest of them into the rat-tletrap of a car that was headed for Don's place.

Don Vinil had already reached home and greeted us in a fake-fur jacket that looked like it had been sitting in a bin at a junk store on Mission Street for the last three hundred years. When he brought out a foil-wrapped nub of heroin, I was queasy and frightened but also hungry to keep going, into the eye of dark-ness.

I'd seen heroin in movies before. I remembered *The Panic in Needle Park*, which was meant to be a warning. But I'd thought it was cool, because the characters seemed separate from soci-ety, and who needed society? It certainly hadn't rewarded me for trying to play by its rules. So I let Don teach me how to smoke heroin, while Brian Eno's album *Another Green World* droned nearby. After the requisite puking, I camped out in the bathroom, staring up at the cobwebs and cracks in the ceiling, feeling comfortable and safe. Eventually he tapped on the door. "Hey, man. You okay in there?"

"Yeah," I chuckled dreamily. "Just fine and dandy." I opened the door, pants and underwear down around my knees.

He laughed. "Want to come to bed?"

"Oh, yes, indeed."

That night I had the sleepwalking dream that had dogged me since childhood: the faceless killer hunting me with his knife. The hallway and closets of the unfamiliar rooms of Don's apartment offered feeble refuge, leaving me exposed to the killer's blade.

I THOUGHT ABOUT STEPHEN a lot during that time, of course. I pictured him in Manhattan in some dark, interesting club down an alley. As the days passed, I longed to hear his voice, but I was afraid to hear that he'd moved on and didn't need me anymore.

The heroin high had barely worn off when I was on my way to the Temple Beautiful with Blackie O and her crowd for another night of hedonism. I wore the pants I'd been fag-bashed in, now badly torn and flecked with bloodstains, pale foundation smeared all over my face and eyeliner to match my new jet-black dye job. *Mass-murderer chic*, I thought. By the time I got there, I was already drunk.

"Highway robbery," remarked Blackie O, putting three dollars into the bouncer's hand. "I remember the olden days when you could get into a show for a buck-fifty. I mean, not everybody has Marin County doctors and dentists for parents."

The Temple Beautiful had surged in popularity in recent months. But because it had been a synagogue with vaulted ceilings and miles of floor space, it never seemed to fill, and there were still plenty of peripheral nooks where you could get up to no good.

Too drunk to join the crowd, I plopped down in one of these deserted alcoves to people-watch. It struck me, as folks in their weekend finery stepped over my outstretched legs, that the punk scene was becoming more sedate. The venues were more crowded, yet the scene was getting diluted, less raw and weird, less sly and smart.

A petite woman I didn't recognize came and sat beside me. In her fake-leather boots and subtly secretarial hairdo, she looked out of place at the Temple Beautiful, but she was friendly. We had the conversation everyone was having at the time, about whether or not we'd gone to the last-ever Sex Pistols show, which had been at San Francisco's Winterland Ballroom (I hadn't; minus Sid Vicious, who'd been kicked out of the band, I didn't really see the point), and she gave me a flyer for an upcoming show. Under the scheduled bands' names was the famous crime-scene photo from the Black Dahlia murder, a naked woman sliced in two at the waist.

I folded it into my pocket. "Does it seem to you like shows are less fun than they used to be?" I asked her.

She laughed. "To tell you the truth, I'm tripping, so everything is okay by me right now."

"Tripping?"

"Yeah," she sighed, sounding very spacy. "Mushrooms. Do you want some? I have more."

I'd never taken mushrooms before (or any psychedelic drugs, for that matter), but it seemed they would be an innocuous amendment to my already raging booze high. Plus, even though they tasted muddy, I was barely eating lately and was thankful for being able to put something edible in my mouth.

Shortly after I'd chewed the handful of leathery buttons, my mind downshifted. Suddenly I was in a cavernous space where the two of us were the only presences, illuminated by a single spotlight. Encompassing us, nothing but murmuring darkness.

By the time the final band played, I was intermittently blacking out, so I was barely conscious for the usual chaotic powwow about who was going where afterward, this time a party at the film collective Target Video, and the usual mooching of a ride from whoever had a car. Tonight's driver was an ex-con who went by Reggie Veggie, a name that I'd heard referred to the horse tranquilizers he favored and which put him in a nearly vegetative state.

I remember being on the sidewalk outside the club, and then somehow we were crammed into Reggie's sedan, a riotous tangle of arms and legs and loud laughter, everybody on somebody's lap. I was on Blackie O's. Fillmore Street whizzed by in a wild blur as we went faster, faster.

In slow motion I watched the white car inching into the intersection before we slammed into it at top speed, then spun crazily. My head cracked against the window.

When everything came to a stop, I instinctively lifted my hand to my scalp and saw blood on my fingers. *Chunk-chunk* of car doors opening. We all filed out and stood in stunned silence.

Two passengers emerged from the other car, cholo dudes wearing low-slung Dickies. Gangsters, I assumed. I could barely comprehend anything anyone was saying, but I got the impression from what they were yelling that someone inside their vehicle was gravely injured, maybe even dead.

I saw Reggie Veggie's face stark and drawn as he whirled to tell us, "My car's stolen. We need to go!"

"But someone's hurt," I said.

"We need to go," he repeated, and tore off running down Fillmore Street.

Someone shouted, "They've got a gun!" and we bolted after Reggie, all of us.

The next thing I knew, Blackie O and I were squatting beside some trash cans somewhere. She looked scared and vulnerable, which frightened me.

"I don't know how we're going to get to the party, Jimmy," she said in a small voice.

"I'm bleeding, I'm bleeding. There's blood all over me," I moaned.

She took my hands, examined them, pushed them away. "No there isn't. You're fine."

"There's blood everywhere. Help! I need a doctor! Help!" I grabbed her by her dress, and she shoved me off. I toppled like a bug onto my back, whimpering, "I need a doctor. Please."

Next the two of us were walking into the Target Video party, as vast and overwhelming to me as an amphitheater, a loft full of baying strangers.

I approached each and every person there, begging, "I have to get to a doctor. I'm bleeding to death. Can you help me?" Everyone edged away as though I had a contagious disease.

"Someone needs to get him to the ER." The words rolled toward me on a cloying plume of cigarette smoke. "He's tripping. It's like the sixties all over again."

Another voice shot back, "Fuck the sixties. Fuck hippies. Hippies can suck my *dick*."

It's because we let Mary Menace die, I thought. *I'm being punished for killing Mary.* Fighting my way to the center of the room, I screamed, "Help! Won't someone help me? I'm dying!"

My cry was so loud it pierced the music. I heard Blackie O's voice. "Somebody needs to call his mother."

SOMETIME LATER, I remember, I was walking out of a hospital in an unfamiliar winter coat. My sister was propping me up on one side, my mother on the other. They looked exhausted.

A nurse called after us, "Ma'am? Are you sure you don't want to keep him here for observation?"

"We can take it from here," said Julie, and they brought me home to sleep it off.

My mother told me later that the nurses in the emergency room had given me Thorazine. On the one hand, the idea of being given a drug reserved for psychotic people made me see myself as worthy and interesting. On the other hand, it made me ashamed. My future wasn't merely not promising, it was dwindling to a vanishing point.

And yet only a few days later I was back at a show. As soon as I got to the club, I felt truly out of place. I was certain I wasn't imagining it—the punk scene really was becoming straighter, more macho, more homogeneous.

"Hey, you! Yeah, you!"

I looked up to see Bruce Loose, the lead singer of the band Flipper, leaning over a banister leering at me. To me, Bruce, with his shaved head and his thuggish, hypermasculine attitude, completely embodied what the shows were morphing into: just another place for straight white dudes to pick a fight with a stranger.

"I know you!" he yelled. "You're the guy who thought he was bleeding to death!" He laughed. "What happened, man? Were you having your period?"

Beside him one of his bandmates shrieked in a cruel falsetto, "'Somebody help me! I need a tampon!'" The tiny world that was the punk rock scene was getting smaller, almost as claustrophobic as the normal world.

I left without even saying good night to my friends.

EVENTUALLY MY DESIRE TO TALK to Stephen won out over my fear of rejection. We set up a time and spoke.

I could tell by his tone that he was happy to hear my voice and that all my gloomy conjecture was unwarranted. *Why'd I think that stuff in the first place?* I wondered. *What benefit is there in doubting myself so much?*

He talked about his loft, which was on the top floor of an old office building that he and his roommates had divided into separate living spaces. As he told me about his view onto Trinity Place, about the rickety freight elevator, and the way the smell from the lousy Chinese restaurant on the ground floor permeated all eight floors, I tried from my perch by the bedroom window to imagine every single detail. It made me sad that all I could see were the same scrubby hills outside my window.

That night my mother came home in a bad mood. A friend of hers at work had been fired, and she was feeling grim and tense, setting two pot-roast TV dinners down with the brusque announcement, "This is all we can afford, and it's all I have time for. I don't want to hear any lip. I had a coupon for it."

For a while we watched TV in silence, until the familiar trapped, suffocating sensation began to overwhelm me. During the first commercial break, I said, "Mom, I want to go to New York City. Would you let me?"

"How would I pay for it? You need to learn that money doesn't grow on trees. You have to work for the things you want."

"You sound like you're teaching a 4-H class. Are you saying I can't go?"

"How can you go without money? I can't just fly you to New York and have you gallivanting around when your father won't even send us rent money."

I sighed. "Oh, for fuck's sake."

"Don't say cuss words to your mother. That's very rude. You need to treat me better. And anyway, you're not going to the other side of the country and leaving me all alone."

There was a book on the coffee table about impressionist painters. I had found it years ago in the remainders pile at the B. Dalton bookstore, and I loved it very much. Now I picked it up and threw it across the room.

Her stare was so intense it bordered on creepy. "You're not my son," she whispered.

"No kidding. How amazing you just figured that out."

"You have no respect," she said, still whispering.

"You're right about that, too." I met her eyes. "And I don't care."

She swung at me. The punch missed my face and landed on my neck. It was a forceful blow, and it hurt.

Within seconds it was like a barroom brawl. I slapped her face. She slapped mine back. I spit at her face. She spit at mine. Throw pillows went flying. A glass of milk got knocked off the coffee table. She grabbed my shirt and yanked. When I heard it rip, I stopped, overcome and out of breath.

She covered her face and started to cry, and the sound set my own tears to flowing. At last I sat on the sofa and embraced her. We wept in each other's arms until there were no tears left.

PART III

24

FLY THE FRIENDLY SKIES

read the letter for what must have been the tenth time. Even its physical presence in my hands, the paper creased from repeated unfolding and refolding, didn't make it seem more real.

Hey, buddy. Your mom says it would mean a whole lot to you to visit New York. Enclosed is a check that should cover the airfare, plus a little walking around money. TWA is having a holiday special, so better buy your ticket soon.

Merry Xmas from your old Dad

In my perch on the window seat, I read the letter yet again. Outside, a cat prowled through the tall grass in pursuit of some invisible prey.

How could my father be capable of such a generous act? In my mind he'd become a monster, a being so heartless that he could abandon his child almost literally on the side of the road and fly off into the horizon. I couldn't connect the dots. I was thrilled, yet convinced that at any moment it could all fall apart, be taken away. To keep disaster from sinking its claws into this stroke of good luck, I had started getting more compulsive again, making sure to spit as I left the house and stepping over luck-destroying cracks in the sidewalk.

I tucked the letter between the pages of my journal and resumed cramming clothes into a pair of Samsonite suitcases that hadn't seen the light of day since the cross-country trip we'd taken to get to California. I had no idea what to expect from a New York winter. Drifts of snow? Icicles hanging off my face?

"Are you sure you're not packing too much, honey?" my mom said from the threshold. "I mean, you're not going away forever."

Don't remind me, I thought.

"I know you like your friend very much," she continued, "but I don't know if this is a good idea, you being in New York with someone I don't know very well. . . ." She trailed off.

I was about to snap, *He's not my "friend" and you know it,* but something in her voice made me stop. I could see from her expression that while she wasn't able to say the exact words, she did understand.

Fidgeting, she continued, "I just don't know what I'm going to do when you're gone. I'm going to be so lonely. Do you really have to go?"

I added my camera and my journal to the pile in the suitcase. "You'll be fine, Mom. We'll talk on the phone."

"I don't know what I'm going to eat without your wonderful cooking. You must have picked up your father's cooking genes."

"I don't think that's scientifically possible."

"Oh, family works that way. You pick things up."

"I guess I'll have to take your word on that one," I said, and threw my weight on the suitcase in an attempt to get it to shut.

Just before I stepped onto the Jetway at SFO, she held me tight. I'd only been on an airplane a couple of times in my life, and she'd made sure to alert every adult in uniform within a thirty-foot radius to keep an eye on me.

"Come back soon, honey. I'll miss you so much." She hugged me tightly once more, then drew back and smoothed my hair, which made me flinch—it had taken me some time to get it to spike up in front properly. She gave me a wan smile. "Please don't be so angry. Please let go of some of your anger."

By the time my plane was making its descent into JFK, my teeth were grinding in sets of four while my mind got busy churning out scenarios of potential disasters. The plane would go careening off the runway and slither right into the icy water of the Atlantic. Stephen's subway car would crash on the way to the airport. He'd have forgotten I was coming. TWA would lose my luggage.

To soothe myself I excavated from my carry-on my latest prized possession, the Sony Walkman I'd gotten as an early sixteenth birthday present (for which my mother had splurged hugely, augmented by my savings), and slipped on the head-phones. Darby Crash, the lead singer of the Germs, was on a downward spiral and his band was dissolving, and I'd had a bootleg cassette of one of their live shows on replay ever since. It was inexpertly recorded, barely coherent, but as soon as I pressed the chunky silver Play button, it transported me to the familiar crush of bodies and the smells of a punk rock show.

Stephen was, of course, there at JFK waiting, and his welcoming hug was enveloping. Outside, he hailed a yellow Checker Cab, which looked to my eyes like a cartoon illustration of a taxi, and joined a stream of sluggish traffic, flurries of snow swirling over the windshield and cars honking all around us.

When the taxi wound its way through a warren of cobble-stoned streets and neared an old office building downtown, I recognized it at once from Stephen's descriptions. There, as promised, was the dumpy Chinese restaurant on the ground floor. Its architecture was more grand and imposing than I'd pictured, with lots of gothic details. The street was filthier than I'd pictured, too. Dog shit festooned the sidewalk, and giant mounds of garbage flanked the entrance of his building like shiny black Hefty-bag topiaries. Seeing my expression, Stephen gave me a wry smile. "You're not in Kansas anymore, Toto."

The cabbie lifted my suitcase out of the trunk and roared away. I heard foghorns and seagulls. On the curb was a man with a boom box balanced on his shoulder, nodding his head to the radio as though in a trance. There were bits of fluff and lint stuck to his Afro, and his army jacket was threadbare. He was sort of groaning along that he loved the nightlife, he had to boogie at the disco.

"Is that your doorman?" I asked Stephen, dragging my suitcase through the vestibule.

"Oh, Dwayne? He's the neighborhood welcoming committee. Coke casualty. It's too fucking cheap, that's the problem. Now that you can buy it with spare change . . ." The elevator came rumbling down, landing with a thud and opening its doors to reveal cracked linoleum. "Watch your step. Sometimes there's a gap in the shaft. Somebody nearly fell in last month."

Unlocking a complicated sequence of padlocks on the eighth floor, he assured me, "This is much easier than it seems once you get used to it."

We stepped into a cold and uninviting space. It did smell like greasy Chinese food, plus dampness. Streetlights filtered through the thick windowpanes. Beside a futon on the floor was a small Christmas tree. The bathroom was a toilet with a cracked and leaking tank and a sink crookedly attached to the wall. A plastic shower stall with a torn curtain completed the picture.

I turned on the faucet to wash my face, but all that emerged was a hiss. "I guess there's no hot water?"

"Nope, not here," he said, fetching a pair of tin camping cups. "We're living here illegally."

"Living here illegally . . . what does that mean, exactly?"

But he just smiled and fixed us a pot of coffee on the hot plate. Feeling a bit shy, I perched on the bed and gazed at the tree, which glittered with a homely beauty. What were those strange ornaments? I knelt to examine them closely. Among the colored lights and tinsel were dozens of tiny sealed jars filled with liquid and a spongy, fleshy-looking substance.

"I see you've found the cats' testicles," Stephen laughed. "My friend Grace Shock works part-time in a vet's office. Doesn't that just give a whole new meaning to the spirit of Christmas?"

That night, jet-lagged and unused to a strange bed, I woke in the small hours and went nude to the window. Looking out at deserted Trinity Place and at the magnificent old office buildings across the street, I thought, *Am I really in New York? Could this be real?*

The next day Stephen took me on a walking tour, after a diner breakfast where the bearded, gruff Greeks behind the counter seemed to know him. We got take-out coffee in blue-and-white paper cups bearing the campy slogan WE ARE HAPPY TO SERVE YOU and walked for what felt like miles. Everything seemed so outsize in Manhattan. San Francisco was a dollhouse version of a city in comparison.

That night he took me to a performance by the Philip Glass Ensemble. It was strange and magical but also boring, and my mind started to drift off. Afterward, while he was introducing me to some friends, I noticed one of the performers, an attractive, chiseled guy, casting obviously cruisey glances my way.

In fact, I'd noticed that pretty much everywhere we went, some guy would be checking me out. Similar to San Francisco, it seemed that men were fucking in every place that was remotely hospitable to a quick hookup. Here, even the cold wind of December wasn't deterring them.

I'd always been aware of the glances and innuendos, but I was discovering that the more comfortable and open I was becoming with my sexuality, the more I seemed to attract the attention of guys on the prowl. It was as though I'd been given the secret password to a world of instant gratification. A certain fixed glance, a casual gesture, the slightest adjustment in one's stance—to imbue these with sexual intention, all you had to do was be aware it was possible.

Stephen seemed oblivious to the electric charge that was building between myself and the men around me, which didn't make sense. He must, I reasoned, have confidence in me as a real boyfriend. Wanting to live up to that, I tried not to return any stares, tried not to get drawn in. But it was both arousing and fascinating—and needless to say, thinking of it as forbidden fruit certainly didn't make it less tempting.

LATE-NIGHT DINNERS at Puerto Rican restaurants, museums, long walks, trips to Bleecker Bob's to peruse newly released albums, sex, midnight screenings of John Waters movies, endless glasses of Valpolicella. All of it felt bracingly adult and sharp.

The art I'd been exposed to as a child, mostly from the glossy books that occupied our glass-topped coffee table, I'd always appreciated: Raphael, Degas, Van Gogh. But as Stephen took me to galleries in SoHo and performance spaces like the Kitchen, other dimensions of artistic practice were opened to me. We visited an exhibition by Walter de Maria called *The Broken Kilometer* that was made of five hundred polished brass rods that spoke to me with far more resonance than the photographic reproductions of painted sunflowers or ballerinas ever had. At a certain point, I realized I could even claim to have specific tastes: the work I liked best was stark and conceptual and had an edge to it that challenged the viewers' preconceptions.

Stephen was eager to turn me on to all the contemporary art and music I could take in. Like the composer Steve Reich, who had a spare and magical style that reminded me of Philip Glass, and Glenn Branca, a musician who somehow managed to make classical music into punk rock. There was the visual-arts collective Colab, or Collaborative Projects, which mounted ambitious exhibitions with ironic names like *The Income and Wealth Show* and *Just Another Asshole*. There were bands I hadn't heard of before, like Throbbing Gristle and DNA, whose music I found both beautiful and upsetting. I discovered writers, too: Gary Indiana and Rene Ricard, whose dryly minimal styles made perfect sense to me. I absorbed every bit of it, even the stuff I didn't love, with an almost physical sensation of horizons expanding.

Stephen's tribe of people, too, consisted of mostly writers and artists. Once we went to visit a friend of his, Lauren, on the Lower East Side, which I'd heard had a reputation for being the murder capital of the country, and I was sure we'd die curled up in some gutter on the way. Among boarded-up buildings and those reduced to piles of bricks, Lauren's place was a filthy and dark edifice that by comparison made even the worst of the slummy buildings I knew in San Francisco's Tenderloin seem like *Architectural Digest* photo spreads.

The interior of her apartment was painted a glossy black, and except for the bare minimum of furniture it was completely devoid of any embellishments except canvases, dozens of them, all depicting the same Chinese deity. Lauren told me she was obsessed with Quan Yin, the goddess of mercy, who listens to all the suffering in the world. I'd asked her what good *that* did. "Through her compassion she gives us hope," she'd replied. "She makes us feel that we're not alone."

"Quan Yin's not her *only* obsession," Stephen added after we left, as we strode along the litter-strewn sidewalks of Alphabet City. "She's into young Chinese men. She's having one affair with a shopkeeper from Chinatown and another with a restaurant-delivery guy."

As I digested the information that gay men weren't perhaps the only ones driven by particular and insatiable urges, we reached the open-air drug market that was lower Avenue B, with seemingly hundreds of street vendors hawking their wares. Pot, speed, smack, coke. It was fantastically lawless, as though any transgression you could think of was suddenly as normal as turning on the TV. A man in clothes so filthy they seemed to be growing on him like moss staggered past us, muttering an incoherent offer.

"Did that guy just offer to sell us a *monkey*?" I asked, laughing, incredulous. New York was making me forget the rapid death spiral of my life back home. I found myself entertaining the possibility of actually residing in this vast complexity. After all, couldn't I reinvent myself again, be an artist or a student? Couldn't I move in with Stephen?

In the moment it didn't seem impossible. My parents had, astonishingly enough, come to some kind of agreement concerning my upkeep, and, even more incredibly, my dad had decided he was doing well enough these days to underwrite my being in New York for a while. I didn't believe he would come through, but I'd received one check already—made out to Stephen, since I was a minor and Stephen had a bank account. It was for seventy-five dollars, and it came with the promise of another just like it in a couple weeks. That would at least keep me in diner coffee and movies.

We could fix up the loft and make it more comfortable, I mused. Who knew? I could probably even convince Stephen to get a couch.

25

REACH OUT AND TOUCH SOMEONE

We spent that Christmas Eve exploring Chinatown, along with the masses of people thronging the cramped byways. I loved the foreignness of the environment, the street names so unlike California street names, the faded lanterns hanging outside narrow doorways spilling forth a cornucopia of souvenirs, the cacophony of languages and cars honking and the displays of battery-operated toys that bleeped, barked, cried, laughed, and meowed in front of every shop; the whole roasted ducks and bright orange smoked squid hanging from hooks in the windows, the carts selling hot chestnuts. San Francisco's Chinatown was nice, but here I tingled with the feeling that we'd been transported to another country.

We wandered into tea shops, supermarkets, apothecaries displaying boxes full of dried objects that were unrecognizable to me—were those mushrooms or scallops, nuts, berries, or stones?—and candy stores, then paused at a busy fish stall on

Canal Street that smelled intense and briny. I was intrigued by the glistening seafood arrayed over crushed ice. Peering inside a crate, I saw frozen soft-shell crabs stacked in careful rows. I recalled having eaten these on one of those trips to Baltimore to see my mother's family; they'd been a treat.

I'd always felt closest to my father when we were together in the kitchen. If he could re-create a festive meal based on dishes he'd eaten while traveling, I thought now, couldn't I do the same?

"I want to make dinner tonight," I told Stephen, who was gazing at a tank full of fish that were swimming against a current of piped-in water. "It'll be my Christmas present to you."

We stopped in at a few other shops to buy vegetables that I thought might go well with the meal, and then, as a special treat, we stopped at Ferrara's in Little Italy and had four of their delicious, crisp-shelled cannoli boxed up and tied smartly with red-and-white-striped string by a counter girl who was so harried by the line of people waiting to place their holiday orders that she didn't even look at us. I'd never even heard of cannoli before coming to New York, and they'd become my favorite dessert. As we crossed onto Trinity Place, a light snow began to fall, and the general air of holiday spirit buoyed my own.

"Will you take the groceries in?" I asked him. "I need to make a call, and then I'll be right up."

He knew I meant the phone booth across the street, which is where we made all our calls, and he gave me a wave as he mounted the steps to his building.

Light-headed with nervous excitement, I dialed the operator. "I need to place a person-to-person collect call to Minnesota, please," I said. "To Larry Oseland. From Jim." Reciting the number, I fumbled a cigarette out of the pack and lit it with trembling fingers.

"One moment while I connect you."

COKE KILLS! was scrawled inside the booth in marker. Some-body had neatly crossed out KILLS and written over it RULES. The phone book had been ripped out, leaving only the binding and some paper shreds that fluttered as I pulled the glass door closed.

Faintly I heard my father say, "Yes, I'll accept," then, loud and vibrant, "Jimbo? That you?"

I twisted the length of metal cord around my hand. The re-ceiver smelled like aftershave. "Yeah, Dad, it's me."

"Hey, buddy. I haven't heard from you in a while. Merry Christmas!" His voice sounded lower, deeper than I remem-bered. With a jolt I realized I hadn't heard it since that long-ago day at my sister's apartment in San Jose. I had the sense that I'd entered a dream.

"So how are you doing? How's New York treating you?"

"It's amazing, Dad."

Spurred on by the warmth in his tone, I found myself over-flowing with the desire to share with him everything I'd seen, to tell him about Stephen's chilly loft and the lousy freight elevator, about the bustle and crush downtown, about seeing the Monet water lilies at the Museum of Modern Art and how standing in front of that huge canvas had made me feel, inexplicably, like I had a place in the world. About how the people here walked faster, talked faster, dressed differently from people in Califor-nia. About how I felt like maybe I was starting to become one of them.

And I really wanted to tell him how my plan to cook from memory a special meal made me feel close to him today, despite the thousands of miles between us and how long it'd been since we'd spoken.

But just as I began to speak, he interrupted. "I spent a lot of time there in the fifties, you know. I used to go for these confer- ences the Swingline stapler people used to hold. Quite the shin- digs, those conferences! I remember one night one of the boys got this idea—that was Bob, he was half in the bag by then— that we'd all show up for breakfast in our secretaries' clothes. And vice versa! I'll tell you . . ."

In his pause I heard the clink of ice cubes in a glass, and it dawned on me that what I'd taken for affectionate warmth might be the glow of an alcohol buzz. "Dad," I interjected, "I just wanted to tell you something. Today when I was—"

"Well, hang on, Jim, I'm telling you a story," he said eas- ily. While he continued to reminisce, chuckling to himself, I watched a squeegee man step in front of an Oldsmobile and swipe at its windshield with a filthy rag.

Swerving away, the driver laid on his horn. It was deafening, like the klaxon of a sinking ship, and I startled. "Jeez, what was *that*?" said my father. "Anyway, New York's a great city," he con- cluded. "Great city."

"Yeah. It really is." My voice sounded as though it had a hole in the middle of it.

"I'm happy to pay for it," he added. "Sometimes your old dad's not too shabby when it comes to presents, right?"

"Yes, thank you very much," I said, all the energy draining out of me, as though I'd been holding a big, dumb balloon full of enthusiasm and he'd just popped it. What could I ever tell him about my life that he would actually care about?

As if to prove my point, he said, "So listen, Jimbo, these calls are pretty expensive. Did you want me for some special reason, besides Christmas?"

"Uh, yeah. I bought these soft-shell crabs today. I wanted to cook them for dinner, but I don't have a recipe."

"Oh, sure, that's pretty easy," he said, his pleasure at being consulted as an expert immediately discernible. I heard the ice cubes clack again as he took another sip of what I guessed was Tanqueray and tonic. "You just dust them in a little flour and then sauté them in oil. But you've got to clean them first, you know that, right? You've got to take out the little lungs."

"Ugh, you have to *what*?"

"You know, the gills. The devil's fingers. What you want to do is . . ."

As he paused to think it through, I could sense his brow furrowing in concentration. I was pierced with a longing to travel back in time and be the little boy admiring his daddy's competence, free of the sludge of bad feeling that was rising in the center of me right now like a backed-up drain.

"Cut off the top, where the eyes are, with a knife," he continued. "Pull up the shell, you'll see the gills, beige pointy things. Rip those out. Then flip it over and pull off the flap. Then rinse the whole thing off. It's not that hard."

"Oh. Okay. I think I can do that," I said, picturing the hot plate upstairs and the thin, unsteady trickle of cold water from the tap.

"Hey, it's good to hear from you. We used to have a good time, you and me. Why don't you come out and see me sometime?"

"Maybe I can. That would be cool."

We were silent for a few moments before he spoke again. "Well, listen, merry Christmas." He wanted to get off the phone, it was clear.

"Merry Christmas," I echoed. "I'll let you know how the crabs come out."

"You do that. And keep your eye out for another check. There's one in the mail."

I placed the receiver, now warm and damp from my breath, into its cradle. Crossing back to Stephen's building, I was so dazed with confusion and hurt and sorrow that I didn't remember to look both ways, and a taxi had to stop short to keep from smacking right into me.

"Watch it, kid!" yelled the cabdriver as he peeled off.

I stubbed out the cigarette on the street, wondering if Stephen would think less of me if I threw the crabs in the garbage and asked to go to a restaurant for dinner tonight. According to him, going out for Chinese food on Christmas Eve was a New York tradition.

Great city, great city, said my father's voice in my head, and I felt myself fighting back furious tears.

26

THE BEST A MAN CAN GET

We rang in New Year's Eve at the Mudd Club. Compared to the anarchic, thrown-together Deaf Club, this place felt like it was run by grown-ups. I was catching on that the punk scene in New York was much artier and more self-aware than it was in California, less about social rebellion and more about a kind of disenchanted intelligence that had turned lethal.

On this night we'd come to see a No Wave band called Teenage Jesus and the Jerks, whose music was, I thought, the personification of violence and rage, so forceful that I was stunned by it. The lead singer, a powerful, diminutive figure named Lydia Lunch, played slide guitar using first a knife, then a beer bottle. At the end of the set, she prowled toward where I was leaning against the front of the stage and pressed her thigh, bare under her leather miniskirt, against my face. It left me feeling anointed.

We celebrated the first day of 1979—once we finally rolled out of bed—with a field trip to the gay-porn theater, where Rusty, Stephen's old roommate from San Francisco, worked the projector. I'd never been in one, so the mere idea of just actually going was exciting.

When the RR train came, it was covered in graffiti, a patchwork of indecipherable whorls both inside and out. Utterly opposite to the sterile banality of the trains of the Southern Pacific, the train car was like a rolling jail cell. The women wore their purse straps slung around their shoulders, the better to clamp them under their arms; but we saw a little kid pickpocket a guy as the train pulled in to the station and then hop out onto the platform and melt into the crowd. The whole thing was over before I'd even absorbed what I'd witnessed, but in retrospect I realized that Stephen had clocked it with detached amusement.

Why hadn't he said anything? I wanted to know as we trudged up the nonfunctional escalator.

He shook his head, still chuckling. "You've got to live here to understand. Oh, hey, get over—the left side's for people who walk faster."

You could've warned the guy. It was just a kid—it's not like he could've hurt anybody, I thought but didn't say. I felt kind of bad for thinking critically of Stephen, but little things, like the horrendously stingy tips he left at restaurants, were starting to bug me. On his turf he was ruder, and he bitched more, too.

Emerging from the Hades-like subway into midtown was a relief. On Fifty-First Street, the buildings were even more majestic than they were downtown; the people walking by were smartly dressed, fresher, stepping briskly past the detritus of the previous night's New Year's Eve street party. "I never go uptown," he told me. "You're getting special treatment."

The Adonis was a captivating mixture of sleaze and grandeur, the façade looking as though it had emerged from the pages of an Edith Wharton novel, but with a grimy marquee stuck on like an afterthought. After Stephen exchanged some words with the ticket taker, we passed through a grand old lobby filled with the gluelike smell of amyl nitrate, then went into the projection booth. There Rusty was sitting on a stool, smoking a cigarette and paging through a copy of the *Village Voice.*

"Hey, Jimmy," he said without enthusiasm. "Happy ass-end of a decade."

"That's a dreary way to put it," remarked Stephen.

"Oh, child, what's the difference, we're in *here,*" Rusty said with a sigh.

I laughed, and Stephen said, "Don't believe the act. Rusty's convinced that the Adonis is the cultural capital of Manhattan."

Rusty turned a page, blew smoke. "Isn't it?"

I excused myself to go to the men's room, more out of curiosity than actual need. I wanted to check out the scene. Clambering back down the ladder, I headed to the concession stand first, out of instinct. In place of the usual neat rows of jujubes and Raisinets, there were neat rows of lube and cock rings—and were those *poppers*? Well, that explained the smell.

Did I want anything? the bored concessionaire wanted to know. No thanks, just looking! I padded next down a dim corridor that smelled like urinal cakes and bleach. In the men's room, a scrawny white guy was giving a scrawny black guy a hand job. In a doorless stall sat a spooky transvestite in lingerie. "Excuse me," I said, and then felt silly.

The auditorium was pitch-dark. On-screen a queen with a mustache was getting fucked to a muffled disco soundtrack. As my eyes adjusted to the lack of light, I realized that the theater was mobbed with men, most of them engaged in some manner of sexual activity. The place was like a darkened church of sex. One of the men was standing close enough to touch. Fiftyish, with a graying beard, leather pants. Reflected shapes from the screen played on the surface of his aviator eyeglasses.

Without breaking his gaze from the movie, he stepped closer, cupping my crotch as casually as a shopper in the produce aisle testing for ripeness. I couldn't help getting an instant hard-on, but I could have moved away. Instead I hesitated.

Having a boyfriend was like a protective cloak. However, I had an animal curiosity to explore my limits, take any unmarked path. This thought passed through my mind in a flash—which was all it took for the stranger to undo the buttons of my Levi's.

He knelt in the darkness in front of me, and I let him. The whole thing was over in two minutes, at which point I thanked him. When I emerged blinking back into the lobby, Stephen was right there.

"Having fun?"

"Totally. This whole place is like the fall of the Roman Empire," I said. "I wish so much I'd thought to bring my camera." Inwardly I was panicking, certain he knew what I'd just done. My hand brushed the crotch of my jeans to surreptitiously check for damp spots, but I couldn't tell.

"'Scuse me." To my dismay it was the guy who'd just blown me, choosing that particular moment to leave the auditorium. Forced to step aside, I avoided looking at him.

Stephen's eyes slid over the man as he passed. His expression was opaque as he held up my pea coat. "You left this in the projection booth."

Thanking him, I shrugged it on, grateful that it covered my waist, just in case. "I'm ready for lunch, are you?" I suggested brightly.

Stephen's response was a nod and an unreadable silence, which I filled with chatter. "Can we get that Japanese thing—what's it called? Sushi? It's supposed to actually be pretty good. Plus, raw fish, that's just too weird not to try at least once, right?"

THE NEXT DAY Stephen seemed irritable, but he didn't bring anything up, so I pretended not to notice. Once he'd left the loft, I put on my Walkman headphones, pressed Play, and was plunged midsong into a mix tape that Blackie O had made me as a going-away present. I sang along to Human Sexual Response: "'I eye everyone I meet, I want to follow them all home . . .'"

Outside was all of Manhattan, waiting for me. I gathered the set of keys that Stephen had left me and threw the Canon into my messenger bag. Then, suddenly overcome with exuberance, I pogoed around the room, leaping onto the bed and springing off again like a little kid, singing along at the top of my lungs.

I hadn't yet been out on my own, and even though it was lonely to be walking the windswept sidewalks without Stephen's sheltering presence, there was something exciting about it, too. I headed uptown on foot, using glimpses of the Empire State Building to guide me. I thought of all the people Stephen had told me he'd seen walking around on the streets of this city— Debbie Harry! Richard Hell and Tom Verlaine! William Burroughs! Nina Hagen! Who knew what was out there waiting for me? Whatever it was, it wasn't San Carlos.

The thought of this dealt a judo kick to my usual anxiety, and I felt blessedly free of the impulse to carry out any protective rituals or otherwise tie myself up in neurotic mental knots. When I happened upon an old stone chapel with a churchyard, I didn't stop to worry whether or not it would be okay to wander in; I hopped over the rusty iron fence.

The tombstones were tilted with age under the bare tree

branches. California tombstones were never this old. I took photos there most of the afternoon, flipping over the cassette in the Walkman at thirty-minute intervals, until my fingers got too numb from the cold to work the camera. Then I stopped in at a greasy spoon where the windows were painted for the holidays with a scene of elves and reindeer dancing around a menorah. There I sat in a booth and wrote a couple of poems, warming my hands on a cup of bad coffee.

Afterward, while I was walking back downtown, a car came too fast along Broadway and made a sharp right, its tires squealing as it took the turn, and from the window a male voice shouted, "Yo, FAGGOT!" as the car screamed off across Broome Street.

I stopped short, startled, and then continued through the crosswalk, mentally scanning my reaction, like checking for broken bones after an accident. I'd assumed this bullshit didn't happen on the East Coast, so I was surprised. But more astonishing was that while I was upset and my blood pressure shot up, the terror I usually felt, especially since that dreadful night in North Beach—that internal bracing for the sound of a car door opening—wasn't occurring.

Whatever happened, I thought, even if the car *did* circle the block and come back for me, I felt in some way cushioned. I'd be hard-pressed to explain exactly what it was that provided the buffer, but it had to do with being in New York City. Of course it was a more crowded place than San Francisco, and things like getting beaten up didn't usually happen in crowded places. But more to the point, it was my impression that the city generally saw different and freaky people like me as somehow necessary to the social fabric, not as enemies of the state as was the case back in California. Not to mention that there were *a lot* more versions of people like me here than out west.

That night Stephen was still somewhat distant, and I wondered again if he'd guessed what had happened at the Adonis. I showed him the poems, hoping for a change in mood, and he seemed to approve of them. Then we went on a gallery crawl. There was something different, I noticed, about going to look at art after I'd spent the day taking pictures and writing poems. It wasn't that I thought I was an artist exactly, but I knew I wasn't *not* making art either. Something in the way I carried myself was subtly altered. Maybe I was holding myself a little taller, or maybe I was just more engaged in what was going on, but in any case I felt a change.

At some point during the crawl, probably with some assistance from the never-ending plastic cups of lukewarm Chablis, Stephen and I got separated, and I found myself taking a breather in the industrial stairwell of some repurposed factory or another. The metal steps clanged as someone descended, and then a pair of Cuban-heeled boots appeared beside me.

"Oh, hi," said a male voice.

I scooted over to let him by.

"Gee, thanks." There was something familiar in the flatness of the tone, and I looked up to see Andy Warhol gazing down at me with his disconcerting, oblique stare.

"Hi!" I said to his retreating back, a beat too late. *Shit! I could've taken a picture!*

Still, that cemented it. I was really in New York City.

27

BETCHA CAN'T EAT JUST ONE

J anuary gave way to February, a short, sleet-flecked month dominated by gossip about the possible closing of Studio 54. Then it was March. Amazingly, my father kept the checks coming every couple of weeks, made out to Stephen, with *"From Dad"* written on the memo line.

I called my mother with increasing frequency, telling myself that it was for her sake and had nothing to do with my missing her. As usual, we'd talk about current events, worrying together about the nuclear accident at Three Mile Island or the freakish number of plane crashes (I joked that when I did return to California, I'd be better off walking there, which she didn't find funny). Or we'd bicker about movies ("Honey, the last thing I want to see is a movie about divorce," was her reply when I told her *Kramer vs. Kramer* was brilliant, but we agreed on the merits and faults of *Being There* and *All That Jazz*), and argue over whether "I Don't Like Mondays," the Boomtown Rats song about the sixteen-year-old girl in San Diego who'd shot up her school, was an appalling (her) or creatively inspired (me) response to the tragedy.

The last time we'd spoken, she delivered the sad news that Peewee the turtle had finally died. She'd buried him on the hill out back. Then she'd asked, somewhat plaintively, when I thought I might ever come home. I evaded the question, having settled comfortably into life on the East Coast. "It's the lifestyle I've always dreamed of," I told her.

I certainly wasn't going to tell her about the other side of it, which was that I was wigging myself out with the amount of cruising I'd been doing behind Stephen's back.

The stranger at the Adonis had been just the beginning. Soon after that I'd followed a beautiful young Asian guy to the far corner of a subway platform. The calm, sure way he pushed me back against the dirty tile wall took my breath away. With almost balletic formality, he unzipped my jeans and released my cock into his hands as the RR train roared into the station, blowing dirt and hot air onto my closed eyelids.

Other than the physical thrill of the experience, the precise nature of its rapture was elusive, like a complex and hard-to-place flavor I wanted to keep tasting until I could name it. Each interlude was a fascinating and excitingly unpredictable adventure. And the only way to taste it all again was to have sex with the hot, balding Latino guy in the black-denim vest who cruised me in the men's room at the Mudd Club. And then with another stranger. And then another.

I'd toyed with confessing to Stephen, but it was all so tawdry that I'd convinced myself it wasn't exactly real, more like a passing fantasy I might've had while masturbating. But in fact it was becoming compulsive. I'd started making a cryptic little hash mark in my journal after each encounter, and I was ashamed of how many of these marks had accumulated. Once, while at the Whitney Museum on a free Friday night, I let myself be felt up by a much older man while Stephen was in an adjoining gallery. When the guy asked for my phone number, I panicked and wriggled away, and he turned abruptly hostile. Afterward I felt deeply ashamed and depressed, but I dodged all of Stephen's attempts to get me to explain why I'd fallen into a funk.

I didn't want to tell my mother about any of that, of course, nor did I want to admit that Stephen and I had had a big blowup one recent rainy afternoon.

When the flow of my dad's checks had begun to peter out, I wasn't remotely surprised. Following through was hardly his specialty. But on that morning, while Stephen was out getting us a couple of bagels and the Sunday *Times*, I'd been looking for some Scotch tape to affix a flyer from a Gang of Four show we'd just seen into my journal, and there in the drawer among the X-Acto blades and markers I found a neatly rubber-banded bundle of cash. When I counted it out, it matched the amount my dad would have sent.

Instead of asking Stephen, I'd just taken the money, folding it into my wallet without mentioning it. But later that day when he discovered it missing, he'd flipped out and confronted me. I was totally taken aback. It was meant for my upkeep, after all.

Yes, he'd responded, it was for my upkeep that the checks were intended. "Which is exactly the point. You forget who the adult is here," he'd said angrily. "That would be me. And you're staying in *my* house. So yeah, I'm controlling the cash. All your needs are tended to, so what's your problem? If you need more pin money, get a fucking job."

"And mop up jizz at the Adonis like your friend Rusty? Sign

245

me up. You don't get to control me. It might be your house, if you want to call this place a house, but it's my money, from my father."

"Right, from your *father*. Because you're a kid, Jimmy! A kid who still needs his mommy and daddy. Having adult vices doesn't alter that fact," he had added coldly.

Adult vices? Was he just referring to pot and booze, or did he know about the cruising? Had he been peeking at my journal and decoded the hash marks? To get us quickly off that track, I'd stuck to my line of reasoning, but he'd stuck to his, too, and we'd ended up in a screaming match.

"You let me believe my father doesn't care about me!" I'd cried.

"You use everyone you meet," he'd snarled.

We'd eventually made up with sex and a walk in the rain, stopping first to buy a pair of flimsy umbrellas, and the next day we were both contrite and careful to watch what we said. And, of course, he promised to resume signing the checks over to me. But the tension had not yet dissipated. I kept feeling like there were still some ugly things he hadn't voiced that he was thinking. And if I were honest with myself, maybe that was true for me, too.

I reflexively thought of us in romantic terms, but the bald fact of it was, we were starting to grate on each other. I was discovering, it seemed, that having a lover didn't automatically mean feeling loving or feeling loved.

THAT WASN'T THE ONLY HARD LESSON I'd learn in New York. One morning Stephen stopped in the middle of sex and rolled over muttering, "Oh, for the love of God."

What had I done now?

"You've got discharge. Are you aware of that? Does it hurt when you pee?"

I was, actually, and it did. I suspected it might have something to do with a busboy from a nearby luncheonette I'd fucked in a bathroom stall during his lunch break and whose hygiene was less than stellar. "Um, yeah, a little."

"You've got the *clap*, Jimmy. Jesus *Christ*."

What followed was an embarrassing trip to a seedy health clinic in Hell's Kitchen, accompanied by a silent and unsmiling Stephen. While he read back issues of *Esquire* in the waiting room, a registered nurse gave me a long lecture about the prevalence and variety of venereal diseases (which was admittedly an education I actually needed), the crucial importance of staying away from "fast girls," and a prescription for antibiotics. Which meant that Valpolicella was one thing that was off-limits for the time being. Likewise getting a blow job.

None of it diminished my unslakable thirst for anonymous sex. As soon as I was free of symptoms, I was right back at it. This time around I was more discreet, and Stephen seemed to grudgingly forgive me for my previous transgressions.

PERHAPS AS AN OLIVE BRANCH, he took me out to meet his friend Anya, the lesbian poet he'd told me about when he was first enticing me to visit. She was something of a big deal in the poetry world, having had a few volumes published by a prestigious small press and some high-flown literary journals, and I was nervous about being introduced to her.

On the way to the coffeehouse in Greenwich Village where

we were slated to meet, Stephen said, "I showed her a couple of your poems—you know that, right?"

"What? Oh no. She'll think I'm an idiot."

"Get out of here," he said, giving me a gentle sock in the arm. "I wouldn't have done it if they weren't any good."

"Well, now I'm *really* nervous," I said. But as soon as we came in, Anya rose from the table and warmly clasped both my hands in hers.

I'd pictured someone wiry and wild-haired, in torn jeans, a Patti Smith type, but Anya was trailing miles of expensive-looking black linen, offset with huge pieces of African jewelry. Her hair was in a knot secured by a pair of silver chopsticks. Over Turkish coffee and almond croissants, she and Stephen exchanged gossip about the various denizens of the art scene. While I didn't know most of them, there were enough famous names to pique my interest, and it was fun to hear about other people's forays into adultery, public tantrums, and drunken brawls at gallery openings. Once they'd exhausted their supply of schadenfreude, the subject turned to her latest publication, and I told her I'd liked it so much I had then devoured all her books, which Stephen had lent me.

"I didn't think I could like any poetry better than Sylvia Plath's," I told her, "but when I saw yours, it was like a bell rang in the center of my being."

Laughing, she turned to Stephen. "Is he always this flattering?"

"Hardly," he replied sourly.

"Well, Stephen showed me some of *your* poems," she told me, whisking croissant crumbs off the table.

I covered my face. "I know, he told me on the way here. I'm so embarrassed."

"Don't be. I liked them! They have soul."

My poems had soul! I stammered my thanks, unable to formulate a way to express how much that meant to me.

Had I, Anya wanted to know, ever thought about art school?

"No way!" I exclaimed. Disparaging art-school students whenever we spotted them at a punk show was one of Blackie O's favorite sports, and I usually joined her. They were easily identifiable, their wealth and privilege broadcast by their carefully curated thrift-store looks. Pretentious trust-fund poseurs and wannabes, was our verdict, and we weren't the only ones on the scene who thought so.

"School's not my thing," I amended, not wanting to be rude to Anya.

"Really? But you're so bright."

I scoffed. "Tell that to my teachers. My grades gave new meaning to the word 'suck.'"

"Well, I think you should consider it anyway. I think being around kindred spirits might open up a whole world for you."

Kindred spirits. The phrase struck me as magical, like a glowing sunlit cloud floating into a cloud bank, melding with its source. But I couldn't imagine how, for me, the art-school crowd fit that description. Maybe nothing could.

They broke the mold after they made you, kid, my father used to tell me. I'd never much liked the sound of that—it seemed to condemn me to being alone. But I'd come to believe that he was right. Not to mention, the whole idea of going back to school sounded completely insane, like escaping from prison and then returning later to ask if you could pretty please have your old cell back.

Anya and Stephen were looking at me expectantly. I tried to

think of a response that would shut down further discussion. "I'll take it under advisement," I said finally, with a bland smile.

It was what my mother would say to Avon ladies and Jehovah's Witnesses who knocked on the door when she wanted to be left alone.

28

ASK ANY MERMAID YOU HAPPEN TO SEE

B y the end of April, I felt like a seasoned New Yorker. The truth was, though, that I hadn't ventured outside our bohemian safety zone below Fourteenth Street—not until Stephen proposed a trip to Coney Island.

The subway ride from our Manhattan digs took forever, and I spent a lot of it going in mental loop-de-loops about our relationship. After the cash incident, it had gotten harder to trust Stephen, and the little things about him that got under my skin were starting to actively chafe.

As the subway car swayed and racketed down the tracks, I asked myself questions that were previously unthinkable. For instance: If he really thought I was so childish, what was he doing with me? And if I loved him so much, why was I compelled to keep having sexual encounters with strangers? What kind of loyalty was that?

He nudged me. The train had emerged from the ground and

was crossing over the East River. "Look, you can see the Statue of Liberty."

You could, but so small it looked like a souvenir on a key chain. Having reached the Brooklyn side of the East River, the train remained on elevated tracks, moving through neighborhoods that were nothing like any I'd ever been to. Miles and miles went by where the only people I saw were Orthodox Jews in cake-shaped fur hats and black coats. Then long stretches where all the signs were in Italian and many of the guys who boarded the train looked straight out of *Saturday Night Fever,* actually wearing their hair in greasy pompadours, with gold medallions gleaming on their barrel chests. The signs changed to Russian, and the subway rattled on and on.

When we got there, a cold fog was sweeping around the Stillwell Avenue subway terminal. Bums and winos were scattered on the floor asleep, bundled in layers of filthy clothes. I saw a woman who'd secured wadded-up newspaper around her feet as makeshift shoes. "Best not to stay here too long," Stephen said, as though I might want to linger to take in the ambience. I bit back the urge to say, *Duh.*

Outside, on Surf Avenue, the main drag that ran parallel to the beach, the light was a dull gray, as though the sun, too, were huddled somewhere in a dirty blanket. The storefronts looked like they'd been bombed, with plywood nailed up over windows and graffiti in layers. Everywhere I looked, there were figures bunched up in doorways or lying across subway gratings like corpses. The fog carried the smell of sewer gas, spoiled garbage, and ocean water.

It reminded me of something I'd read by Kathy Acker, a punk writer who'd been handing out photocopied broadsides at a Misfits show we'd been to recently. Her depiction of New York City was of an apocalypse already well under way, of disease-ridden people living in piles of garbage and packs of feral dogs tearing at human flesh. It occurred to me now that maybe the scenes of depravity and horror she portrayed weren't fiction at all. Maybe she was just describing her neighborhood.

Something crunched underfoot, and I lifted my shoe to see a bloodied syringe. "Jesus, it's like the fabric of civilization has been torn to shreds."

"Exactly," Stephen said, not unhappily. "Let's hit the board-walk. Watch out," he added, extending an arm to stop me as I moved to cross the street. "People tend to ignore red lights down here. Too many carjackers, so it's not safe to stop. Oh, hey, goody, it's open—c'mon, you've got to come see this place."

He meant the one shop that was still surviving in the ruins, directly across from the terminal. WILLIAMS CANDY ICE CREAM POPCORN, its sign read.

We stood looking at the window display with its colorful array of cotton candy and pinwheel lollipops. "It's been here since forever. It's basically the one and only thing that remains of old Coney Island. Check *that* out," he said, pointing.

"What on earth am I looking at?" I tried to puzzle out what I was seeing, a mysterious row of shish-kebab skewers bearing glossy, maraschino-red-lacquered blobs. "It looks almost like . . . but no, that'd be too gross."

"It is, it is!" he said with glee. "Candy-coated marshmallows on a stick! Satan's own seaside treat. Want some candy, little boy? Come on, it's a tradition."

"Oh Lord."

Standing on the boardwalk five minutes later, my teeth crack-ing into the bizarre and cloying confection, I could tell that Stephen was having fun, but I didn't understand why.

The boardwalk featured an amusement park with all the amusement drained out of it, a closed midway of decrepit hot-dog stands and sideshows where apparently you could pay seventy-five cents to watch some guy nail a board into his face. The video arcades looked more like places to score heroin than play Atari. Above us rose the faded pastel skeleton of the Wonder Wheel, its empty gondolas creaking in a creepy way as they swayed in the cold air. It looked as if a fistfight was in progress next to a public bathroom that nothing in the world could have induced me to enter.

"I feel like I'm walking around inside my own depression," I said. It made Stephen laugh, though I hadn't meant it as a joke. There was a time when I would've been fascinated by this level of squalor, but today it was just accelerating the sense I had that everything was in free fall. I thought of a line from a Joan Didion book I'd read: "The center was not holding." At the time I hadn't really understood what it meant, but now I got it.

We shared french fries from Nathan's, which made me better understand what Stephen liked about the place—eating the piping-hot, crunchy fries with the little two-pronged fork they came with, the delicious warmth a pleasant contrast to the chill in the air. But when he suggested that we go check out the scene under the boardwalk, I wasn't into it. "You can't come to New York and not see how the other half lives," he insisted.

I threw the trash from Nathan's onto a refuse heap that might once have been a functional garbage can. "I've seen plenty, thanks."

"I guarantee you've never seen anything like this. It's the underworld. 'Under the boardwalk, down by the sea-ee-ee,'" he sang jokingly, leading me under the pilings.

In the damp, dark, sandy world beneath the wooden planks was what I assumed was a homeless encampment that seemingly stretched for a mile in either direction. The stench was overpowering, and I had to struggle not to throw up. There was broken glass everywhere and unspeakably disgusting mounds of what had to be human shit. A woman whose hair was one gigantic dreadlock was cooking something over a trash fire.

When we'd been getting ready to leave the loft for the day, Stephen had advised me not to take my camera. I'd seen it as a protective gesture and thought it was sweet. Now, though, I wondered: Why bring me here in the first place?

"Hey, honky, you got a dime?" called a voice from the darkness. Instinct told me not to respond, and I was glad I hadn't when another voice laughed, an unfriendly chuckle that scared me.

And yet Stephen was leading me farther along. I found myself grinding my teeth and exhaling in sets for the first time in recent memory.

"You got a dime, I said," the voice called after us. "How 'bout a nickel, then!"

"Forget about Three Mile Island, *this* is the end of the world, right?" whispered Stephen with excitement. His eyes gleaming in the firelight struck me as manic, as if he were taking pleasure from my discomfort. Or did he think I would actually enjoy this in some nihilistic way? *I don't actually love misery,* I thought.

I turned around and headed back, following the band of gray sunlight. "I want to go home."

"Okay, okay," he said, catching up with me. "We're actually pretty close to Brighton Beach down here. We can catch the West Eighth Street stop."

"No. I mean," I said, only realizing it was true as I was saying it, "I want to go *home*."

MY SUITCASES WERE PACKED and waiting by the front door, their bulging forms secured with twine. Stephen and I had lugged the stuff I'd accumulated—records, stacks of photographs I'd had developed—in cardboard boxes to the Prince Street postal station, to be shipped ahead to California. It would've cost a fortune, but I had written TEXTBOOKS on each box and so was charged the special book rate, no questions asked. ("Pulling a fast one," Stephen had commended. "Well played. New York has schooled you in the art of the hustle.")

Now I was standing at the window, taking one last photo of the view from the loft, when the buzzer blatted. Stephen exited to let Anya into the freight elevator. Even though this was our last few hours together, we were both relieved to have a third party present. It had become glaringly obvious that there was only one cure for the tensions in our relationship, which was to put three thousand miles between us.

"I've got to get to the Village for a reading in just a few," Anya announced as she came through the door, "but I couldn't let Jimmy leave without saying good-bye. Though I will have a quick glass of wine. Even if you *are* going to put it in one of those vile little tin cups."

This last comment was directed to Stephen, and he looked abashed. I felt a twinge of satisfaction. While he poured a glug of Valpolicella into one of his blue-speckled camping mugs, Anya set to rummaging through a purse crammed with manuscript pages, eventually fishing out some kind of catalog.

"Also," she told me, handing it to me, "I wanted to drop this by. Something to read on the plane."

As I read the title, Stephen looked over my shoulder and grunted with approval. *The San Francisco Art Institute Course Catalog*.

"You went out of your way to get this for me? How come?" I asked.

Above the rim of her cup, she gave me a disingenuous look. "So you can take a gander, is all."

"Anya!" Stephen said. "Are you Svengali-ing Jimmy?"

"Maybe just a little," she told him. "Come on, you know we aging lezzies love to dispense advice to other people's kids. It's spinster-aunt syndrome." She set the mug down on the counter. "Well, that was fortifying. Jimmy, walk me to the elevator?"

"If you'll sign one of your books for me first."

In the corridor she gave me an embrace that smelled like musk, then pulled back and gave me a long look. "You're going to be just fine," she said. "I know it doesn't seem that way, but you are. You are a great kid. Trust me."

I SPENT THE FLIGHT BACK to California watching the green patchwork below me go by, feeling like a very small X on a very large map. *You Are Here*, I thought. Here, moving away from Stephen at five hundred miles an hour, thousands of feet above the earth, flying home to the familiar nest.

I didn't want to stay there long under the wing of my mother, as safe as it was. On the other hand, though, where could I go, what could I do?

Restless in my cramped coach-class seat, I kept returning to the catalog Anya had given me, which now bore brown rings from my airplane coffee cup. Truth be told, since I'd never understood the allure of college, the catalog was kind of blowing my mind. Its glossy pages painted a picture of an educational environment that was completely unlike school as I understood it. The photography department at the San Francisco Art Institute was founded by Ansel Adams! You could study experimental filmmaking with George Kuchar! I must have seen George Kuchar's strange short film *Hold Me While I'm Naked* a dozen times. I kept recalling the phrase "kindred spirits," hearing it in Anya's voice.

THEORETICALLY, I KNEW what culture shock was, but I didn't truly understand what the term referred to until I stepped out of the San Francisco airport onto what felt like the soil of another planet, wearing a leather jacket perfect for a May evening in Manhattan but much too heavy for the West Coast.

My mother pulled up to the passenger loading zone in the used Honda Civic that had finally supplanted the ancient Dodge Coronet. Funnily enough, she'd managed to find a better and more modern car in the same Harvest Gold color as the station wagon. It seemed fitting that even the vehicle that met me at the airport should be changed in some way. While she exclaimed how happy she was to see me, how much older I looked, how she hoped Stephen had gotten me to quit smoking, and other maternal cluckings, I tried to come to grips with the strangeness, the way the very air tasted different. But I couldn't shake the sense that I was a stranger in a strange land. Craving some totem of selfhood, I got my camera out.

"Jim! You can't take my picture with my hair like this," she protested from the driver's seat. "I'm a mess! Let me put on some lipstick at least!"

"No, Mom, you look great." I couldn't explain what I meant by "great." You look like you. You look like home. You look like California in this moment, the one familiar element of this new version of my life.

29

CALIFORNIA ÜBER ALLES

t had been strange to set my bags down in my suburban bed-room after sharing a loft with a lover, strange to sit down to frozen pizza and TV with my mom after nights of wine and after-parties, strange to sleep alone. So as soon as the opportu-nity presented itself to go to a show with Blackie O, I took it, and bused up to the Mabuhay Gardens for a double bill head-lined by Black Flag.

It was a bumpy evening. My old friend greeted me brightly on Broadway, having already procured our ritual vodka milk shake to share, but almost immediately our connection showed signs of wear and tear. As we walked, she asked me "what the boys of New York" were like, and I tried to tell her the truth, that as hot as it had been to have sex basically whenever I wanted it, it had also been disturbing and driven a wedge between me and Stephen besides.

"So much dick, so little time" was her breezy reply.

I'd always known she lived inside a carapace that kept emo-tions at a distance. And I was still bothered by the flip way she accepted news of Mary Menace's having died basically right in front of us. But for the first time, I felt my own real desire to connect bouncing off that shiny, impenetrable shell.

It *was* a beautiful shell, though—as always, she was dressed in a style that while totally of the moment was also all her own. And I'd learned that relating to someone or something from behind the viewfinder of a camera was a way to be less at the mercy of it. So I aimed the Canon at Blackie O, who mugged obligingly before saying, "You really shouldn't have brought that, you know."

"Why not?" I snapped another photo as, in her prim way, she dabbed milk shake off her lips with a vintage handkerchief.

"These shindigs have gotten wilder in your absence. The hardcore boys have taken over. They prefer their musical entertainment with a side order of mayhem."

"It's always been like that," I said, adjusting the focus for a closer shot of her face. "We *enjoy* mayhem."

"You can't step into the same river twice, sonny boy. Trust me, it's different now."

I was trying to capture, through the camera's eye, the guarded look I perceived beneath her bright exterior. "Eh. I can handle it," I replied.

In response she put her hand over the lens. "Suit yourself."

As it turned out, though, she had been understating the case. As soon as we walked through the doors, I sensed an unfamiliar and threatening volatility in the room. We made our way through the scrum of bodies to the bar while the opening band played its set. Some elements were familiar—the eardrum-crushing decibels, for example, and the damp, smoky smell of the place—but other components were missing. Gone were the drag queens and freaks, the Asian-American, black, and Latino kids. The whole bar was populated by what looked like a uniform mob of white guys displaying the plumage of punk rock machismo: shaved heads and bare chests crisscrossed by Union Jack suspenders, clumsy swastikas tattooed onto biceps.

I'd always felt that the scene was a multifarious Us, shielded from the Them outside, but tonight I got the distinct sense that They had invaded. As we tried in vain to catch the bartender's attention, I saw myself and Blackie O through a stranger's eyes, and for the first time we looked out of place.

I leaned in close so she could hear me over the opening band, which sounded like a train derailment. "Is it weird to be, like, the only black girl at a show?"

"Oh, am I a black girl? I hadn't noticed."

Her intention to deflect was so obvious that I couldn't even fake a laugh. "Seriously. Is it tripping you out? It's tripping *me* out. I mean, there are so many swastikas in here it's like a fucking Hitler Youth rally."

"You sound like my mom. Hey! Can I get a shot of well scotch?"

I gave up and tried to watch the opening band, but then Blackie O zeroed in on the inevitable cadre of art-school students at the far end of the bar, sharpening her tongue on the topics of their spiffy clothes and towers of pomaded hair. For once, though, her pithy diatribe didn't strike me as funny.

Okay, yes, admittedly, they *were* posturing. But then again wasn't everyone in the room? And now that I understood that when they weren't at clubs, they were creating films and paintings and such . . . well, they had their shit more together than either of us. "Why do you hate them so much?" I blurted.

She looked at me with suspicion, then winced as the opening band concluded its set in a gale of squealing feedback. In the scattered applause and whoops that followed, the bassist grabbed the mic and announced, "So, hey, I heard there's some cocksucking going on in the men's room."

This was met with a chorus of jeers and catcalls. The bassist wiped sweat off his face and said, "Go back to the fucking Castro, man." Then he shoved the mic stand over, and it clattered to the stage floor.

Somebody threw a beer bottle onstage, which shattered in a spray of wet glass. "Fuck the fucking Castro!" somebody shouted.

"Eat shit," the lead singer mumbled, kicking the heap of broken glass directly back into the audience. A gob of spit hit his face from somewhere in the mosh pit.

I rounded on Blackie O. "What the fuck is going *on* here?"

She shrugged. "Can't say I didn't warn you."

Less than an hour later, she returned from the pay phone looking preoccupied. "Mommie Dearest wants me home by midnight," she said, hunting through her purse for bus fare. "And you know when she summons, I must obey."

"Seriously? The headliners haven't even shown up yet." *And aren't we getting too old to be running home to our mothers?* I thought about saying, but I knew how beyond hypocritical that would be, coming from me. Still, I could almost see the tie that bound us fraying right in front of me.

She drained the last of her scotch and set it neatly on the bar. "Well, fulfilling one's filial duties isn't easy, but you know what Confucius said about it."

I laughed despite myself. "No, what did Confucius say about it?"

"Hell if I know, I was asking *you*," she deadpanned, and disappeared to catch a bus back to Berkeley.

Alienated and annoyed, and pissed off at Blackie O for reasons that I sensed were more complicated than the inconvenience of being left alone at a club, I kicked back a few beers and, when Black Flag took the stage, threw myself into the mosh pit. Moshing wasn't something I'd been doing in New York, and it was even more bruising than I recalled, the floor soon slick with beer and crimson droplets from other people's bloody noses. I responded with equal violence, elbows akimbo, shoving and being shoved with the abandon I remembered, but then some guy head-butted me so hard it sent me careening right into the art-school students. They fell like bowling pins.

"Shit! You guys okay?" Even shouting at the top of my lungs, I could hear my words being obliterated by the music.

As they picked themselves up and dusted themselves off, only one of them, a guy with a handsome, gaunt face framed by Julius Caesar bangs, actually responded to me.

"No broken bones!" He nodded toward the camera case slung around my neck. "Your camera survive?"

Surprised at the question, I unzipped the case. The Canon looked unscathed, but Blackie O had been right—I never should've brought it here.

"I think so! Thanks for asking!" It was so exhausting to scream over the music that I suddenly wished I were at home. Or anywhere else, really.

He leaned close to my ear. "I need a cig! Want one?"

"Yes! Jesus!"

Outside, our ears ringing, sharing an unfiltered Lucky Strike, he told me his name was Brian Anderson. As it turned out, his concern for my camera wasn't incidental: he was a photographer, about to finish the graduate program in photography at the San Francisco Art Institute.

"Our final show is hanging next week," he said. "You should come to the opening. Hold on, I think I have a flyer. . . ."

Somewhere I could feel Anya smiling.

30

TWINKIE THE KID

n my mind a college campus resembled an overgrown high school, except for maybe the Ivy Leagues, which I mentally decorated with clock towers and greenswards. So I was more than a little surprised when I walked through the entrance of the San Francisco Art Institute and found myself in a fairy-tale courtyard girded by trees and bound by Spanish Colonial arches. In the center a fountain splashed softly into a mosaic-tiled pool in which carp were making sinuous passes around a cluster of Egyptian papyrus plants. The monkish sound of earnest conversation echoed from somewhere. *This* was a college?

I followed signs to the photo department's final show, but I was early and the gallery wasn't open yet; the students were in a huddle with a bespectacled man in jeans and a sweater, who I assumed to be a professor. Brian Anderson spotted me and waved. *See you soon,* I mouthed, and wandered off to explore the campus.

The courtyard wasn't the only surprising part. There was an extraordinary mural by the Mexican artist Diego Rivera, of whose work I had seen only reproductions. The main plaza was built into the rooftop and overlooked the whole San Francisco Bay, which the setting sun was turning a coppery electric blue, and Coit Tower on its hill. When a young woman in a bespattered apron emerged from a doorway to dump a bucketful of coffee grounds into the trash, I saw the kitchen behind her and realized I was standing in front of a café, so I went in, thinking I'd grab a coffee before the show.

The first thing that struck me about the café was the unbelievable view—you could see Alcatraz Island from every seat in the house. The room glowed pink with sunset. I tossed my jacket over a chair in the back of the room, to save a seat where I'd be able to observe everything without attracting notice. Maybe I'd spy one of the cool faculty members Brian had told me about, like the performance artist Laurie Anderson or the activist Angela Davis.

I did feel out of place in this world, although I was admittedly warming to it. During a meeting we'd had earlier that week, Brian had shown me how to process film in the darkroom he'd built in his flat near Dolores Park, and afterward he'd introduced me to his roommates, most of them other SFAI students. One of the roommates, Debora Iyall, fronted a band called Romeo Void that I'd seen play a couple times and liked. It was a marked contrast from the other shared households I'd seen— clean, airy, with wood floors painted battleship gray and white walls to showcase the residents' artwork. I had to concede that while maybe they weren't as authentically miserable as the people I knew who were sunk deep into the punk rock scene, they weren't necessarily hollow poseurs either.

As I threaded my way around the tables to the café counter, I noticed that a huddle of people were clustered at the front, apparently listening with concentration to a transistor radio. I saw one of them, a handsome young guy, put his arm around the shoulder of his friend as if comforting him.

I came up to the register to place my order, but the girl in the apron shushed me, gesturing toward the radio.

"What's going on?" I said, as quietly as I could.

The handsome boy, lips pale with fury, told me, "They just announced the verdict on Dan White. Fucking Twinkie Boy got voluntary fucking manslaughter."

His friend, who I now saw was weeping, looked up to say, "He could get four years! It's a slap on the fucking *wrist*."

It took me a second to remember who Dan White was, but then I heard the words *"Harvey Milk," "Mayor Moscone,"* and *"assassinations"* emerge from the radio. Right. The G.I. Joe doll who'd shot San Francisco's first gay official.

"Tomorrow would've been Harvey Milk's birthday," muttered the woman at the cash register. "What can I get you?"

THE PHOTOGRAPHY SHOW WAS GOOD, but I was especially impressed by my new acquaintance's pictures. Some of Brian's images, of compellingly weird yet ordinary people, reminded me of Diane Arbus's work. My favorites, though, were of places and objects, like a window display of mannequins modeling formal menswear that were static and disembodied yet seemed full of metaphorical power.

I tried to visualize myself hanging my own photography show, or reading an important book over a cappuccino, looking out at that view of Alcatraz, or engaged in an intellectual discussion on the rooftop plaza with some handsome painter. It wasn't entirely easy to insert myself into the picture. Everyone there looked better groomed than I was, richer, slicker, more self-assured. I doubted any of them lived with their mothers in dull suburban towns, eating Stove Top stuffing for dinner because she had a coupon for it, or found themselves having to scrounge under the sofa cushions for train fare. But the sense of mental stimulation in this environment was like a jolt of caffeine, and something in me moved forward to meet it. In a funny way, it reminded me of my first punk show, a hundred lifetimes ago, hearing Tuxedo-moon and feeling like *This is what I've been waiting for.*

I wished I had someone to share these thoughts with, and I even considered telling Brian. But while he was glad to see me, he was also swarmed with well-wishers vying for his attention.

"Hey, Jimmy, it's sort of crazy now," he said when we finally did get a chance to say hello, "but we're all going to North Beach for drinks afterward. The Savoy. Will you come?"

Of course I would come, I said, but as visitors gathered around the wine-and-cheese table, news of the Dan White verdict began to circulate and the plan seemed to be changing. When I went to refill my wineglass, the pretty boy from the café was there at the table, spearing a chunk of cheese on a toothpick, and with a self-important air he informed me, "If you were going to the Savoy after this, don't. Everyone's going to the Castro now, to show support."

Although I'd never been fired up by the idea of public protest, this situation seemed to require my involvement, and anyway, Brian and his friends were going, and I didn't want to lose my connection with these people. So when the show wrapped up, I followed them down the steep sidewalk to Columbus Avenue, where we all caught the next Castro-bound bus.

Everyone was deeply involved in conversation about the White case. It was a discussion I couldn't quite join in, having been away from California for so long, but I learned more on the bus as it lumbered up Market Street. A sweet and very butch girl in a motorcycle jacket explained the debacle to me, including the unbelievable fact that at one point in the trial the defense lawyer argued that White couldn't help committing a double homicide because he'd been eating so much junk food—the Twinkie Defense, it had been dubbed. Even to me that sounded like the world's most pathetic excuse.

When we spilled out onto the street, the neighborhood was already more crowded than usual, with people milling around on the main intersection of Castro and Market with grim purpose and clustered outside of the bars and bookstores in urgent conversation. Shopkeepers were putting CLOSED signs in the windows. Our crowd of SFAI graduates, bedecked in their most flamboyant art-school finery, stood out among the plaid shirts, denim jackets, and hankie-coded Levi's like an entire squadron of sore thumbs.

It was Brian's idea to lead us to a gay bar called Elephant Walk on Castro and Eighteenth Street, which was loud and hectic, and for a minute, as we lined up at the teeming bar, it looked as if things might be more or less turning into a graduation celebration, with jittery social overtones. But just as we were all carrying our cocktails to a table, there was a commotion of sound and movement outside, and everyone hurried to the window.

Coming down Castro Street, fronted by a makeshift banner reading STOP ATTACKS ON LESBIANS & GAYS, was a huge mass of people, drumming, shouting, and blowing whistles. As they came toward the intersection, they chanted, "Out of the bars, into the streets!" The whirring of helicopter rotors stirred the air overhead, and in the distance sirens began to wail.

A young guy broke ranks to jog over and tell us, "We're marching on City Hall. Let's go!"

After that all pretense of a graduation party was over. Indeed, within moments every single person in the bar was gulping drinks, gathering jackets, and heading for the door. The SFAI students, awkwardly encumbered with graduation gifts, took a while to collect themselves as the Castro clones streamed out to join the fray.

Brian picked up a bouquet of tulips someone had given him and turned to me with a wry smile. "I guess the bartender's going home with a lovely floral arrangement," he said, jamming the stems into an abandoned beer pitcher.

"Maybe you can stick them in a policeman's gun, like a hippie," I said.

"Right, and then he can use his pretty flowered gun to smash my faggot face."

I trailed after him and his cohorts as they made their way outside. More and more people were pouring onto the streets from all directions, hundreds of them. Some were carrying candles as though in a funeral procession; others pumped their fists in the air or waved placards. I'd never seen so much anger in one place. It seemed to rattle the air like a sonic boom. When the chant rose up—"Kill Dan White! Kill Dan White!"—a cold shudder went down my spine, and I had a sudden understanding of the phrase "out for blood."

Only Brian and I remained on the sidewalk; the SFAI students had melted into the crowd already. The heavy rumble of motorcycle engines, the shriek of whistles and sirens, and the rhythmic clapping of the marchers were so loud I couldn't catch what he was telling me. "City Hall," I heard, and something about "teach those motherfuckers they can't . . ." Then a pair of strapping leather daddies shouldered past us, and my friend was swallowed up into the crowd.

I stepped into the shelter of a doorway, overwhelmed. Some part of me was conscious that this terrifying mob was on my side, but I couldn't focus on it; my hands were clammy, and I felt faint with anxiety. All my instincts were telling me that violence was about to explode in my face, and whether or not it was supposedly "my" side—whatever that meant—who held the whip hand, it was freaking me out. In my mind's eye, I saw Stephen's misshapen face smeared with gore, felt my skull crack against the stucco wall. "One," I whispered to myself, and ground my teeth helplessly for the first time in weeks.

As the mob surged past on the street, I thought of what my mother would do if she saw this. She'd jump into that Honda Civic and comb the city streets looking for me, the sight of cordons and police cars making her ever more hysterical. Considering how many nights I'd kept her awake worrying, the countless times she'd come running when I was stranded, that awful night she'd had to pick me up from the emergency room . . . I wasn't the only one, it occurred to me, who would be genuinely frightened if I stayed and got involved.

Just then I saw a man carrying a baseball bat. His teeth were bared in rage, and his voice, hoarse and ragged, rose above the others': "Kill Dan White! Kill Dan White!"

My guts contracted with raw fear. I had to get out of there before the time bomb went off. Cutting down Eighteenth Street, I walked alone to my usual SamTrans stop on Mission.

The streets were soon clogged with patrol cars and cordoned off with barricades, and it took an interminable amount of time for the 7F to inch its way out of San Francisco. By the time I was coming up the front walk on Torino Drive, it was nearly midnight. No sooner had I gotten my key into the lock than my mother, in her flannel nightgown, flung open the front door crying, "Oh, thank God! Jim, I was so worried!"

Behind her the news was blaring on the TV. "They're rioting, it's terrible," she said, returning to the living room. "They're burning down the *building*! People are getting hurt!"

"Burning down . . . ?"

On the screen a blond guy was smashing a pole into the gilt-edged double doors of a municipal building. I could practically feel the fury in his body as he brought it crashing through the glass again and again. Flames and smoke were billowing out of the windows of City Hall. Police cars were engulfed in flames like logs in a campfire. Cops in riot gear were advancing on fleeing civilians, in a din of barking German shepherds—I heard a cop shout, "Let's go, Marys!"—and there was screaming as a canister of tear gas rolled across the sidewalk, spewing a thick white cloud. A woman staggered out of frame holding a blood-soaked cloth to her face.

A moment later I watched as police marched toward a corner building that, even in the grainy darkness, had a familiar look. While I struggled to figure out what the sign on its awning said, a phalanx of cops descended and started smashing its windows. Just as I realized it was the Elephant Walk, I saw a guy being dragged out of it by a pair of cops. Their arms rose and fell as they beat him with truncheons. The newscaster was speaking over the sound of screams and shouts.

"Oh my God, I was just there," I whispered. "I can't believe I was *just there*." I began to tremble uncontrollably, feeling the blood drain from my face.

For the first time, Mom looked away from the horrors on the television, aghast. "What?! I thought you were at an art show!

Why would you want to let yourself get mixed up in something like that?"

There was, of course, a retort on the tip of my tongue. But I was too weary to get into it, and I let it slide. Probably if I cornered her, she'd have to admit that gay people had a lot of good reasons to "get mixed up in something like that." But did she really *need* to be cornered? Would it change anything?

Well, maybe she did, and maybe it would. But I was too damned exhausted.

I changed into pajamas and curled up in the window seat with my journal and a cigarette, intending to use my last scrap of energy to jot down my impressions of the day. Writing calmed me, and I needed calming.

I'd been keeping the catalogue for SFAI tucked between my journal's pages, and now it fell onto the carpet. Retrieving it, I ran my eyes down the amazing course list. You could get a degree in *performance art*! I glanced, not for the first time, at the application form printed on the back. By now I'd practically committed the guidelines to memory. All you needed was a high school diploma (I'd passed the California High School Proficiency Exam—check!) and to have filled out the essay question: "On the lines below, please submit no more than 500 words stating your reason for wishing to attend the Art Institute."

I opened my journal. *"Tonight was totally fucking insane. It started with Brian Anderson's photo show,"* I wrote, then fell into thought, tapping ash out the window. From the living-room television, the sounds of people clashing in the streets roared and rumbled.

I tore out the page and started again.

"To the admissions board," I wrote.

"I always thought I had no future. I thought nobody did—that

every citizen of the USA was programmed to be a mindless robot of consumption. That belief filled me with frustration and anxiety and rage. For a long time, I assumed the only thing to do with those feelings was connect with people who felt equally shitty."

I crossed out "shitty" and replaced it with "enraged." From the other room, I heard the popping of tear-gas canisters or gunshots, then an ad for Löwenbräu beer.

"But I get it now: you can consume, sure, but you can also create. It's time for my anger to be turned"

I crossed that out and paused, imagining how Mrs. O'Hagan might phrase it before resuming. *"It's time for my rage to be transmuted into creativity. I want to learn to be an artist."*

31

YOU'RE GONNA MAKE IT AFTER ALL

Many months went by. The San Francisco Art Institute's Film Studies I class was held twice a week and had a start time at 9:00 A.M.

Needless to say, I wasn't a morning person, and getting my butt from San Carlos into a seat twenty-five miles away at such an ungodly hour posed a challenge. My mother had finally managed to shed the title of Kelly Girl for a staff secretarial position that held the promise of career advancement, and she was carpooling with her fellow secretaries to the Round Table Pizza corporate headquarters in the city. It'd only taken me one attempt to get to school on time via public transportation before I started tagging along with her.

I was grateful for the free ride but I found the car-pool ladies to be depressing company: their bitter gossip, their polyester-heavy wardrobes, and their cut-rate salon hairdos all seemed to advertise a life of diminished expectations. For my mom's sake, though, I quashed the frequent urge to cannonball into their watercooler chatter with stories about all the anonymous sex I was having. And for their part, they tolerated my incongruous presence by ignoring me.

Tuning me out was easier these days. Over that summer I'd become gradually less interested in using clothing and personal style to make a statement. For one thing, having to be ready to walk out the door at seven o'clock in the morning wasn't especially conducive to complicated makeup experiments or crafting bizarre accessories. For another, now that I'd taken out a student loan, I was a lot more conscious of where my money was going. And I had fewer occasions to put effort into dressing up because I was going to fewer punk shows. My drifting apart from Blackie O was partly responsible for my waning presence on the scene, but aside from that I was just less into it. In my opinion the bullies had taken over. And I'd had enough of bullies—whether or not I was their intended target—to last me a lifetime.

In any case, I still looked identifiably *other*—I just didn't feel the need to push it to extremes. Good thing, too, because I doubted that the collected administrative assistants of Round Table Pizza would've borne it in silence had I shown up with, say, a fresh Manson family X carved into my forehead.

Not that there was ever silence anyway. Michael Jackson's *Off the Wall* was as omnipresent as fluoridated drinking water, and the car radio penetrated even the thick headphones of my Walkman, volume adjusted to maximum. Lately—this morning, for instance—I was exploring the sludgy, droning strains of No Wave music, which I'd been interested in since Stephen had turned me on to it. The Contortions, Theoretical Girls, Mars. Atonal, dissonant, and avant-garde in the extreme, to me it was the sound of New York City imploding. But it tended to bring memories of him that, like his occasional phone calls, I often felt the urge to cut short.

A song by Teenage Jesus and the Jerks called up a recollection of our New Year's Eve at the Mudd Club. I hit the Eject button and popped the cassette out of the Walkman, allowing in a burst of office complaint ("I told her it's just common courtesy, you don't help yourself to somebody else's yogurt!") before slotting in a tape of Ravel string quartets. I was discovering classical music for real, and my passion for Joni Mitchell had rekindled, too. Sometimes I felt bad for having ever put such wonderful music on the back burner, as though I'd forgotten to write to an old and important friend.

By the time we got to my destination, my legs had cramps from occupying the middle seat and my clothes held the cloying aroma of office-lady beauty products. But as I walked through the enchanted courtyard of SFAI, all my discomfort began to evaporate, as it did every time.

True to my original fantasy, I was taking my beginning film-studies class with one of the Kuchar brothers in Studio 8, a black-painted box of a room that functioned as a classroom, screening room, and movie studio. Though it was his brother's films I'd been more familiar with, George's fraternal twin, Mike, was an esteemed filmmaker himself, with an engaged but relaxed teaching style that put me at ease among my classmates, all of whom were older than I was, and more educated.

So far the lion's share of class time had been spent watching projected experimental films Mike found noteworthy, usually shot in 16- or even 8-millimeter. This Thursday morning was no exception. Fingertips scrabbling through his long gray beard, Mike yawned, then addressed us. "Morning, everybody.

I'm running a little behind, just gotta make some copies quick. Curt, can you do the screen?"

My classmate Curt Thomas rose to pull the movie screen down into viewing position and then returned to his seat beside mine. "You smell like ladies' night at the Tonga Room," he whispered to me.

"That's the Summer's Eve douche," I whispered back. "Strawberry aroma. With Summer's Eve, freshness has never been simpler." He tried and failed to stifle a horselaugh. From the first day of class, Curt and I had been instant friends, and by now, three weeks into the semester, we were inseparable. He'd initially caught my eye with his cute looks and faintly preppy uniform of pegged black jeans, a turtleneck, and a too-small denim jacket, to which his Kansas background added a wholesome, sincere vibe. But it was his gentle nature that I was most powerfully drawn to, his unfailing politeness, the attentive way he listened.

When I figured out he was gay, I was over the moon for about a week. We went on a spree of coming-out revelations after that; I even confided to him about how, when I was twelve, I used to call gay movie houses on the phone and then hang up when they answered, just to see if they actually existed, which Curt deemed "cute, in a pathetic way." But as it turned out, he had a boyfriend, Ron, a much older man. Moreover, they'd been together for years, sharing a one-bedroom in the Tenderloin. I hung out with them together once or twice and even spent the night on their couch a few times after nightclubbing in the city, but I suspected that Ron's reserve was just a cover for a more entrenched uptightness, and I thought Curt deserved a better match—me, for example. Once I got over the initial disappointment, though, it was sort of nice to remove sex from the equation, bypassing its complications and delving right into companionship.

It wasn't as though I was especially needy for a sexual relationship anyhow. While I wasn't as sexually compulsive as I'd been in New York, I was still cruising and having one-night stands; I'd just gotten more seasoned at it, more intentional, more selective.

Mike was back with a handful of photocopies. "Everybody settled? Can somebody hit the lights, please?" One of the many foreign students, a tall, handsome dyed-blond German guy named Wieland Speck, got up and darted over to hit the switches.

"Mike, is this another Brakhage flick? 'Cause I just ate breakfast," said Curt in the ensuing darkness.

Everyone laughed. Tuesday's lesson had centered on watching *The Act of Seeing with One's Own Eyes,* an intricate study of autopsy procedures. According to Mike, the filmmaker Stan Brakhage had made it in order to understand and confront his fear of death. The film was presented without sound and composed of close-ups so intimate that everything fell away except lurid colors and shapes, but then sometimes the camera pulled back for a disturbing and crystal-clear view of the particular cadaver being operated on. The overall effect was profound, even reverent, but also utterly nauseating. I liked it. I saw it as a further rejection of the forms of film I was accustomed to.

Mike chuckled. "Nah, don't worry," he said in his sardonic New York accent. "This is one of my brother's pictures. He made it . . . oh, in 1967. The cast is mostly folks we knew from the Bronx. And according to George," he advised us, "it's painful to watch. But, you know, it's only about twelve minutes, so you'll live. Okay, folks, this is *Eclipse of the Sun Virgin.*"

I loved the sense of expectancy that settled over the room as the opening credits rolled, loved the shushing sound of students settling into their seats. Then, in a swell of music . . . a nerdy young man gulped alcohol, then coughed it up. Another young man and his mother played separate pianos in a cramped, tacky apartment. The mother's piano was tiny, almost a toy. *It's like my relationship with my mom*, I thought.

As a formal voice-over dictated the biblical-sounding rituals one must enact to experience "true humility," the first young man pushed through a large pile of plastic fruit to find his own reflection in a mirror. He cleared away the pears and bananas and grapes and gazed at himself. The visual wordplay lit up my mind: *Fruit. Faggot.*

At once I grasped not just that subtle and personal associations *could* be expressed through the medium of film but *how* they could do so, how film could be a genuinely poetic medium. In that moment it dawned on me: I'd been consuming movies as though they were magic tricks, mildly curious about the underlying mechanics, but ultimately I'd been content to just sit back and enjoy the show. All the art I'd ever seen had been trying to teach me this—how had I not understood until today? As George Kuchar's marvelously rich images played on the screen, my mind began to teem with ideas.

When I was little, there'd been a toy called a Slip 'N Slide, a track of slick plastic that you attached to a garden hose, which turned it into a sluice. On a hot summer day, you'd run toward it full tilt and then leap, landing on your belly or your back, sliding down the slippery track. For some reason I flashed on this memory now: that frictionless slide into a sunlit realm of pure play.

LATER THAT DAY I SAT in the Oasis Café across from Curt, chattering with excitement. Just as I'd pictured, the café at SFAI had fast become one of my favorite hangouts, even though the coffee was so strong it caused an instant stomachache in anyone who drank it. The soundtrack was the David Bowie album *Lodger,* which was being played for what seemed like the hundredth time that week, at a volume that made anyone trying to study take his or her reading outside instead. *"When you're a boy, other boys check you out!"*

"I've seen nonnarrative filmmaking before, but I've never been moved like this," I rhapsodized. "Those were the most life-changing twelve minutes of my life."

Curt looked amused. "Yeah, it was cool." He preferred the abstractions of the filmmaker Michael Snow to the work of either of the Kuchar brothers. Snow's *Wavelength* was his favorite film, and even though practically nothing happened in it, he could parse the nuances of its technique for hours.

"Not just 'cool,'" I continued. "It was pure creativity! Pure possibility!"

He laughed. "Okay, okay, it was mind-blowingly life-changing." He leaned in with the attentive expression I loved. "Can you explain a little bit about why, though? I'm interested. I didn't know you were capable of being so . . . enthusiastic."

Gathering my thoughts, I gazed out over the bay. My surging emotions seemed reflected in the distant whitecapped waves and the wisps of cloud that swept around the towers of the Golden Gate Bridge.

"For the first time," I told him, "I'm thinking . . . *I* can do this. *I* can make a film." I clapped my hand over my mouth. "Oh my God, did I just say I could make a film?"

"Yup, you sure did. But that's what we're here for, isn't it? Or did we take out student loans for the awesome view?"

"Well, it *is* awesome, you have to admit. No, you're right, I just didn't entirely believe it could really happen, I guess." Mulling this, I gulped the remaining coffee from the bottom of the cup. Then I slumped, realizing I'd forgotten a major practical aspect. "Oh shit, Curt, I'm such a klutz with the technical stuff. I don't think I can handle that part. I can barely figure out the lenses on my camera."

"Oh, don't worry about *that* stuff. I can totally help you."

"You would really do that for me?" I studied him a moment. "Why?"

"Why not? To be honest, that's the part of being in art school that *doesn't* freak me out."

"I didn't think anything about school freaked you out. You always seem so totally at ease."

He looked embarrassed. "I dunno, I'm a little shy about the artistic process, I guess. It's easier to mess with the equipment."

I felt overwhelmed with gratitude for Curt's candor and generosity. How was this my real, actual life? To be here, at the art institute, seventeen years old, with the best friend I'd ever had, talking about a film I would make!

I pushed back my chair and rose. "I feel like I have to give you a gift. Please let me get you something," I told him. My hands were trembling, I noticed, yet for once it wasn't anxiety coursing through me, but joy.

Curt smiled up at me. "Well, I wouldn't say no to a piece of pie."

32

BOYS KEEP SWINGING

As to what the topic of my film would be, I barely had to think about it. For months I'd been completely sucked into a series of investigative articles in the *San Francisco Examiner* about a teenage murderer and molester named Jimmy Fisher, a deranged young Bay Area man whose mug shot showed a pale, confused boy with tousled hair and swollen lips.

Fisher had lured children, male and female alike, into his home to have sex. He'd only been caught after killing his final victim, a little boy. His trial was upcoming. His saga, with its echo of my recurring childhood sleepwalking nightmare of being hunted by a knife-wielding man, had a hold on my imagination that I couldn't shake, and I was convinced that he had to be the subject of my first film.

My fascination with the case had led me to read an academic tome called *The Personality of a Child Molester: An Analysis of Dreams,* which I'd found in a free pile outside a Goodwill and which I pored over looking for inspiration. And which, not surprisingly, gave me further unsettling dreams. The dreams gave me specific ideas about the visual style I wanted the film to have. I envisioned Fisher pursuing his child victim in slow-motion in a spooky meadow, slashed with knee-high wild grasses, under a black sky. I pictured Fisher's hands parting the long grass as they sought the boy. I pictured the movie as being in black and white, like a nightmare sequence from some Hollywood 1940s film. And I would be the star of it. I would play both parts, the murderer and the victim.

I KNEW MY MOTHER THOUGHT that attending college to learn avant-garde filmmaking was a total waste of time. And as I predicted, she saw the choice of subject matter for my first film as grotesque. ("The world is hard enough. Why don't you try adding a little sunshine to it?") I also knew, however, that she was a sucker for a good craft project, and sure enough, when I solicited her opinion about whether there was any way to create a meadow indoors that would look realistic, she jumped right in.

Together we drove to fields and creek banks around the peninsula to hunt for long grasses that were sturdy enough to be stuck into Styrofoam blocks. She went with me to secondhand stores to pick out costumes, too. And while the sight of me dressed as the schoolboy victim made her sigh and shake her head, when I showed her how I stuffed my cheeks with big wads of tissues to round out the sharp planes of my face and make me look younger, she couldn't help but laugh and then grudgingly praise my inventiveness.

One night, after staying up late reading, I had another dream that centered on the image of a woman's disembodied arms silhouetted against a white backdrop, one hand using a knife to slice into the palm of the other. I woke in a cold sweat. In the past a nightmare like that would've left me with residual anxiety for the rest of the day. Now, though, my only thought was that I absolutely had to depict it in my film. Moreover, I discovered that concentrating on matters like what was the best stand-in for real blood was so absorbing that it redirected my general feelings of dread. Finally my restless brain had something better to do than turn on itself.

"Jim, nobody wants to watch gory things like this!" Mom protested later as I poured another gout of Hershey's chocolate syrup into her palm. The lighting I'd chosen for this scene was harsh, and she blinked at me reproachfully.

"I promise you, there are people who want to watch gory things like this. Okay, can you do that again, but this time push the blade down a little more, so the syrup kind of oozes up around it?"

"Oh, honey. You are the most morbid young man I have ever known."

"I know. Hey! No licking the syrup till we're done!"

As game as she was, she had nothing in the way of musical talent so was no help at all with the score. But serendipity intervened, and one day while Curt and I were exploring around Fort Mason, we ended up waiting for a bus with five teenage girls who had a pop group and rock-star dreams. They thought being involved with a student film sounded totally cool, and later that week they came to SFAI and let me record them singing an angelic, high-pitched, one-chord chorus, which I planned to loop over the visuals.

TIME FLEW BY, and as the Thanksgiving holiday weekend approached, it was time to film the main scene.

Even though my mom's tentative, grandmotherly driving still drove me crazy, I was holding out on learning to drive, stuck on the notion that it would somehow normalize me, make me start thinking and behaving like other people. So my mom drove me, the props, the costumes, and the set up to the art institute in her little Honda, complaining the whole way that the long grasses piled high in the back were obscuring her view out the rear of the car. In Studio 8, which I'd rented for the day, she started helping me put the "meadow" in place as Curt, true to his word, set up the lighting equipment.

While my mother arranged the Styrofoam chunks, I stowed a shopping bag full of props under a ladder. "Uh, Mom?"

"Hmm?"

"Do you remember that haunted house I put together in the garage in fifth grade, when we lived in Oklahoma?"

"Aw," said Curt.

"Sure I remember, with the bowl that you put peeled grapes in so that people would think they were touching eyeballs. You put a lot of effort into it. Jim was always creative like this," she added for Curt's benefit.

"Well, I just remembered it myself," I told her. "I was remembering how when Halloween came, not a single person showed up. I have the horrible feeling this is going to be like that."

"How could this be like that?" Curt laughed at the same time as my mother said, "Oh, honey, I'm sure *somebody* came."

"Not one person. Unless you count you and Julie."

It would not, in fact *could* not, be like that, they assured me. Doubtful, I pulled on the beige winter coat that was part of my schoolboy-victim costume. "Okay, if you say so."

By midafternoon my mother had left for her new bridge club with the Round Table Pizza secretaries. When day turned to dusk, Curt and I ordered takeout and ate it on the quadrangle, letting the evening layer of marine fog refresh us. Then, limbs sluggish with exhaustion, we resumed filming.

When I came home that night, I was bone tired. The apartment was hushed, my mother sound asleep. As burned out as I was, though, I could never resist a piece of mail with my name on it, and there was one on the counter by the front door, where my mother had clearly set it aside for my notice. Even in the darkness, I recognized my father's slanted, all-caps handwriting.

I fixed myself a piece of bread and butter and took the letter to the kitchen table, drawing out the moment. Finally I opened it, slitting the envelope carefully with the butter knife.

Dear Jim,

> *I was glad you went to New York. It is a great city.*
> *Wish I could see you. We used to have a good time together.*
> *I don't want you to think that your mother and I did what we did because of you. It was because of her and me, not you.*
> *I mean it, please come out and see me.*

> *Love,*
> *Your old Dad*

I turned it over, even though there was obviously nothing on the back, just in case there was something I was missing. Then I read it again. Six lines, not counting *"Dear Jim."* Well, seven, if I counted *"Love"* as its own line.

Every sentence called up an instant rejoinder. *"Wish I could see you."* Well, why does that have to just be a wish? I'm not dead, I just live in California. *"We used to have a good time together."* And we can't anymore because . . . why? *"Come out and see me,"* but no suggestion of buying me a ticket to fly out and visit. And the way he said *"your mother and I,"* as though Mom had any part in deciding to bundle us off like used clothing into a donation box. New York City got five more descriptive words than I did, although I noticed they were the same five words he'd used last Christmas.

I crumpled up the letter and tossed it onto my plate. Then, seized with immediate remorse, I smoothed it out again, using a napkin to blot the smear of butter that had left a transparent oblong between *"Love"* and *"Dad."* Then I read his words yet again, as though new information could be wrung out of them. But there was only the same vague aura of distant, affectionate regret, as though all the events of our lives had been beyond his control.

The sound of the refrigerator's compressor kicking into life interrupted the thick nighttime silence. Headlights moved across the kitchen ceiling to the wall, and I realized how long it'd been since a car had gone past. It must be very late. I put the note back into its envelope with a feeling of heaviness.

But there was some other layer to my emotions, too, I pondered as I used a dollop of my mother's rose-scented Pond's cold cream to remove the thick makeup covering my face. Something less familiar than the usual heartache that contact with my dad typically imparted. I washed my face and looked at my reflection. My eyes were bloodshot from exhaustion, long hours of concentration, and exposure to movie lights. But they were dry. Tearless.

I felt sorrow, I realized, walking into my bedroom, but I didn't feel up for crying. I felt anger, but I didn't feel up for expressing it. I felt longing, but I didn't feel up for diving headlong into it.

The only thing I really wanted was to get a good night's sleep, so I could return to my project tomorrow, refreshed and clear. After taping the envelope into my journal, I shed my murderer/victim costume and slid under the bedclothes. I had just enough consciousness left to register how surprisingly easy, considering the emotional impact of the letter, it was to fall asleep.

As I drifted into slumber, I thought, *How unlike me. I like it.*

33

BREAKFAST OF CHAMPIONS

O ver that Thanksgiving break, Curt and his boyfriend, Ron, had a bitter, protracted argument that led Curt to move out. I was sorry the acrimonious breakup left my companion with sad feelings, but I was secretly happy that he (and by extension our friendship) was now free of what I perceived as Ron's dour and constraining presence. Curt moved into a railroad flat in the Mission where one of our classmates lived—Wieland Speck, the gay Berliner whom everyone at the art institute had a crush on, myself included. Rumor had it he was *actual friends with David Bowie!*

The flat was located on a stretch of Sixteenth Street that was used by the local vagrants as a combination latrine and place to stow shopping carts full of stolen goods. It was undeniably squalid, a state that for me no longer held the allure of the unknown. There was a stench of human urine near the building entrance, the mailboxes were always getting pried open, and it seemed like every other week there was a mugging within a one-block radius. Inside, its brown shag carpeting needed vacuuming at all times, but the only vacuum cleaner on hand would, while sucking up a few crumbs, vigorously spit out dust at the same time. Still, I always looked forward to being there.

Part of it was purely practical: it was ten times closer to SFAI than my mom's place in San Carlos, of course, and none of Curt's roommates seemed to care if I slept on his bedroom floor most nights, as long as I brought over a big bottle of booze every so often. And hanging out with my best friend had become my favorite pastime.

Plus, the revolving roster of housemates made for an atmosphere that both amused and inspired me. Originally a three-bedroom, the flat was occupied by at least five young gay men at all times, who'd transformed almost every square foot into a place to sleep and/or entertain sex partners. One of them spent his short tenure there building a partition in the living room made entirely out of empty cereal boxes. The visual effect was undeniably cool: the vivid colors and cartoon mascots, the rows of Bruce Jenners athletically shilling for Wheaties. However, empty cardboard boxes don't muffle sound, and while there was something unintentionally funny about hearing him and his boyfriend du jour going at it behind a wall of Count Chocula and Cap'n Crunch, eventually it got him kicked out.

Even the small utility closet off the kitchen had been turned into a kind of sleeping nest, the standpipe that ran through it functioning as a place to hang clothes. Not surprisingly, that room attracted the most transient characters. One of its occupants was a one-time Christian who'd made a beeline for San Francisco after getting kicked out of Bob Jones University. According to him, there were a thousand transgressions that could get one expelled from the evangelical college, including masturbation, but the reason for his own expulsion was the discovery of a pack of cigarettes in his dorm room by the provost. He'd told me and Curt about it one Sunday afternoon over Bloody Marys made with one of my vodka-as-rent offerings.

"I got called to the dean's office," he told us, "and I was like, 'Sir, I am *so* sorry about the pack of Camels.' I did *not* apologize for all the *cock* I was sucking at the time." When we laughed, he said, "What? They didn't bring it up!" He lasted for about a month before he met a sugar daddy who swept him off to a seaside ranch in Mendocino County.

And Wieland Speck, who not only did know David Bowie but was a backup singer on his last tour, was always a pleasure to hang out with. Sometimes the three of us SFAI students would take the bus back from North Beach together and turn the 24-Divisadero into a rolling filmography class, dissecting the Kuchar brothers' latest forays into cinema weirdness. My favorite time with him, though, was spent sitting at the sticky kitchen table, watching him cook his signature meal. This consisted of eggs fried sunny-side up in butter, two per person, sprinkled liberally with pepper and the contents of every dusty, crusty jar of dried herbs in the cupboard. It shouldn't have been so absolutely delicious, but it was. On one such morning, he asked me if I'd like to participate in the film he was making for class.

"You're kidding," I said, digging into my share of fried eggs. "Of course! What's the film about?"

"Ah, *sehnsucht*. There's not really a good word for this in English! Maybe 'yearning'? It's called *David*, meaning Bowie, *Montgomery*—Clift—*und Ich*, 'and Me.'"

"Cool. What do I have to do?"

"It's not difficult. You will be the star. You will watch two men make love from across the . . . ah, what do you call it, the *luft-schacht*, the long place outside, like so?" He gestured to the dank, narrow space outside the kitchen window.

"Air shaft?"

"*Ja*, just so, the air shaft." He set down a plate for himself and pulled up a chair. "The lovers will be in one room and you will be in the other. With the air shaft between you, you will be watching them, full of *sehnsucht*." He made a silent-movie face of desperate longing, then laughed, biting into his toast with evident pleasure. "Or anyway, that is how I see it in my mind. It never really looks the way you think it will, no?"

"Totally," I said. Actually, due to Curt's technical skill and the simplicity of what I'd set out to do, I was pretty sure my own movie was coming out exactly how I pictured it. But of course I wanted to agree with Wieland.

In any event, being in Wieland's film didn't require much more of me than emoting a lot of homosexual angst while wearing a black turtleneck. But it was tons of fun, certainly more amusing than my senior year at San Carlos High would've been, and was an excellent outlet for my crush.

Plus, once word got out that I was game, I was invited to be in any number of films. I got to play, in Divine-like drag, the role of the Greek goddess Circe for Mike Kuchar's short of the same name, and, most memorably, I was called upon to masturbate in a helicopter as it rotored over the Pacific Ocean for my friend Mary Bellis's film *Bowlahoola*. For that one I was clad in a tuxedo.

I SLEPT AS MANY NIGHTS as I could at that place in the Mission, but I availed myself of other options, too. If a one-night stand invited me to crash at his place, I always said yes. I stayed with other friends—like my dear friend Thor, whom I met through a personals ad in the *Advocate*—when they felt up for it. And if there was no other alternative, I'd sleep at my mom's; of course, I still kept a lot of my belongings in my old bedroom. But in general, San Carlos was beginning to recede in the rearview mirror. The city of San Francisco was becoming my daily life.

Because Curt liked his liquor and was especially happy to go out for a drink or three in the wake of his breakup with Ron, part of that daily life meant hitting the gay bars with him. I'd go along, because anything could be fun if I was doing it with Curt, but I'd usually just prop up the bar, gulping Cape Cods and checking my watch.

I got approached by men all the time on these outings, but I repelled almost all their advances. The fetish themes and costumes—leather, western, muscle daddies, nellies, and dungeons, and sailors, and bears—struck me as being as artificially constructed as the rides at Disneyland. To my way of thinking, they leached the wonder and intrigue and mystery out of sex, too fixed on one specific fetish to leave room for the interesting variations of chance I liked best. I got the sense that the bars were fulfilling some long-held fantasy of gay desire for many, but I didn't really relate. I was more turned on by the egalitarian randomness of the cruising scene, where a young Mexican gardener could hook up with a waspy college professor. And who knew? Maybe they'd strike up an interesting conversation afterward.

So my days were spent finishing my film, which I'd titled *Fisherisms*, followed by nights drinking with Curt at the Stud or the Tool Box, or cruising for sex. I wondered sometimes if its constant availability could possibly have unintended consequences in the long run. Could too much sex be a bad thing? It was an unusual thought to explore, but I didn't bother. It was fun, that was the main thing, and on weekends there would be messy, cozy, hungover mornings at the Mission flat that smelled like coffee and young male bodies and overflowing ashtrays and cheap incense from the botanicas on Valencia Street.

34

THE BEST PART OF WAKING UP

As Christmas vacation neared, I was almost done with my film. There'd been a moment of panic when I found out what it was going to cost to have it printed, but my father stepped up at the last minute and offered to pay for it as a Christmas gift. I assumed he was glad to have something to do that, while requiring no more effort than writing a check, would maintain his likely image of himself as an excellent parent. I didn't have to feign gratitude, though, as it kept me from having to take out another loan.

Now, with nervous anticipation, I fed what existed so far of the edited film through the Steenbeck flatbed machine.

Curt's lighting and camerawork perfectly conveyed the eerie menace of the meadow, the same slow-motion tension and beauty I'd had in my dreams. The killer parting the grass, seeking his prey. The terrible vision of a knife's blade sinking into a wrist. I felt like I could've stayed in that chair in the dark forever, breathing in the vaguely electrical scent of the editing bay, floating suspended on my elation. "I made this," I whispered to no one in particular.

I spent that night in San Carlos on my mom's sofa, drinking acrid Folger's coffee and watching the obligatory moth-eaten Rankin/Bass animated holiday specials on TV. I snuck into the bathroom to fire up a joint, which made me feel fourteen again, blowing smoke into the fan vent.

But watching stop-motion Kriss Kringle take his jerking dance steps on *The Year Without a Santa Claus*, I felt pride. I'd made a film about something intimate and real. *"Put one foot in front of the other,"* sang the little puppet, *"and soon you'll be walking out the door!" Yeah, or directly into the path of a convicted child molester,* I thought. I didn't say it out loud, though. My mother was never keener for me to "add a little sunshine" than during the holidays, so I refrained from provoking her.

The next day she was eager to take me to a restaurant in San Francisco's Chinatown, one recommended by a fellow Round Table secretary. Halfway through the first course, she had a formal announcement to make.

"I was hoping we could have a real family Christmas this year. You, me, and Julie. It's been years since we were all together like that."

"Mom, Christmas is like ten minutes from now." I slurped up a wonton. It never failed to amaze me how much better everything tasted outside San Carlos.

"Are you saying you have other plans?"

"Well, no," I admitted. "But I mean, me and Julie . . ."

Don't get along, I was about to say, but she misunderstood, maybe on purpose. "You and Julie are plenty of company for me. I don't need anyone but my two beautiful children to have a wonderful time!"

I shrugged. "Okay. I'll come down and stay for a couple days."

She shook her head, confused by my lack of resistance. "Well, the thing is, though, Julie says she doesn't want to come. She wants to go with her boyfriend—what's his name?"

"The latest one? Uh, Eric, I think."

"She wants to go to *Eric's* family's house. I told her, 'Fine! Bring Eric over!' But she said, 'Mom, please, I just want to do my own thing.' I don't know why she always chooses to run away from her own family."

"Really? I do."

"Don't start," she warned, brandishing a barbecued sparerib.

"I'm not being facetious." *My God, I'm really not,* I thought, surprising even myself. "I'm just saying that I can understand why. Maybe you should try to understand, too."

"I don't see what there is to understand. It's simple. I just wanted us to have a family Christmas for once." She wiped hoisin glaze off her fingers with exasperation.

Usually this would be my cue to lose my temper. But Mike's class had trained my eye, so instead I tuned in to the visual metaphor of the sparerib she was now gnawing on. *Once this woman gets an idea between her teeth, she never lets it go,* I noted. *She worries it like a terrier with a bone.* It struck me as funny and revealing.

And even though she continued to restate her complaint until after the Hunan-style cucumbers with fresh garlic had been consumed, I couldn't get worked up about it. Julie would or would not come for Christmas, and then the holidays would be over.

The making of *Fisherisms* would be over. The whole year, for that matter, would be over.

ON CHRISTMAS EVE, Curt and I went down to my mom's to lug the pine tree lashed to the roof of her car onto the sidewalk and into her living room, where we helped decorate it while bingeing on Danish butter cookies that my mother bought at Woolworth's. Then we hightailed it back to the city and hunkered down in Studio 8 with a bottle of red wine to film the title cards, the last step before we could strike a print.

It was harder than either of us had expected, the light either bouncing off the cards in ugly white spots or so subdued that the words weren't legible. While Curt swore under his breath and fiddled endlessly with the C-stands, I sat tailor fashion on the floor in a drift of discarded pieces of white poster board and Avery press-on lettering.

From years of playing with the office supplies my father gave me at every holiday, I excelled at the arcane process involved in using press-on lettering, so practiced that I didn't even need to make guidelines with a ruler. I had a favorite typeface, Franklin Gothic Condensed, which I was using now. I knew the paramount importance of even spacing and the frustrating way the edges cracked if too much pressure was applied. The letters gave off fumes with a subtle but distinct odor, which as a child I'd enjoyed but which was probably in fact *eau de cancer*.

At this point I was so exhausted that the fumes were getting me a little high. "I don't know why I'm blanking on this," I said, laying down the *u* in "Curt," "but it's 'Thomas' with a *Th*, not *To*, right?"

"Oh, gosh darn it. Sorry, not you. Yes."

"I love it when you try to swear. Do it some more."

"Be quiet and go add a little sunshine to the world." He'd found my mom's reaction to what *Fisherisms* was about priceless, and he quoted it at every opportunity. He thought she was "a hoot," and she thought he was the nicest young fellow she'd ever met. She seemed to acknowledge his gayness by tactfully failing to ever mention it, as though he had a distinctive facial birthmark.

This was, I reflected as I lit a cigarette, her chosen tactic with me, too. I wasn't sure how we'd arrived at an unspoken agreement to leave the topic alone, but I was certain of one thing: There wasn't a doubt left in her mind about who I was, and maybe she was even getting more comfortable with it.

I set down letters spelling out "A FILM BY," pressing on each character with the tip of a pencil I'd brought especially for this task, its point dulled to precisely the right level. Then I paused and ashed the cigarette into an empty coffee cup, pondering. It was strictly forbidden to smoke in Studio 8, but whoever made the rules had obviously never spent a weekend in San Carlos listening to John Denver's *Rocky Mountain Christmas* on an eight-track tape player. Sometime later I'd laid down the letters for JIMMY NEUROSIS.

"Finally!" Curt exclaimed. "I got the lights figured out. Thank God. I was just about ready to jump off the dang roof."

"Don't do it. Then I'll have to go to your funeral, and you *know* that my mom and I will fight about me wearing a suit."

He yawned. "It's so good to know that somebody really cares. Gimme a drag."

I handed him the cigarette, which was nearly down to the

filter. He ferried it outside to stub out the butt and then stood at the door, flapping it gently to clear the smoke. "You ready with the title cards?"

"Actually, just give me a few minutes." I ripped up the card I'd just finished, tossed it onto the reject pile, and began again.

A FILM BY JAMES OSELAND.

I drew back and looked at it. Yes, that was right. "Okay, come back," I told my friend. "I'm ready."

ACKNOWLEDGMENTS

The events and experiences described in this book are true and have been written, to the best of my ability, as I recall them. Some names, identifying characteristics, and circumstances have been altered in order to protect the privacy of the people involved. In some instances, composite characters have been created or timelines have been compressed. Many individuals helped in the writing of this book. I would in particular like to express my gratitude to editor and guide Jenna Leigh Evans, publisher Daniel Halpern, editor Denise Oswald, David McAninch, Michele Schroeder, Jill Goodman, and Denise Shannon. I would also like to thank Francine Prose, Carter Lyon, Sreelesh VK, Justin Tanner, Betty Fussell, Pamela Kaufman, Sofia Perez, Susan Traylor, Laura Cohen, Robin Brewer, Merrie Lawson, Alexis Scott, Vivian Cohen, Noreen Hennessy, David Plotnikoff, Tracie MacMillan, Amanaa Rendall, William Andrews, Harris Salat, Maureen Sugden, Dog Swan, Nicole Panter, Dave Weaver, Emma Janaskie, Sanford McCoy, Naomi Duguid, Vijayan Swami, Bill Jacobsen, and Julie Oseland, who in the years since the matters accounted in this book has become my closest friend and confidant. And thanks, especially, to James Roper.